THE MANAGEMENT AND PRACTICE OF PUBLIC RELATIONS

Norman Stone

MACMILLAN
Business

First published 1995 by
MACMILLAN PRESS LTD
Houndmills, Basingstoke, Hampshire RG21 6XS
and London
Companies and representatives
throughout the world

ISBN 0–333–60975–1 hardcover
ISBN 0–333–60976–X paperback

A catalogue record for this book is available
from the British Library.

10   9   8   7   6   5   4   3   2   1
04 03 02 01 00 99 98 97 96 95

Copy-edited and typeset by Povey–Edmondson
Okehampton and Rochdale, England

Printed and bound in Great Britain by
Antony Rowe Ltd
Chippenham, Wiltshire

THE MANAG
PUBLIC RELA

■ Contents

List of Tables   xii

List of Figures   xiii

List of Portfolio Cases   xiv

List of Portfolio Checklists   xv

List of Portfolio Guidelines   xvi

List of Abbreviations   xvii

Foreword by Norman A. Hart   xix

Acknowledgements   xx

Introduction   xxii

1   **What Public Relations Can Do**   1
   What Public?   1
   Managing PR   2
   The Personal Portfolio of PR   2
   Setting Realistic Objectives   4
   Supporting Business Objectives   5
   Awareness and Perception   5
   Pulling People In   6
   Internal PR   6
   Caring PR   7
   PR and Marketing   7
   Change as an Objective   8
   Ask a Policeman   8
   The Timescale of Change   9
   The KAP Hypothesis   9
   No Bouquets   10
   An Unusual Objective   11
   Planning and Programmes   11
   Assessment   13
   What PR Cannot Do   14
   The PR Perspective   17
   An Unwritten Law   17

2 **Choosing and Using Public Relations   18**
   A Management Function   18
   Symmetrical PR   19
   Some Management Issues Affecting Stakeholders   20
   Recruiting   21
   In-House versus Consultancy   23
   Outputs, not Inputs   26
   Matching Client to Consultancy   27
   What Consultancies Earn   27
   Staff Deployment in Consultancies   28
   Managing Consultancies   28
   When In-House and Consultancy Combine   30
   Reassurance   32
   The Slow Burn   33
   PR across Frontiers   33
   Managing Information   34
   Policy and Operations   34

3 **Public Relations and Marketing   35**
   A Difference in Perception   35
   Topicality, Credibility, Involvement   36
   The Business Market   36
   Existing Products, Existing Markets   37
   New Products, Existing Markets   37
   Existing Products, New Markets   37
   New products, New Markets   38
   A Target of Three   38
   Changing Markets, New Techniques   40
   Re-organised Products, Re-organised Markets   40
   New Products, New Methods   40
   Own Products, Market Awareness   40
   Refreshing the Brand   40
   Brand Positioning   42
   The Dinosaur Effect   43
   Cause-Related Marketing   44
   Marketing Support for Intermediaries   45
   Product Placement   46
   Quality Upgrade   46
   One for the Money, Two for the Show   47
   The Overall View   49

4 **Research and Public Relations   51**
   The Purpose of Research   51
   Research Planning   51
   Kinds of Research   52

Types of Data   54
Research Techniques   54
Telephone Research with a Difference   55
W. A. Muzack   56
No Material Risk   56
Using Research Results   57
An Attitude Survey   57
Probing, Tracking, Evaluating   57
Multi-Dimensional Perception   59
Presenting Information   60
Change Means Opportunity   61
Cost-Free Research?   62
PR Auditing   62
International Research   63
Pseudo-Research   64
One More Questionnaire   65

5 **Corporate and Financial Relations   66**
Image or Identity?   66
Who Takes Charge of Identity?   67
Corporate Values   68
Corporate Design   68
Brands   69
Sponsorship   72
The Financial Arena   76
Privatisation and Flotation   76
Distinctiveness   79
Management Buy-outs   81
Writing Reports   83
Personal Finance   85
New Markets   85
Reputation   87
Briefings   88
Speeches   88

6 **Government Relations   91**
How it all Began   91
Putting Pressure on Government   92
The Government and Other Audiences   95
They Ought to Make a Film about it   95
Winning Contracts   96
Lobbying   98
The Woman on the Clapham Omnibus   98
Select Committees   98
Local Government Relations   99

Performance Indicators: Opportunity or Threat?   100
The European Dimension   102
Europe and You   103
Mind Your Language   105
Pan-European PR   106

7   **Employee and Community Relations   109**
Company and Community   109
Communication Styles   109
The Toyota Way   110
Communicating with Staff: Four Principles   111
TSB Goes On-Line   111
Sound and Pictures   112
Two More Principles of Staff Communication   115
Mobil, *sans frontières*   116
The Seventh Principle   116
The RAC   116
Another Three Principles and a Final Thought   117
The Community   118
Social Contribution   119
Educational Involvement   119
Educational Material   121
The American Experience   122
Consultation   124
What Made Banbury Cross?   125
Conspiracy or Cock-Up?   126
Cleveland Supertram   126
The Environment   127

8   **The Third Sector   129**
Understanding the Economy   129
Public and Private   129
The Other 10 per cent   130
Control and Benefits   130
Building a Higher Profile   130
Correcting Misconceptions   131
Co-operative Bank Financial Advisers   132
The Law Society   132
Strategy Shift   133
Non-Profit Organisations   135
Media Relations   137
Internal Communication   137
House Journals   138
Events   138
Sponsorship   138

Third Party Endorsement   139
Advertising   139
Exhibitions   139
General Expenses   139
Training   140

9   Customer and Consumer Relations   141
We are all Customers   141
The User-Friendly Bus   142
Quality and Value   142
Enhancements   143
A Customised Magazine   143
Educational Leaflets Add Value   144
Will the Cow (& Gate) Jump over the Heinz?   146
Skipjack   146
Family Decision Making   147
Industry Decision Making   148
Influencing Workforce and Customers   148
Key Buyers   150
Voters are Customers   151
Internal Customers   151
When is a Customer not a Customer?   152
Southern Electric   153
Competitors as Customers   153
Professional Users   154
Customer Centres   156
Influencing Perception and Increasing Consumption   157

10   Media Relations   160
What Story?   160
Know your Media   160
The Press   162
Radio and Television   170
Interviews   172
Media Events   172
Taking the Product to the Media   174
The Essex Brewer   175
Advertorials   175
Infomercials   177
No Guarantees   178
Sponsorship Credits   178
Sponsorship in Regional Newspapers   180
Deadlines and Provisos   180
An Insidious Practice   181
A Sense of Proportion   182

11 Organising and Training for Excellence   183
What Kind of Organisation?   183
An Excellent Partnership   184
Professional Organisations   186
Identifying Skills and Attitudes   186
Training for Performance   188
National Vocational Qualifications   190
Writing: A Fundamental PR Skill   191
Getting it Right   192
Creativity Training   193
Reference Banks   193
Skills for the Future   195
Unix to Apple   197
Train Everybody   197

12 Paying for Public Relations   198
'Just Put in What you Think'   198
Principles of Budgeting   199
Budget Brackets   201
Informed Guesswork   208
Cost Justification   208
Costing Procedures   209
Salary Costs   210
Paying for Consultancies   211
Cost of Materials and Services   212
Budget Checks   212

13 Public Relations in a Crisis   214
What Qualifies as a Crisis?   214
Disaster: Piper Alpha   215
Recovery   215
Disaster: Commercial Union   216
Learning from Experience   218
Not always Sudden   219
Not just Firefighting   219
Product Tampering   220
Product Purity   221
Hostile Take-Over Bids   221
Inner Strength   222
Staying in Control   222
The Ultimate Rollercoaster   223
Kwik-Fit   223
Other Crises of Business Life   224
Some Principles   224
After a Crisis   226

14 Evaluation   228
What is Evaluation?   228
Results that Can be Measured   229
A Weighty Decision   230
Results that Cannot be Measured   230
Methods Used to Measure and Assess   231
Media Measurement   232
Equivalent Advertising Value   234
More to Life than Media   236
A Campaign to Change the Law   239
The Royal Tournament   240
Getting Results for Charity   241
Evaluating Community Relations   242
Accelerating a Revolution   244
A Really Significant Figure   247
Verification   248

In Conclusion   249
The Final Portfolio   249

Appendix A: Sources of Information   251

Appendix B: Additional Information Sources   255

Appendix C: Professional Conduct   265

Appendix D: Bibliography   282

Notes and References   285

Index   292

■ List of Tables

2.1   Purchasers' expectations of individual services   24
5.1   Timetable for flotation   78
6.1   EC information programme: material available   108
10.1   Media statistics   161
11.1   Toyota's UK public relations   184
11.2   Toyota public relations interfaces   185
11.3   Brent's training programme   189
12.1   In-house salary costs   210
12.2   Consultancy salary costs   210
14.1   Expectations of service quality   231
14.2   Insurance check programme summary   237
14.3   Cost per visitor of major media, Royal Tournament, 1993   241

■ List of Figures

2.1   Earnings of top 150 public relations consultancies   28
2.2   Staffing levels in top 150 public relations consultancies   29
3.1   Summary of benefits   39
4.1   Perception analysis chart   60
6.1   Schematic of decision making in the European Commission   104
7.1   Which presentation media?   113–15
8.1   Control/benefit relationships   131
10.1 Slicing the triangle   166
10.2 Public relations input the nationals prefer   169
10.3 Public relations input the regionals prefer   170
10.4 Readers' perception of advertorials   176
14.1 Classic FM: analysis of press coverage   235
14.2 Banana consumption, 1972–93   236
14.3 The community relations triangle   243
C.1   Sample contract   276

List of Portfolio Cases

1.1 Thoughtful, not impulsive   12
1.2 A classic plan   12
1.3 The obscene monster   13
2.1 Junior Champs   30
3.1 Selling the benefits   38
3.2 One to get your teeth into   41
3.3 Academy wins awards   43
3.4 From 2 per cent to market leader   46
3.5 The Royal Tournament   47
4.1 Launching Shell Select   58
5.1 Putting factoring in the frame   80
5.2 Success is no accident   86
6.1 The first modern pressure group   92
6.2 Devonport versus Rosyth   96
6.3 Worth every penny   101
6.4 A complex, coordinated consumer campaign   106
7.1 The business class   120
8.1 Rescuing the rescuers   133
9.1 Insurance checks   144
9.2 Beating them on paper   149
9.3 Doing the business, instantly   154
9.4 A sensitive subject   156
9.5 Add a banana   157
11.1 Anglo–Japanese cooperation   184
11.2 Cascading to excellence   188
12.1 Something to show for the money   203
12.2 The scent of success   205
13.1 Crisis timetable   216
14.1 Bail bandits   239
14.2 Huge celebrity involvement   242
14.3 Open Systems are go   244

■ List of Portfolio Checklists

2.1   Stakeholders   19
2.2   Management in the twenty-first century   21
2.3   PR knowledge   22
2.4   PR skills   23
2.5   Choosing a PR consultancy   25
2.6   How to run a consultancy   29
4.1   Key questions about research   65
7.1   Choosing and using sound and pictures   112
7.2   Opportunities for community relations   118
10.1 Media crediting   178
11.1 Knowledge and skills   187
11.2 Visual reference bank   194
11.3 Managers in the twenty-first century   196
11.4 Training in the twenty-first century   196
14.1 The acid test   248

■ List of Portfolio Guidelines

1.1   Realistic objectives   4

4.1   Ringing the bell   55

4.2   Choosing a chart   61

5.1   Good sponsorship   75

5.2   Financing a BIMBO   81

5.3   Reports: arranging your material   83

5.4   Writing speeches   89

6.1   Decision making in Europe   103

7.1   Staff communication: summary   117

7.2   Business sponsors of educational material   121

7.3   Talking to family and neighbours   128

9.1   Gaining credibility inside your firm   151

10.1   What the journalists say   162

10.2   What kind of press notice?   163

10.3   Writing a press notice   165

10.4   Writing a feature article   167

10.5   Media provisos   180

11.1   Writing style   191

12.1   Task-directed, zero-based budgeting   201

13.1   Crisis on the shelf   220

13.2   Crisis management   225

■ List of Abbreviations

ABC	Association of Business Communicators
ABFD	Association of British Factors and Discounters
ABSA	Association for Business Sponsorship of the Arts
ACBE	Advisory Committee on Business and the Environment
BA	British Airways
BAIE	British Association of Industrial Editors
BDHF	British Dental Health Foundation
BIMBOs	management buy-outs and buy-ins
CAD	computer aided design
CBFA	Co-operative Bank Financial Advisers
CBI	Confederation of British Industry
ccm	column centimetres
CCTV	closed circuit television
CDC	Cherwell District Council
CERP	Confédération Européenne des Relations Publiques
COTS	cumulative opportunities to see
CPS	Crown Prosecution Service
CURM	Commercial Union Risk Management
DML	Devonport Management Limited
DMU	decision making unit
DTI	Department of Trade and Industry
EAV	equivalent advertising value
ECU	European Currency Unit
EPOS	electronic point of sale
ETUC	European Trade Union Confederation
EU	European Union
fmcg	fast-moving consumer goods
IES	Institute for Employment Studies
ILR	Independent Local Radio
IM	Institute of Management
IMS	Institute of Manpower Studies
IPR	Institute of Public Relations
ISBA	Incorporated Society of British Advertisers
IT	information technology
JSI	Jones Stroud Insulations
LCTC	Lambeth Children's Theatre Company
M&S	Marks and Spencer
MBI	management buy-in

MBO	management buy-out
MORI	Market Opinion Research International
MU	Mothers' Union
NCC	National Consumer Council
NOP	National Opinion Polls
NPCA	National Peanut Council of America
NT	New Technology (Windows)
NVQ	National Vocational Qualification
OHP	overhead projector
OS	open systems
OSI	Open Systems Interconnection
OSiS	Open Systems information Service
OTS	opportunities to see
OXY	Occidental Petroleum (Caledonia) Ltd
PACE	Police and Criminal Evidence Act
PRCA	Public Relations Consultants Association
QTV	Queue Television
SVQ	Scottish Vocational Qualification
TMAB	Toyota Members' Advisory Board
TMC	Toyota Motor Corporation
TMME	Toyota Motor Europe Marketing and Engineering SA
TSB	Trustee Savings Bank
UNICE	Union of Industrial and Employers Confederation of Europe
VNR	video news release
WDC	Wycombe District Council

■ Foreword

I was very pleased to be asked to contribute a Foreword to Norman Stone's *The Management and Practice of Public Relations* because the actual practice of the business is moving so fast that it seemed to me that a really up-to-date text was exactly what was needed at the present time.

There are, of course, a large number of existing texts, but many of them, sadly, are dated and to some large degree based simply upon personal experiences and recollections.

The Management and Practice of Public Relations is noteworthy in a number of respects. It is obviously extremely well researched over a very wide range of subjects, and is accompanied by a host of practical examples. Furthermore it discusses PR matters from the point of view of today's practice rather than yesterday's. The range of authorities and references is comprehensive and makes it an ideal book both for practitioners and students. It really is a book for the 1990s and beyond.

Finally it is written in a down-to-earth style which makes it eminently readable, and is structured in such a way as to enable the reader to find readily that particular part which is of special interest.

This is Norman Stone's second book on public relations. I look forward to his next one.

NORMAN A. HART
Chairman, International Public Relations Foundation

■ Acknowledgements

Ritchie Calder, who was just about the best science journalist I ever knew, used to say that every book has its grandparents and godparents.

The grandparents are those people whose knowledge, experience and attitudes you absorb almost without realising it; they should be acknowledged. The godparents are those whose brains you pick, whose ideas you crib, whose words you quote direct, and who must be acknowledged without fail.

I am indebted to the chief officers and senior staff of the following professional institutions, industry associations and representative bodies for permission to quote from their codes of practice, guidelines, publications and other documents: Institute of Public Relations (John Lavelle); Public Relations Consultants Association (Colin Thompson); Institute of Management (Christine Hayhurst); Association for Business Sponsorship of the Arts (Andrew McIlroy); Incorporated Society of British Advertisers (Ken Miles); Association of Business Communicators (Pida Ripley); National Consumer Council (Ruth Evans); and British Institute of Professional Photography (Philip Way).

A remarkable number of consultancies gave me substantial assistance and very detailed information. These included Beechey Morgan Associates (Jane Beechey), Bruce Naughton Wade (Alastair Bruce), Cohn & Wolfe (Peter Halliday), Counsellor (Niki Caidan), Flora Martin PR (Lesley Fleming), Infopress (Dermot McKeone and Tricia Boyd), Kestrel (Roger Haywood and Janine Hood), LeFevre Williamson (Joy Williamson), Livingstone Guarantee (Barrie Pearson), Media Measurement (David Phillips), Northern Lights (Victoria Tomlinson), P Four (David Miller and Louise Thompson), Paragon (Julia Thorn), Price Waterhouse (Peter D. Smith), Radio Lynx (Simon Hughes), Scope: Communications (Jonathon Howard and Jenny Reid), The Rowland Company (Judy Ditchburn), Two-Ten (Ricky Faw) and Welbeck Golin/Harris (Alison Clarke). Chapter 8 draws on the knowledge and goodwill of Jane Hammond (Trident Training Services), Frances Walker (Co-op Bank Financial Advisers) and Peter Welch (MultiStrategies). For Chapter 13 I was fortunate to learn from the frontline experience of Kate Graham (Kate Graham PR), Ray Morley (Commercial Union) and Julia Thorn (Paragon).

Expertise in local government was contributed by Vaire Cheadle (Shropshire County Council), Anne Clarke and Alison Davies (Cherwell District Council), Peter Heaton (DTW Group), Mark Oaten (Westminster Communications), Eddie Russell (Wycombe District Council) and John Walker (Brent Council).

For insight into their own particular problems and opportunities, I am grateful to Leo Allo (Kymi), Adrian Berkeley (*The Photographer*), Gordon Blain (Jones Stroud Insulations), Clea Caisley (Tommy's Campaign), Raymond

Cook (Lambeth Children's Theatre Company), Penny Hallett (Avon and Somerset Constabulary), Peter Judge (Technology Appraisals) and Sue Kistruck (Mothers' Union).

Throughout the book I have quoted copiously from newspapers, magazines, publishers and media organisations, notably *IPR Journal* (Harvey Smith), *PR Week* (Stephen Farish and Ed Charles), *Management Today* (Charles Skinner), *Professional Manager* (Westerly Donahue), *brand strategy* (Joanna Perkin), National Magazines (Tracey Richards and Joanne Thomas), Benn's Media (Karen Roffey), *Intermedica* (Ian Swash), NTC Publications (David Roberts) and Reuters (Steve Garvey).

Nor does my indebtedness end there; and I gratefully acknowledge the help of Rosemary Arnold (Deddington Public Library), Nigel Bain (Nigel Bain Consultancy), Michael Bland (Michael Bland Consultancy), Amanda Bowman (Business in the Community), Di Burton (Cicada), Meriel Cook (Casstallack), Natalie Corren (Scope: Communications), Helen Dyer (ABSA), John Fowler (Burson Marsteller), Peter Gerbrandy (NCVQ), Warren Greaves (DTI), Anne Gregory (Leeds Business School), Keith Hopkins (KBH), Malcolm Hurlston (Malcolm Hurlston Corporate Consultancy), Sir Dennis Landau (Unity Trust Bank), Bénédicte Martin (Media Appointments), Mandy Merron (Willott, Kingston, Smith), Tracey Metchear (IPR), Tracey Mullins (The Radio Authority), Ashley Sollitt and Sue Stapeley (The Law Society) and Anne Wilson (Livingstone Guarantee).

The Macmillan team of Norman Hart, whose advice I always value, Stephen Rutt, Jane Powell, Keith Povey and Gloria Hart have been supportive and patient. My wife, Angela, continues to control my manuscripts and see them through to completion and delivery.

To all these, and the many others whose names ought to be there, I can only say 'Thanks, I couldn't have done it without you.'

NORMAN STONE

■ Introduction

To be without method is deplorable, but to depend entirely on method is worse.

Wang An-chieh of Hsiu-shui[1]

Take any four weeks in the last twelve months. Study the national, regional and trade press. You are likely to find 100–150 announcements of public relations (PR) contracts, or of substantial amendments to existing contracts, or of appointments of in-house public relations professionals. That's at the rate of at least 1200–1800 per year. There will have been many more such contracts and appointments which were not announced, but which happened just the same.

As in the course of those twelve months, so in the next or any future year; pretty well every type of business will be engaged in public relations, from airlines to art galleries, lawyers to local government, shoes to show business.

It has to be said that in a few of these instances public relations will be used as whitewash, and in one or two as pure eyewash. But mostly you will find the management and practice of public relations playing an increasingly important and successful part in the management and practice of business.

According to many respectable and respected authorities, public relations is solely about organisational representation, corporate image and corporate identity, while everything else is something else, and not PR. That clear distinction has an austere logic that is easy to understand, and I would not even try to persuade anyone otherwise. It is, however, too restrictive, pure and hard-edged for our purposes. This book is about the management and *practice* of public relations. In my experience, it is not theory, concept or principle that constitutes and defines practice, but what the practitioners actually do.

The Institute of Public Relations (IPR) recently added to its formal definition of public relations practice as the planned and sustained effort to establish and maintain goodwill and mutual understanding between an organisation and its publics.

One additional definition is that public relations is about reputation: it is the result of what you do, what you say and what others say about you.

The other new definition is this: 'Public relations practice is the discipline concerned with the reputation of organisations (or products, services or individuals) with the aim of earning understanding and support.'[2]

For the next couple of hundred pages we will explore that practice in breadth and in depth. Theoretical boundaries will be crossed and every specialism plundered – advertising, direct mail, graphic design, media relations, product promotion, whatever – as we learn how mutually beneficial relationships are developed and sustained between the people who affect an organisation's activities and those affected by these activities.

Success in the practice of public relations is recognised annually by the Public Relations Consultants Association (PRCA) in their Outstanding Consultancy awards and by the IPR Sword of Excellence awards to individuals and organisations. Submissions for the IPR awards have to cover:

- *information*: analysis, research and definition of operational objectives
- *planning*: drawing up a strategy and costed action plan
- *action*: communicating and carrying out the programme
- *measurement*: monitoring and evaluating progress, results and budgets; reassessment and modification of programmes as necessary (this should preferably include evaluative comment from the chief executive of the organisation for which the programme was designed)[3]

These four stages give us the basis of an approach to public relations that will be methodical enough to satisfy Wang An-chieh while leaving room for creativity and opportunism.

Every chapter in this book is relevant to one or more of these stages, with what I hope you will agree is just the right amount of method (neither 'deplorable' nor 'worse').

Chapters 1–4 deal with broad functions: what PR can do, and what it cannot; comparisons between in-house PR and consultancy; the relationship between PR and marketing; and the role of research in PR.

Chapters 5–14 are about public relations in action. Corporate and financial PR; government relations; employee communications and community relations; that sector which is neither commercial nor public, known as the third sector; relations with customers and consumers; the media; organisation and training; budgeting; crisis PR; measuring results.

There is an essential minimum of theory, and a good deal of practicality. There are case histories, of widely different kinds, each authenticated by a protagonist. Many of these have won IPR, PRCA or other awards. In addition, plenty of brief examples are quoted, drawn from the experience of numerous different practitioners. You will be helped to put together your own personal portfolio of public relations practice (more about that in Chapter 1). The book's Appendices are full of reference material, and the Index should help you to home in on a particular point quickly.

Guidelines and checklists summarise some of the lessons I have learned over the years and others I am still learning. Two guidelines come before all others, and the first one is this: in public relations, always tell the truth. You have options about how much of it you tell at any one time, to whom you tell it and when, but if you are to succeed in the management and practice of public relations, you must tell the truth. There are five powerful reasons for this:

- telling the truth protects and enhances your own credibility, and that of your company or client
- if you don't tell the truth, the way is open for somebody else to, and so damage your credibility
- journalists will look to you – and, by extension, to your company or client – as an authority in your subject area
- it is an encouragement to your company or client to do right
- you don't have to remember what you said last time

The second guideline is equally uncompromising: whatever the pressures and temptations, never deceive yourself. Come to think of it, that also means tell the truth (in this case to yourself).

I hope *The Management and Practice of Public Relations* will answer many of the more common questions about what working in public relations is like and how PR can permeate every aspect of a business. But please do not rely only on my answers. Challenge them and check them out.

If this book is to be of lasting use to you, it must encourage you to find your own answers, and, more important still, to ask your own questions.

CHAPTER 1

What Public Relations Can Do

Of course, we might not be able to trace the simple steps that constitute a perception or an opinion, or precede or bring about an action: but underneath there is no doubt that they are there.

P. W. Atkins[1]

■ What Public?

Every business has a range of publics. These include the institutions and individuals who provide the finance for the business, the men and women who work in it and the families living near it. The customers who buy from it and the suppliers who sell to it, the consumers who actually use its products or services, and the competitors who want those customers and consumers for themselves: these, too, are publics.

Nor should we ignore, even if they'd let us, the politicians and officials who legislate on the business and who take taxes from it. All these, and more, are publics. With each and every one of them the business has a relationship, either direct or through intermediaries, who are also publics in their own right.

A very important public, though not always as important as they think, is that amalgam of press, television and radio known collectively as the media.

What determines the success or failure of the business is the way these publics behave towards it, and this behaviour is determined, or at any rate influenced, by attitude and by perception. These in turn are shaped by reputation. Managing the causal linkage between reputation, perception, attitude and behaviour is what PR is all about.

It is not a matter of choice. PR is the one business function that organisations cannot decide to do without. Their only option is whether to manage and practise PR as a conscious and deliberate activity, or to leave it to chance and hope for the best: a sure route to the worst.

Public relations can:

- support business objectives
- explain policies

1

- increase awareness
- focus attention on issues
- encourage informed discussion
- help to change perception, opinion and behaviour
- influence attitudes
- motivate staff
- reinforce the marketing and sales effort
- build and sustain a reputation, over time
- help to restore credibility
- have some effect on the values of a particular group or of society as a whole

■ Managing PR

To do any of these things successfully, PR has to be managed, and the way to do that is fundamentally no different from the way any other business activity is managed:

- realistic objectives are agreed
- a programme to achieve the objectives is put together, and costed
- adequate resources are assigned and responsibilities agreed
- the programme is carried out, to a timetable
- reliable methods are devised for measuring programme performance and verifying that objectives are attained
- emergencies are anticipated (which means that not only are they expected but that forestalling action is taken)
- results are evaluated and fed back, so that all six previous steps are continually repeated in an endless cycle of constant improvement

■ The Personal Portfolio of PR

Public relations consultants and in-house practitioners like to get involved in the planning and programme stages. It gives them lots to do and makes demands on their expertise. In doing so, especially at the less senior levels, they run the very real risk that they not only can't see the wood for the trees, they can't see the trees for the twigs.

You won't want to get yourself in that position. Here's what you can do. Start developing a PR portfolio of your own. Put together summaries of PR projects and programmes, including ongoing activities. You don't have to be involved in them directly yourself: as long as they are by or for your company, into the portfolio they go.

You will probably find it helpful to categorise each summary into a few broad types, such as:

- corporate PR
- customer relations
- internal PR

In each category, each summary should show:

- business objectives
- PR objectives
- budget
- strategy
- programme
- PR techniques
- key events
- timings
- responsibilities
- evaluation methods
- results

A simplified version of this structure is used in most of the cases in this book. You could add those cases to your portfolio, too.

The better you build your portfolio, the better you will see and understand the total PR function and your part in it. But don't worry if your entries are less than perfect: do the best you can at the time and improve the information as and when.

Using the portfolio will enable you to check that PR strategy is consistent with overall business strategy. You should be able to compare the scale of effort on PR – money, time, and other resources – with that on other mainstream activities and with turnover. You will get an idea of cost/benefit and also of cost/risk ratios. By measuring gains achieved against those intended, you will know where the shortfalls are and what to do about it.

Your portfolio should have lots of practical entries:

- *press contacts* – the key people for you: who and where they are; telephone numbers; deadlines; type of material they like; and so on
- *contractors* – who; where; specialisms; strengths; weaknesses; who else they work for
- *budgets* – typical costs: for example, how long/how much to produce a press notice? What does a minute of finished video run out at?
- *guidelines and checklists* – encapsulations of lessons to learn, good ideas to borrow, mistakes to avoid

Take whatever information is useful from wherever you can find it.

Physically, the portfolio could be a Filofax or similar, but it doesn't have to be. An ordinary A4 ring binder, of the sort you get at the cut-price stores, is fine; plastic pockets to fit; 2–hole pads; an indexing system. You could put most of the information on a personal computer – which makes it easy to weed out and update – but in some cases, such as colour samples, there is no substitute for the real thing.

Later chapters in this book suggest ways of developing your PR personal portfolio into a working tool of life-long value. There are case histories, checklists and guidelines – look for the identification **PORTFOLIO**. Here is the first one.

■ Setting Realistic Objectives

What do we mean by realistic objectives? Opinions will differ and it is easy to let enthusiasm over-rule realism. These guidelines will help you take a detached, professional view.

PORTFOLIO
Guideline 1.1 – Realistic objectives

1. Be definite and precise. Always set specific objectives.
2. Specific objectives work best when they are action-orientated (a named person doing something).
3. Specific and action-orientated objectives need to be quantified. How many? How much?
4. PR objectives are only worth pursuing if they make a contribution towards the attainment of specific action-orientated and quantified business objectives.
5. Make sure that your objectives are clearly and simply stated.
6. They also need to be known and understood by all concerned.
7. Objectives must actually be attainable within an acceptable timescale. Short term objectives are those you intend to achieve within, say, six months and certainly within a year. For medium term objectives, your timescale might be two or three years. Anything over that is a long term objective, to be worked towards, without prospect of early attainment.
8. However, by the very nature of things, long term objectives become medium term objectives over time, while medium term objectives become short term objectives quite rapidly. Before you know it you can be at panic stations, dealing with an emergency or crisis, whereas you ought to be properly prepared for anything that could happen. The two crucial points are that 'long term' doesn't mean 'never', and 'short term' doesn't necessarily mean 'now'.

9. 4 If your objectives meet all these criteria – none is more important than another, and none less – they will be verifiable.

■ Supporting Business Objectives

Public relations objectives should always bear a relationship to business objectives, and the closer that relationship is, the more effective the programme will be. Third Wave advertising agency Elgie Stewart Smith had four very clear business objectives: to acquire new clients; to take initiatives in the financial sector; to target financial institutions; and to sustain long term business growth. Their PR objectives were equally clear: to attract potential clients; to create awareness of Elgie Stewart Smith's business initiatives; to promote the agency's expertise in financial advertising; and to raise and sustain the profile of the agency over time.[2]

Robert Worcester's objectives for Market Opinion Research International (MORI) associate reputation with performance: to earn a superior reputation; to provide an outstanding level of quality; to create a satisfying working environment; to enrich the wider community's knowledge and understanding of research.[3]

The British Maritime Charitable Foundation claimed to be the only organisation undertaking detailed research across the wider maritime economy. The Federation looked 'to demonstrate the industry's contribution to the overall British economy' – said to be around £30 billion (thousand million) a year – and to 'halt the current decline'. Can I be the only one who thinks that the first of those objectives was more realistic than the second?[4]

■ Awareness and Perception

In Shandwick's 1992 programme to introduce the new 10p piece, the key objective was to raise awareness of the coin as legal tender among the general public before its introduction on 20 September. Sub-objectives were to orchestrate a smooth transition to the new coin, encouraging acceptance and negating any criticism of Ministers, and to generate positive perceptions.

The four main programme elements were as set out below.

1.   1200 information packs were issued to a wide range of media, resulting in extensive coverage in September 1992. The kits contained a short news release; photographic comparison of old and new 10p coins; Royal Mint background leaflet: Questions and Answers; and a *Did you know?* bullet points list.

2. Four months earlier, the Royal National Institute for the Blind was issued with 1000 of the new coins, to aid familiarisation amongst blind and visually impaired people.

3. Building societies and major multiple retailers were asked to include information about the new coin in their house magazines and also to display on-site posters provided by Shandwick. Sixteen out of 20 top building societies and 10 out of 12 top multiple retailers agreed.

4. A taped interview with the Deputy Master of the Royal Mint was syndicated to local radio stations, and 24 ran it. In addition, over 70 other interviews were set up and used on television and radio.

All objectives were achieved.[5]

British Airways' (BA's) PR objectives were nothing less than to achieve worldwide recognition and approval. It may well be that BA achieved one but, to judge by the so-called dirty-tricks episode, it could have been at the expense of the other.

■ Pulling People In

It is sometimes argued that PR can influence opinion but cannot actually shift goods off shelves or put bums on seats. The Harrogate-based Northern Lights consultancy wouldn't agree: they have proved that PR can pull visitors in. Their campaign for the launch of Eureka!, the first UK museum for children, achieved the full-year objective of 200 000 visitors in the first three months, and on the tightest of budgets (see Case 12.1, Chapter 12).

The organisers of the Royal Tournament likewise had a specific, numerical, objective: they needed to achieve an attendance of at least 10 000 people for every one of the 21 scheduled performances, at a time when awareness and understanding were falling off, and when fewer and fewer people had Service connections. How Kestrel Communications tackled that, and what results were obtained, are dealt with in Case 3.5, Chapter 3, and Table 14.3, Chapter 14.

■ Internal PR

Political, military and market changes forced British Aerospace's Military Aircraft Division to make tough decisions on site closures and redundancies which could only be carried through if the workforce understood and accepted their reasoning. A communications programme was devised, with half-a-dozen interdependent objectives: enhance the flow of focused information; create a climate of openness; get all on the payroll to understand and commit themselves to Military Aircraft's business plan; develop wider opportunities for upward communication; involve employees, their families and local communities; and maintain cost-effectiveness.[6]

■ Caring PR

To help recruitment of nurses, Hampstead Health Authority wanted to overcome a local shortage of suitable accommodation available to staff. Dr Barnardo's decided to correct misunderstandings about what the charity actually did, and in the process dispel any stigma there might be about being helped by it. Hands up those who think Hampstead set themselves a more realistic objective than Dr Barnardo's.

By a programme of face-to-face contact, posters in health centres and GP surgeries, Open Days, liaison with a major building society, local advertising and a 24–hour inquiry service, Hampstead won a 60 per cent increase in the amount of accommodation offered to the Authority.[7]

Dr Barnardo's change of name campaign was quite successful temporarily, but since then a revamped strategy proved necessary, with Fishburn Hedges as the chosen consultancy.[8]

■ PR and Marketing

Whoever it was who first defined marketing as 'the entire business seen through the customer's eyes' probably thought that was an unreservedly good thing. Companies that are marketing-driven focus on the customer to the exclusion of almost all others who have a stake in the business. Clear customer strategies; well thought out programmes for customers; tightly controlled, customer-weighted budgets; saleable, customer-friendly products; good outlets in places convenient for customers; prices acceptable to customers; when firms which do all this are successful, they can be very successful indeed.

During economic recessions, when budgets are tight, there can be an increasing tendency to use PR to launch niche products, premium products and new concept products. This objective is most likely to be attained when PR is part of a balanced marketing strategy.

There could hardly be a more narrow product definition than premium brand ice creams. Häagen-Dazs's television and cinema ads campaign raised the brand's 1991/93 market share from 9 per cent to 20 per cent. But what got the brand to its 9 per cent position in the first place? Public relations. Biss Lancaster had the job of educating a public to pay 40 per cent more for Häagen-Dazs than for the market leaders like Walls and Mr Whippy.

If premium brand ice cream is a narrow product definition, what about self-assembly salad dressing? HP Foods salad vinaigrette 'Just Add Oil' was launched by Welbeck Golin/Harris, using media relations.

According to Alison Clarke, Deputy Managing Director of Welbeck:

> Our objective was to generate third party endorsement through leading food and cookery journalists, but we had to do it under the banner of education. This is the first salad dressing product on the market that requires an element of what you might call self-assembly, and we needed to communicate that fact. Therefore in launching to journalists we created heavy tasting opportunities in addition to simple communication of our message.

Chapter 3 examines the relationship between PR and marketing in more detail.

■ Change as an Objective

All these objectives are different from each other, but they all have one thing in common: they are intended to bring about a specific change or changes in awareness, knowledge, understanding, perception, opinion, belief, attitude or behaviour. The changes are achieved by means of an appropriate campaign or programme, within a given timescale and to a budget.

Some changes may be easier than others. According to Robert Worcester, founder of the MORI research company:

- *opinion* is shallow and easily changed
- *attitudes* are the stronger currents beneath the surface
- *values* are the deep tides of public mood; slow to change, but powerful[9]

■ Ask a Policeman

However, there are occasions when the whole purpose of a PR campaign or programme is to oppose change and maintain the status quo; but, strangely enough, that also involves change.

For example, the Police Federation, which represents 125 000 lower-ranking officers in England and Wales, allocated £1m to a campaign to keep the same structure and organisation, the same system of remuneration, the same responsibilities and reporting procedures; in short, no change at all. What the campaign was really about, however, was not just opposing the government's reforms, but actively persuading them to change their minds and their policy.

The most comprehensive overhaul of British policing since the war was derived from four major pieces of work: a White Paper on structure, a consultative document on discipline, the Sheehy Report on pay and conditions, and the Royal Commission on Criminal Justice. The Police Federation was not overjoyed with any of it.

The Federation's objective of safeguarding its own central negotiating role was endorsed by sister organisations in Scotland and Wales. That is hardly surprising. Less predictable, perhaps, was the backing from the Police Superintendents' Association; until you realise that one of the proposed reforms was to abolish the rank of Chief Superintendent. A former Prime Minister joined in – he had been an Adviser to the Federation – plus a Chief Constable or two. Opposition MPs and Government backbenchers weighed in, largely because they wanted to see the same police/government partnership in London as applied everywhere else.

This consortium of dissenters, advised by Westminster Strategy, ran a PR programme that included full-page advertisements in selected national newspapers, a huge rally at London's Wembley Arena, local press advertising, Parliamentary lobbying and ear-bending of the main political parties at their annual autumn conferences.

■ The Timescale of Change

Some of the changes we have discussed were supposed to happen in a relatively short time; others had a longer timespan. If you want change to happen, make every attempt to see changes through the eyes of the people involved. That is essentially the PR approach.

Nothing can be taken for granted amid the uncertainties of business. If a change is significant, can it be anything other than disturbing? It is pretty well bound to put some people's noses out of joint. Better to accept that change is disruptive and that some people lose out, but make sure that your company or your clients are not among them.

The curious thing about change is that there is never as much of it as we would like in our lives, but neither is there as much stability. This paradox explains why the cycle of change – status quo . . . awareness . . . encounter . . . reflection . . . letting go – is often interrupted. It is because a conflict develops between a conscious desire for change and an unconscious desire to avoid change.

■ The KAP Hypothesis

The well-known KAP hypothesis of the process of change – knowledge . . . attitude . . . practice – may be too linear to accord with our practical experience, as this example illustrates.

Suppose Jon is about to purchase a new car. All the research through reading car magazines and talking to friends (knowledge) might point to model X being the 'best buy' in the view of the experts. So, on a bright Saturday morning, armed with this knowledge, Jon sets out to buy his car at the local showroom. It also just happens to be his mother's birthday. On the way to the showroom he passes another garage selling model Y, which advertises a free bouquet of roses for anyone taking a test drive that morning. Jon needed a present for his mother, and taking a test drive does not take much time, so Jon stops . . . There may now be a problem.

What if, despite his (cognitive) knowledge that model X is the 'best buy', he drives model Y purely for the free gift, but then falls in love with model Y, experiencing enjoyment in its handling, comfort and general smoothness of ride? Even after going on to test drive the original model X, the feeling of 'rightness' for model Y persists, and as the price is similar, Jon ends up buying model Y.

He might then go back and research (justify) reasons for his choice, so as to align his own knowledge base with the experts. His *practice* (buying the car) was directly affected by his *attitude* (falling in love with the car) but this in turn changed Jon's explanation of his reasons for buying (*knowledge*).

Thus the KAP theory, as a simple, linear, individually centred model, is severely limited as an explanation for why we make the choices we do.[10]

■ No Bouquets

One of the functions of PR is to provide the motivational equivalent of that bouquet of roses. If Ford could have done that, one of the best known disasters of the motor car industry might have turned out very differently. This is what happened.

The Edsel Ford was more thoroughly researched, engineered, styled, marketed and promoted than any car before it had ever been. It was also a flop.

Not enough people bought the Edsel even to cover the development costs, let alone show a return on production and distribution outlay. Nobody knows for sure what went wrong, though there is no shortage of theories. What is sure is that a car programmed to be a winner turned out to be a liability, a real loser.

Would things have been different if Ford had paid more attention to aspects of its business over and above the undisputed need to sell what they believed their customers would buy? Was enough thought given to public relations? What was the perception of a car like the Edsel? Were Edsels too like other cars or too unlike? Cars are bought for some strange reasons (the name can be very important, and Edsel does sound a bit naff) and many more people than the one who pays the bill have an influence on the purchasing decision.

This probably explains why, when Chrysler took over the ailing Rootes Group in the 1960s, they focused PR campaigns on the 'enormous improvements' that took place. These included new models of modern design, higher productivity and improved distribution. In fact, nearly all the 'improvements' were reductions, such as fewer models, cost-cutting in the factories and closing down many dealerships. When the new 'myth exploding' models actually appeared, under the brand name *Avenger*, they were practically indistinguishable from their Ford and General Motors competitors. *Motor* magazine described them as 'dull and ordinary looking', though the reviewer did agree that 'well tried techniques made the *Avenger* unusually refined'. Chrysler/Rootes had produced cars the public wanted at a price they were prepared to pay. The success derived 'not from novelty but from simplicity' and the manufacturer's market share, which had fallen to 10 per cent, reached 11 per cent within two years – an increase of 10 per cent in market share. It is very likely that the macho name *Avenger* made a contribution to the success of a very average car. It was no surprise when, in 1994, Chrysler US resurrected the name. The new *Avenger*, 'a sleek new two-door coupé powered by a 2.5 litre V6', sounds a bit like what the old *Avenger* should have been – but in that case would it have been the success it was at the time?.

■ An Unusual Objective

Some of the PR objectives discussed so far are more realistic than others. The fact that an objective is unusual does not necessarily mean that it is unrealistic, especially if you agree with the purpose behind the objective. What do you make of this?

Cardiff-based Christian charity Care for the Family was considering hiring a PR firm to promote what project manager Dave Carlos described as a moral concept. 'Young people get plenty of information about safe sex', he said 'but I'd like to talk to a PR firm about promoting abstinence.'[11] Any takers?

■ Planning and Programmes

To achieve an objective you need a plan, and to carry out a plan you need a programme. Often a plan will focus on one or two main ideas, whereas a programme is a detailed, operational document which spells out ways and means.

Planning campaigns is a matter of making good tactical decisions from a range of options. The PR practitioner can get good results by using some fairly simple management techniques, not in any sense as a substitute for PR know-how, but to support and reinforce it. Many of the cases in this book exemplify the principle of programme planning. These are the first two.

PORTFOLIO
Case 1.1 – Thoughtful, not impulsive

Toyota's integrated operations – engineering and design facilities, manufacturing plants, public relations, marketing and sales support, distribution through over 3400 dealers – spread from Austria to Hungary, Iceland to Switzerland.

The 1994 PR strategy, created with Scope: Communications, was to:

- develop a distinctive corporate image
- support sales by focusing on messages about quality and good working practices
- strengthen the company's existing market position in the face of increased protectionism in Europe
- maintain support of local community and motivate staff
- reinforce corporate citizenship position through the Toyota Science and Technology Education Fund

The company's style was to be thoughtful, not impulsive, and its PR programmes gradual, not sudden.

Twice-yearly strategic evaluation reviews were built in. Papers charting progress and future planning, prepared and discussed by all concerned in the UK, formed the basis of a consensus which then went to Tokyo for further review.[12]

PORTFOLIO
Case 1.2 – A classic plan

Classic FM was the UK's first national commercial radio station and first 24–hour popular classical music station. Before the licence was awarded there were problems – financial, organisational, personal – and many doubted that the station would ever broadcast at all. So Classic FM's prediction that audiences would be around 2.8 million a week was greeted with scepticism even by those who wished the venture well.

Three months after the first programme went on air, 4.3 million listeners were tuning in. How was it done? By thoroughly planned, strategically timed, carefully targeted and highly focused public relations. There was no advertising until much later. According to KBH Communications consultancy, the priority was to forestall credibility problems, maximise publicity and establish a comprehensive communications strategy aimed at potential listeners and advertisers, the business community and the media.

The detailed strategic timetable was in four phases: preparation and early planning; event planning; launching the station; consolidation and follow-up.

In the first phase, key messages were decided, target audiences defined, action plans drawn up and a press information library established (including fact sheets, photographs and a structured mailing list). A separate campaign was devised for the media and the advertising industry. Early contact was made with key broadcast media and publications with long lead times.

In the second phase, a series of news pegs, stories, photocalls, features, promotions, briefings and other events was arranged. Two key personnel acted as 'spokespersons' for the company, especially in the immediate pre-launch period. They were less available once the station went on air.

Phase 3 was the four-week launch period in August–September 1992, when most of the visible PR activities took place: press conferences, photocalls, interviews, Ministerial visits, television filming and regional promotions, as well as a whole battery of back-up services.

The fourth phase focused on Classic FM's longer term PR effort to sustain interest and get the maximum benefit from the interest generated by the launch. Audience figures were publicised as they became available.

KBH Communications calculated that they devoted some 2000 hours to PR for Classic FM. This was over a period of nine months during which expenses totalled £34 000, covering press liaison, video production, photography, special events, press mailings and office administration.[13] (For Media Measurement's evaluation turn to Figure 14.1, Chapter 14.)

∎ Assessment

Would you think that analysis of everyday crime statistics by a provincial police officer could lead to something new and powerful enough to persuade the government to alter the law? That was the objective of a campaign by the Avon and Somerset Constabulary. To find out what happened, turn to Case 14.1, Chapter 14. There is a lot to learn from it.

But what can we learn from a case that happened over a century ago? That you have to come clean on what your objective really is, before you can tell what constitutes a successful result.

PORTFOLIO
Case 1.3 – The obscene monster

When Emile Zola, the French journalist and novelist, was invited to address the 1893 annual general meeting of Britain's Institute of Journalists, he was sceptical.

'What is this Institute of Journalists?' he asked R. H. Sherard, his biographer. 'Has it any influence? I have no wish to see London and I have no desire to be fêted. If I consent to go, it will be with a view to advancing interest in my books in England.'

'People in England', replied Sherard, 'have been taught to consider you an obscene monster. You will be seen at this gathering of journalists from all parts of the three kingdoms. They will be proud and delighted to have met you and they will make it known what kind of man you are.' He might also have thought that it wouldn't do his own reputation any harm.

Zola accepted and saw a good deal of London – the Savoy Hotel, Drury Lane Theatre, the Imperial Institute, Crystal Palace, the Mansion House, the Press Club – and was fêted everywhere. Well pleased with his visit, he said that the results could only be good. He was not entirely right.

Certainly, Sherard's PR programme achieved Zola's stated aim of stimulating interest in his books in Britain. However, it did not lead to a greatly improved reputation in Paris. Consequently he never attained his true, long term, but unstated, objective of election to the French Academy.[14]

■ What PR Cannot Do

In this chapter we have looked at PR campaigns which had more or less realistic objectives, plans and programmes. We have discussed the success or otherwise of these campaigns and how that was assessed. The assumption has been that what was attempted could actually be done through the exercise of public relations. Just as we need to be clear about that, so we need to be clear about what PR cannot do.

■ Public Relations Cannot Confer Credibility, Unless Content, Source and Method of Delivery are Credible

□ *Content*

Does what is said match your experience and expectations?

Sales of the traditional timber preservative creosote were threatened by knocking copy advertisements for some branded preservatives, which were claimed to be more effective.

The creosote traders set up their own Council and complained to the Independent Broadcasting Authority, the Advertising Standards Authority and Internal Complaints Bureau about what they saw as the scurrilous and inaccurate claims of the brands. At the same time an aggressive PR campaign was launched by the Council.

Knocking copy stopped, but it is not at all clear that there was an associated increase in sales of creosote. Could it be that customers and consumers perceived brands as having user-friendly attributes like ease of application?

☐ *Source*

Do you trust the bearer of the message?

In a MORI survey of believability, a large sample of adults was asked, 'Who do you trust to tell the truth?' Top of the credibility list came teachers and doctors, followed by clergymen/priests. Television newsreaders scored a respectable fourth place, with professors and judges not far behind. Right in the middle of the rankings came 'ordinary people'. The lower half of the table started with the police, then, in descending order, came pollsters, civil servants, union officials, business leaders, politicians and government ministers. Last of all, and therefore seen as the least believable of any, came journalists.[15] PR practitioners were not even on the list.

If the MORI survey were to be repeated after ten years, the pecking order might not be the same, and could be different again a decade after that. But I suspect that then, now, in the future, and every time, the slot at the bottom of the list would be occupied by journalists. That is very curious, because the words spoken by those trusted television newsreaders are written by journalists, who also write at least some of what is said or signed by others who are rated more believable than they are themselves.

☐ *Method*

Do the chosen media and the tone of voice reinforce what is said and who says it?

Advertising cannot do the job of public relations, if only because it has a built-in factor which automatically reduces credibility. Exaggeration, playing on words and excess repetition – these are some of the reasons; but mainly it is because people know that advertisements are controlled and paid for by the advertiser. Testimonial advertising tries to get around this, but third party endorsements work best below the line.

Advertising makes you aware of a product, and if it is one of the cheaper, fast-moving, consumer goods you don't risk much if you buy it, or lose much if you don't like it. For more serious purchases, like hi-fi, computers or financial products, the risk is greater and the cost of getting it wrong is higher. You want to share the decision with others, such as your family, and you look for a convincing demonstration, a good review, an authoritative assessment, or a personal recommendation to help you make up your mind to buy.

■ **PR Cannot Do the Job of Advertising**

'There's no way you can launch a major fmcg [fast-moving consumer goods] product into a mature market without advertising.'[16] PR can support advertising, just as advertising can support PR. And when it comes to launching niche products, PR can work very well, as we have seen. But the basic job of advertising is to tell and sell.

■ PR Cannot Build Reputations Overnight

Media stunts can generate almost instant coverage, or hit the television screens while they actually happen. Sales campaigns produce results within weeks, especially when boosted by massive advertising. Do not expect a quick response from a PR campaign intended to build a reputation, even when it is thoroughly deserved.

■ PR Cannot Sustain a Reputation that is not Deserved

If what your company does is different from what it says, what do you think will be said about your company?

■ Public Relations Cannot Substitute for an Absent or Unconvincing Product

It was reported in February 1994 that leading computer software manufacturer Microsoft owed much of its success to the integration of PR with advertising and direct marketing. Microsoft Windows New Technology (NT) was launched in May 1993 to 5000 potential customers over two days. Although there had been a separate press launch earlier, journalists were invited to 'extend media coverage of the product'. Microsoft, Text 100 and Ogilvy & Mather between them achieved for Windows NT 'one of the highest awareness ratings of any Microsoft product launched'.

No doubt that comment on awareness was fully justified: but what is the advantage of being aware of a product that is not available? Here is a report from the trade press.

> Journalists and other ne'er-do-wells were invited to the official lunch [sic] of Windows NT . . . We did not see NT . . . But we did sit through an interminable lecture . . . then we sat through an equally long live link from Atlanta . . . In between we sat through a very good lunch . . . Windows NT is the most heavily hyped software of all time . . . even though you cannot buy it.

Noting that NT would bring no obvious benefits to a desktop PC user and had cost Microsoft $150m to develop, the reviewer concludes: 'It will have to spend a great deal more before Windows NT achieves respectability, let alone a significant market share . . . So do not expect Windows NT to take the world by storm. Expect a slight drizzle over the next decade.'[17]

■ PR Cannot Explain Away a Bad Policy, or Turn it into a Good one

Roger Haywood, Chairman of Kestrel Communications, was realistic and credible when he pointed out the following.

WE DO NOT	manage our client companies, though we often make positive comments on business plans and add business ideas.
WE DO NOT	win the sales, though we can often help create the environment which leads to inquiries, and confidence in the products and services our clients offer.
WE DO NOT	write the legislation, though we often present evidence to the right levels of influence along the corridors of power to help shape such legislation to meet our clients' best interest.
NOR DO WE	make the shareholders invest, though we can keep them informed to ensure their loyalty and goodwill.
WHAT WE CAN DO	is to evaluate the opinions and attitudes of the audiences upon whom an organisation depends for its success; and structure programmes of communication to help create the best environment within which the organisation can operate.[18]

■ The PR Perspective

The Governor of the Bank of England put the whole thing in perspective when he addressed the IPR's City and Financial Group. 'Company Chairmen', he said, 'cannot assume that paying large sums for a PR consultancy will save them from taking an active and personal interest in how the company's relationships are handled.'[19]

You may wonder who are the lucky consultancies who get paid sums of money that even the Bank of England describes as large, but you can't fault the inference. PR is neither a panacea nor a whipping boy. Chairmen and Chief Executives bear the ultimate accountability for the reputation of their firms, therefore they have to take an 'active and personal interest' in the management of reputation.

■ An Unwritten Law

None of which alters the inescapable facts of business life. An unwritten law states that when a company has a good reputation, it's because its policies are good, whereas a bad reputation is entirely due to bad communications. As they say in horseracing, when you win, you're on a good horse: when you lose, you're a rotten jockey.[20]

Ask any politician.

CHAPTER 2

Choosing and Using Public Relations

Public Relations . . . is the top-level employment of the management function, and colours – or should colour – every action which concerns a public or an attitude or an opinion about the company.

E. F. L. Brech[1]

■ A Management Function

In many cases, a company's introduction to PR can be by way of a PR project. A particular need is identified, perhaps not very sharply, a programme devised and carried out and, once the occasion is past, the PR toolkit is put away until next time. It is a better introduction to PR than no introduction at all, and some effective programmes can arise in this way. However, there is more to be gained by treating PR as part of a policy of ongoing communication: and that is a management function.

Are PR practitioners functional specialists? In the opening stages of their careers, yes, though management responsibilities can come fairly swiftly. More and more are now progressing to top management, as board directors or heads of departments.

The IPR suggests that any or all of the following could be involved in the management of PR.

- Anticipating, analysing and interpreting public opinion, attitudes and issues which might impact, for good or ill, on the operations and plans of the organisation.
- Counselling management at all levels in the organisation with regard to policy decisions, courses of action and communication, taking into account their public ramifications, and the organisation's social or citizenship responsibilities.
- Researching, conducting and evaluating, on a continuing basis, programmes of action and communication to achieve informed public understanding necessary to the success of an organisation's aims. These may include marketing; fundraising; financial, employee, community or government relations; and other programmes.

- Planning and implementing the organisation's efforts to influence or change public policy.
- Setting objectives, planning, budgeting, recruiting and training staff, developing facilities: in short, managing the resources needed to perform all the above.
- Examples of the knowledge that may be required in the professional practice of PR include the principles of management and ethics, sociology, psychology, politics and economics. Technical knowledge and skills are required for opinion research, public issues analysis, media relations, direct mail, institutional advertising, publications, film/video productions, exhibitions, special events, speeches and presentations.[2]

■ Symmetrical PR

Symmetrical PR – better known as two-way PR – is a dialogue between those affecting what an organisation does, and those affected by what it does. In any dialogue the *ear* is the control. Make sure you know what input the ears need from you: and when it is your turn to be the ear, listen; then act.

You will find that there are many interests, pre-occupations, apprehensions, demands and counter-demands to reconcile. It is not a case of just one dialogue, but many. Some will be strident, some restrained. All will involve 'stakeholders': that is, the people and organisations, internal and external, who are the many publics who add up to 'the public'. There are over 100 of them on this checklist.

PORTFOLIO
Checklist 2.1 – Stakeholders

To make a personalised list of your own stakeholders, you could go through those set out below and discard those that you are sure don't matter to you. If in the slightest doubt, leave them in. Pay particular attention to stakeholders who are not on this list and should be on yours. They are *your additions*. Add them.

ACADEMICS	THE BOSS	COMPETITORS
ACCOUNTANTS	BUSINESS CLUBS	COMPLAINERS
ADVISERS	BUSINESS SCHOOLS	CONSULTANTS
AGENTS	CHAMBERS OF COMMERCE	CONSUMERISTS
ANALYSTS	CHARITIES	CONSUMERS
AUDITORS	CLIENTS	CONTRACTORS
BACKERS	COMMENTATORS	CREDIT-RATING AGENCIES
BANKERS	COMMITTEES	CUSTOMERS
BOARD OF DIRECTORS	COMMUNITY GROUPS	DEBENTURE HOLDERS

DECISION MAKING UNITS
DIRECTORS OF
  ASSOCIATED
    COMPANIES
DISTRIBUTORS
EDUCATORS
EMPLOYEES
EMPLOYERS'
  ORGANISATIONS
ENVIRONMENTALISTS
ETHNIC MINORITIES
EXPERTS
FAMILIES (of employees)
FINANCE PROVIDERS
FINANCIAL JOURNALISTS
FRONT-OF-HOUSE:
  COUNTER STAFF
  DRIVERS
  LIFT ATTENDANTS
  MESSENGERS
  SERVICE ENGINEERS
  TELEPHONISTS
  OTHERS
FUNDRAISERS
GOVERNMENT OFFICIALS:
  LOCAL
  CENTRAL
  EUROPEAN
  INTERNATIONAL
'GREENS'
HOUSEHOLDERS
INDUSTRY
  ORGANISATIONS
INVESTORS
JOB SEEKERS
LEGISLATORS
LENDERS

LOBBYISTS
LOCAL COMMUNITY
MANAGERS
MARKETING
  DEPARTMENT
MEDIA:
  LOCAL
  SPECIALIST
  TECHNICAL
  NATIONAL
  INTERNATIONAL
MOTORISTS
NEIGHBOURS
OVERSEAS VISITORS
OWNERS
POLITICIANS:
  LOCAL
  NATIONAL
  EUROPEAN
  INTERNATIONAL
PREDATORS
PRESSURE GROUPS
PRICE CONTROL BODIES
PROFESSIONAL
  INSTITUTES
PROTECTIONISTS
REGULATORY BODIES
RETAILERS
RETIRED PEOPLE
SALESFORCE
SCHOOLCHILDREN
SHAREHOLDERS
SHIPPERS
SHOPFLOOR WORKERS
SPECIFIERS
SPONSEES
SPONSORS

STATISTICIANS
STATUTORY BODIES
STOCKBROKERS
SUB-CONTRACTORS
SUBSCRIBERS
SUPPLIERS
TAX AUTHORITIES
TAXPAYERS
TRADE ASSOCIATIONS
TRADE UNIONS
TRANSLATORS
VISITORS
VOTERS
WHOLESALERS
X-GROUP:
  EX-CONTRACTORS
  EX-CUSTOMERS
  EX-INVESTORS
  EX-STAFF
  EX-SUPPLIERS
YOUR ADDITIONS

Keep your Checklist of Stakeholders under constant review. Make changes as circumstances change.

■ Some Management Issues Affecting Stakeholders

Because PR is a function of management, it will need to take full account of the important issues of the day – and tomorrow, too – which affect and will affect the business, everyone in it and everyone connected with it. In other words, the issues that will affect stakeholders. What are these issues likely to be?

PORTFOLIO
Checklist 2.2 – Management in the twenty-first century

The Institute of Management held interviews with leading opinion formers. These highlighted some key issues likely to affect the future environment in which UK organisations will have to operate. How do you rank them in order of importance?

Persistent high levels of structural unemployment and associated social issues .... □

Standards of education which are inappropriate to the needs of employers .... □

Financial pressures of an ageing population on the state and those in employment .... □

Increasing competitive pressures from low wage economies .... □

Rapid pace of technological change in all aspects of business life .... □

Saturation of 'traditional' markets .... □

Increasing competitive pressures from developed economies .... □

Integration of the European Union leading to further regulations on UK industry .... □

Difficulties of predicting accurately the future operating environment .... □

Changing values in society that influence the balance between home and work life .... □

Rise of well informed, articulate and discriminating customers and consumer groups ...... □

Impact of environmental or 'green' issues on business behaviour .... □

Others (be specific)[3] .... □

The people who will be dealing with these issues are the people you will be working with. What sort of people are we looking for?

■ Recruiting

In the late 1980s, the Institute of Manpower Studies (IMS) undertook research into what companies were looking for when recruiting or selecting management staff. The IMS analysed what criteria were actually applied in the selection process. They found that what most impressed the recruiters was *brainpower*. What did they mean?

Well, *brainpower* is not the same thing as intelligence, which is a quality that in some degree can be measured against agreed criteria. Intelligence tests are a well known fact of life in education, the armed services, industry, commerce and government. You don't hear much about brainpower tests because they have made nothing like the same inroads. You could perhaps describe brainpower as a combination of intellect, intelligence and imagination. All the best managers have it, and early signs of it are eagerly looked for. It may not be easy to define, but it is unmistakable when you come across it.

Next in importance to brainpower in the IMS study came *communication*. No matter how powerful your brain, if you can't get through to people, how can you manage them? Clearly that is important in any business: in the communication business itself it is indispensable. It is, of course, a two-way process: dialogue, not monologue; conversation, not lecture; consent, not command.

Third was *self-motivation*. If you always have to be told what to do, you'll end up either doing what nobody else wants to, or what doesn't actually need doing at all, whereas if you demonstrate that you are capable of starting your own engine and running your own programme, sooner or later you will be allowed, then expected, then trusted to do just that.

The fourth of the key selection criteria is *personal maturity*. What that means is being your age, for your age. Nobody wants 20-year-old greybeards: but being young for your age is only an advantage when you are, in fact, no longer young.

Those are the four top indicators that people look for when selecting junior or potential managers in any business.[4] Over and above that, what do they look for when recruiting into the PR business?

The IPR and the PRCA agree on the need to ensure that all people practising public relations, in-house or consultancy, have the highest levels of skills that can be attained. There are, of course, essential differences between working on PR in a business organisation and in a PR consultancy (this book illustrates some of these); but there are many similarities, and most of the requisite skills serve equally well in either capacity.

The following two portfolios are about the pre-entry requirements as spelt out in the PR Education and Training Matrix of the IPR and PRCA. The first is about knowledge, the second about skills.

PORTFOLIO
Checklist 2.3 – PR knowledge

1.   What do you know about the role of public relations, both in-house and consultancy, in commercial and public sector organisations?
     If you haven't thought seriously about that, why on earth are you trying to get into PR anyway?
2.   Do you have an appreciation of the range of techniques and media available to PR practitioners in the UK?
     You have been, are, and will be, on the consuming end of many of these techniques, so you are equipped to have a view even before you have started working in PR.
3.   How well informed are you on the legal, legislative and regulatory framework of Britain and the EU?
     You can't make sense of what's going on if you don't know the framework.[5]

PORTFOLIO
Checklist 2.4 – PR skills

1. Can you set an agenda for a meeting? Take notes and write them up? Play a constructive part?
   Well-prepared and well-run meetings make a vital contribution; otherwise they are a waste of time.
2. Are your letters clear, concise, effective? There is no such thing as business English.
   Business letters are written in plain English.
3. Can you write a good memo?
   Put down everything that is necessary, and nothing that isn't.
4. Are you happy turning out regular progress reports and turning them in on time?
   All concerned need to be clear on what action is to be taken, by whom, and when.
5. Have you learned how to put a contacts list together and keep it updated? That's pedestrian but important.
   Any business needs contacts. The PR business lives by them.
6. What about the telephone? It's a tool that you can't do without.
   The better you use the phone, the better your overall performance will be.
7. Are you good at working in a team? In public relations, you have to be, whether your co-members are inside the firm or outside (contractors, journalists and so on).
   Although there are some famous solo acts in PR, nobody can do anything entirely on their own.
8. Can you work as part of an organisation? PR can affect every aspect of an organisation's activities, and is central to most of them.
   You have to be able to work with the system.
9. What about planning your own workflow and setting your own priorities? You need to start doing that from Day One, but not in isolation.
   Your workflow has to fit in with and reinforce the workflow of others.[6]

All that is only the pre-entry stage. When you are actually in the team, the requirements are more demanding. We will come on to those in Chapter 11.

■ In-House versus Consultancy

The title of this section is not to be interpreted as meaning that in-house practitioners and consultancies are adversaries. Each have their own strengths and weaknesses, and the decision on which way to go should be made as objectively as possible. Increasingly, the conclusion now is to use both. They can be more formidable in combination than in competition.

The main strength of the *in-house* PR team is that it is part of the organisation and its culture. That is also a weakness. The in-house team is conversant with company policy, structure and procedures, so there is none of that to learn. On the other hand, it can be very difficult to propose credible alternatives from inside.

The main strength of the *consultancy* is a fresh point of view. That is also a weakness. The consultancy can question and challenge every aspect of policy, structure and procedures with an open mind. On the other hand, there is a learning curve to master first.

Another plus for the *in-house* team is that everybody knows everybody and there are recognised lines of communication. On the other hand, consideration of rank and relative status can inhibit freedom of access. A *consultancy* can usually home in on top management, but there is a price-tag attached.

Then there are PR skills. The *in-house* team can be assumed to have those that are wanted regularly and/or frequently. On the other hand, this means that additional skills have to be bought-in at extra cost.

Table 2.1 Purchasers' expectations of individual services

From consultancies		From in-house
1	Media/press relations	1
2	Message of the campaign	2
3	Advice on key issues	5
4	Special events/functions	3
5	Corporate PR	4
6	Problem definition	10
7	Audience determination	11
8	Advice on public affairs	7
9	Crisis management	8
10	Lobbying	16
11	Financial PR	17
12	Input into wider business decisions	9
13	Design services	14
14	Employee communications	6
15	Issues management counselling	18
16	Sponsorship	13
17	Exhibitions	12
18	International	15

Note: The first 14 are thought essential services for in-house departments to provide; only the first five for consultancies.

Source: *IPR Journal*, April 1994. Research conducted by Gillian Hogg for Stirling University supported by IPR's Scotland Group and Scottish Enterprise.

A *consultancy* may be expected to muster a wide range of in-depth skills. On the other hand, this can mean that a client company could find itself paying for more than it needs.

What services you as a purchaser expect depends on your point of view, though pretty nearly everybody puts media services at the top of their list. Table 2.1 shows the results of some research carried out in Scotland in 1994.

In-house salaries and salary costs per hour tend to be lower but have to be paid regardless. A *consultancy* is only paid for the hours actually logged, or services provided, though at a higher price per hour.

Here is a simplified checklist to help steer you through the process of choosing.

PORTFOLIO
Checklist 2.5 – Choosing a PR consultancy

1. Why do you need a PR consultancy?
   added skills
   breadth of experience
   depth of back-up
   creativity
   time
   objectivity
2. What sort of consultancy do you need?
   full service
   subject/sector specialist
   skills specialist
   local/national/international
   hot shop
3. How do you find suitable consultancies?
   personal experience
   own company experience
   experience of comparable companies
   marketing and trade press
   asking journalists
   PR industry sources (see Appendix A)
4. How do you select your contenders?
   agree objectives and criteria with colleagues
   discuss outline brief with long list
   set up credentials pitches, with supporting documentation
   discuss budgets and methods of charging
   shortlist three or four consultancies whose chemistry and fit feel right
   clear all outstanding contractual arrangements with other consultancies
   if there is already an incumbent, do not invite them to pitch if you have
      no intention of re-engaging them

5. The pitch
    tell each of the short-listed consultancies how many are pitching, but not who they are
    do not expect to pay pitch fees unless agreed in advance (for example, for very detailed recommendations)
    give all short-listed contenders exactly the same brief
    tell them who will be involved in the final yes/no decision
    be fair and open about budgets
    expect consultancies to be equally open with you
    decide in advance how much time and information you are willing to provide; be even-handed
    be prepared for initiatives and insights by consultancies; encourage them
    set a timescale (three weeks?) for return of written responses to the brief
    hold presentations as soon after that as you can, and as close together as you can
    the people who make the final decision ought to attend all the presentations.
6. The decision
    work to an agreed checklist as your basis for comparing consultancies
    check on who would actually be working on your account; insist on meeting and talking to them all
    sort out budgets and charging systems
    check references, especially from satisfied clients
    come to your final decision quickly
    tell the winners and the losers[7]

■ Outputs, not Inputs

Quite often a PR consultancy can provide administrative and back-up services more cheaply than you can yourself. That's because they need to have on instant call what you may only require occasionally (such as messengers to take an urgent proof halfway across town or deliver a press notice direct to a journalist). Of course it has to be paid for, and if you ask them, the good consultancies will give you a detailed breakdown of where your money goes. Very good consultancies do it without being asked, but that's part of a tendency to concentrate on inputs, whereas what you need to monitor is outputs, having first agreed them with the consultancy.

Keep a running check.

● Have you got to where you should be at this point in the schedule?
● Have you spent what you should have spent?

- If you are underspending or overspending, how is that affecting the PR programme?
- Are you achieving what you mean to?
- Can the consultancy demonstrate and prove that they can provide what you need better and more cost-effectively than you can do it yourself?
- If not, you shouldn't have hired them.

Note that I said 'what you need', not 'what you want'. You may argue that they're always the same thing, and I hope for your sake you're right. But if you happen to be like most other people, including me, you could use some impartial advice on separating what you want from what you actually need. That is one of the best services a consultancy can offer you.

■ Matching Client to Consultancy

The PRCA's computerised referral system matches client needs to consultancy skills.

From Aerospace to Travel Destinations, by way of Chemicals, Fashion, Insurance and Office Equipment, 77 distinct *sectors of the economy* are listed. Among the 46 PR *functions* identified are Advertising Services, Crisis Management, Media Relations and Speech Writing. Other parameters are preferred *location* of consultancy (choose one from 14); *size* (five options); and estimated initial *PR budget* per annum. From its 150 member companies and registered individuals, the PRCA reckons to come back with a maximum of five recommendations which fulfil the client's requirements. All the recommended consultancies will conform to the PRCA Charter which obliges them to follow an agreed professional code of conduct (see Appendix C).

There is no need, of course, to select a consultancy from the PRCA membership, or to restrict yourself to their recommendations. Other methods of selection are discussed in Checklist 2.5. It would, however, be advisable to require that the consultancy follows the PRCA code.

The more you know about the consultancy industry, the better equipped you are to choose. (See also Chapter 12, on paying for PR.)

■ What Consultancies Earn

In fees and mark-up, the top 150 PR consultancies earned £254.3m in the calendar year 1994, an increase of 15 per cent on the previous year. The top firm, Shandwick, took £23.5m, and the top 10 took £103.7m between them. Nearly 60 per cent of the top 150 earned less than £1m apiece, and only 7 per cent took over £5m each (see Figure 2.1).

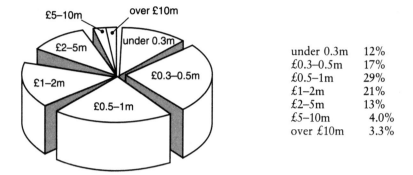

under 0.3m	12%
£0.3–0.5m	17%
£0.5–1m	29%
£1–2m	21%
£2–5m	13%
£5–10m	4.0%
over £10m	3.3%

Source: PR *Week*, 28 April 1995.

Figure 2.1   Earnings of top 150 public relations consultancies

Although the majority of consultancies in the top 150 had their head office in London, about 40 per cent were regionally based, including one in the top 10 and three in the top 20.[8]

■ Staff Deployment in Consultancies

A total of 2998 women and 1476 men were employed in the top 150 PR consultancies in 1994, an increase of 12 per cent on the previous year. The percentage who were executives were about the same for both, at 53 per cent in each case. Part-time staff, including consultants, accounted for 4 per cent of women and 2 per cent of men. The two big discrepancies were at the extremes: 33 per cent of the men were directors or partners, while 34 per cent of the women were support staff; whereas 9 per cent of women were at director or partner level, and 12 per cent of men carried out the support function (see Figure 2.2).[9]

■ Managing Consultancies

Detailed consideration of the management of PR consultancies is outside the scope of this book, but Alison Canning – when Managing Director of Cohn & Wolfe – and Liz Fraser – Managing Director of Tenet Public Relations – boiled down what experience had taught them into a short checklist. This is it.

PORTFOLIO
Checklist 2.6 – How to run a consultancy

1. Have a convincing, professional front person.
2. Set up good financial management.
3. Major clients look for personal service, not being passed down to junior staff.
4. The pitch process can take up to nine months, or more.
5. Be aware of other disciplines when pitching for accounts.
6. Corporate communications has become a board-level function.
7. Be down to earth.
8. Essential personal qualities: be mad; have self-control and self-discipline; and stamina.[10]

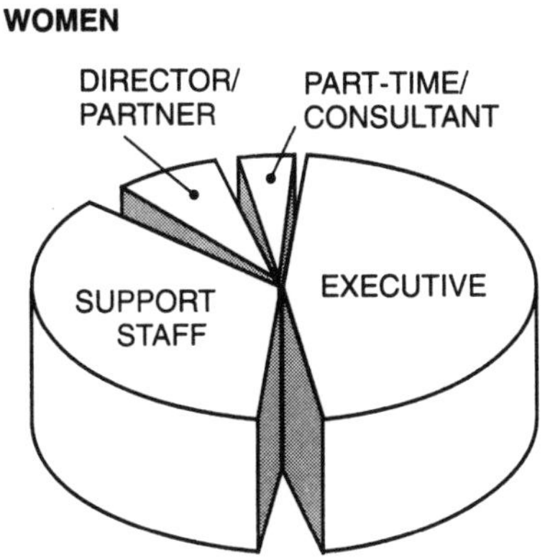

53% executive
34% support staff
 9% director/partner
 4% part-time/consultant

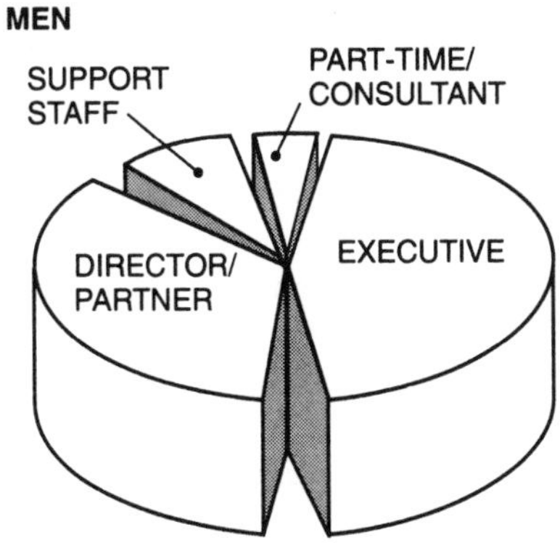

53% executive
33% director/partner
12% support staff
 2% part-time/consultant

Source: PR *Week*, 28 April 1995.

Figure 2.2   Staffing levels in top 150 public relations consultancies

■ When In-House and Consultancy Combine

Increasingly in the 1990s you find that even organisations with perfectly good in-house PR resources of their own go outside to a consultancy. This is not usually as an alternative to the in-house capability, still less in contention with it. But as we have seen, there are some things that PR consultancies do best and some that in-house PR is better at. A mixture of in-house and consultancy is often a good way of using the strengths of both, and neutralising the weaknesses.

Here's how combining in-house and consultancy might work for an upmarket range of casual and sports clothes for children. Let's call the brand Junior Champs.

PORTFOLIO
Case 2.1 – Junior Champs

Before we get into such matters as the budget, and measuring results, we need to ask ourselves four questions.

- Who are we talking to?
- What will we say to them?
- How will we reach them?
- Who does what?

1. *Who are we talking to?*
    There are probably four main groups we need to reach:

    (a) children who will wear Junior Champs
    (b) their peers, who have to accept Junior Champs as OK for the age group
    (c) teachers, trainers, coaches and other leaders from the schools and clubs you want to endorse Junior Champs
    (d) parents, who will actually buy Junior Champs.

    Each of these groups will have different needs and expectations. Each needs to be addressed with a message that is right for the particular group. Each message needs to be conveyed through the most effective channel.

2. *What will we say to them?*

    (a) to the children who will wear Junior Champs, we say that the clothes will not only make them look good and feel good, but can actually improve their performance

(b) to their peers, we say that anybody wearing Junior Champs is instantly recognisable as part of an in-group, which they could belong to, and should

(c) to leaders in schools and clubs we say that the gear is good and appropriate, that there is good back-up and company involvement, and that special deals can be arranged

(d) to the parents we emphasise the reasonable price and high quality of Junior Champs (we might even imply that their children will love them for buying them Junior Champs).

3.   *How do we reach them?*

(a) Children who will wear Junior Champs – mainly consumers, but some will also be customers – can be reached through:

- features, interviews, stories in children's and teenage media
- in-store promotions
- breakfast food tie-ins
- competitions with local press and radio
- Junior Champs touring sportshow
- T-shirts
- endorsement by leading sportsmen and women.

(b) Peer group influencers and potential consumers can be reached as with children, but with emphasis on status and lifestyle rather than product.

(c) Teachers, trainers, coaches, youth leaders (influencers and potential customers) can be reached through:

- joint ventures with youth, sports, and athletics clubs
- sponsorship of clubs and school teams
- competitions
- survey and report on importance of right equipment in improving performance
- features in educational and sports press
- picture stories in general press
- direct mail
- support to sports charities.

(d) Parents, the main customers and (they hope) influencers, can be reached through:

- advertising in women's magazines, consumer and general media
- advertorials and infomercials
- television advertising at key sales periods

- Christmas specials
- 'local kids make Junior Champs' in local media
- direct mail
- support to high-profile children's charity.

4. *Who does what?*

- overall coordination – PR consultancy
- national and specialist media relations – PR consultancy
- local media relations – in-house PR
- charities – direct involvement of Junior Champs staff
- sponsorship – PR consultancy/specialists
- advertising – advertising agency
- endorsements – PR consultancy/specialists
- direct mail – PR consultancy/specialists
- events and competitions – specialist consultancy
- research – independent specialists jointly with an academic institution
- final accountability – the Chief Executive of Junior Champs.

The whole approach to the campaign should be responsible and informative, and non-pressurising. We are not aiming to create Junior Champs junkies, hooked on a high-priced status symbol, are we? We are making a genuine effort to help youngsters improve their fitness and health and reach their own physical potential: aren't we?

■ Reassurance

Mail order catalogues are an established feature of the retail trade. Home shoppers are comfortable with them, placing their orders confidently either through a local agent, who is usually somebody very like themselves, or direct. Clothing, household goods and children's toys predominate, though there is significant business in technical gear like telephones, televisions, calculators, desktop computers and faxes.

Small businesses can order everything, from elastic bands to filing cabinets, direct from catalogues. Prices are low; delivery is routinely within 24 hours, there is nothing much to go wrong, and if it does, instant replacement is normal.

It is different in the world of industrial electronics. Installations and applications are more complex, interconnection and hardware/software conflicts more likely, financial and other risks much higher. In these circumstances, a main function of PR is reassurance.

Black Box supplies communications equipment to large industrial end-users and computer companies, through an international catalogue operation listing more than 6000 stock items. The firm employs 100 engineers worldwide and 80 per cent of their job is pre-sales support. What they provide is information and reassurance before the customer buys. Nearly all their work is telephone-based, but they also carry out on-site surveys and aftersales troubleshooting whenever and wherever necessary.

In the UK alone, Black Box sends out 200 000 catalogues. Each year, seven engineers handle 8000 telephone inquiries apiece, mainly as 'sanity checks'. According to managing director Roger Croft, customers like to confirm that what they have read in the catalogue is right and that what they plan to do with the equipment is correct. 'They want', said Croft, 'a human side to the catalogue.' That human side provides the vital reassurance that pays off in 14 000 orders a year worth £7 500 000.[11]

■ The Slow Burn

The official definition of PR talks of 'planned and sustained effort to establish and maintain . . .'. A good example of this kind of slow burn (or drip feed) campaign is The Banana Group's sustained and relatively low budget PR programme over the period 1983/92. In the decade before the campaign started, banana consumption had remained virtually the same year on year. In the corresponding period since 1983, consumption increased by 84 per cent, significantly out-performing the rest of the fresh fruit market. The story is told in full in Case 9.5, Chapter 9, and Figure 14.2, Chapter 14.

■ PR across Frontiers

When your potential audience tops 340 000 000 people in 12 different countries with nine official languages, you want to be sure that you have a set up willing and able to deliver your programme. So when the Consumer Policy Service of the EC needed to develop a detailed and comprehensive information campaign for consumers, 28 European communications companies – including the Worldcom Group – were invited to submit evidence of interest and capability. Subsequently four organisations were invited to make full recommendations.

The Commission had voted a budget and were expecting proposals for an advertising campaign. Worldcom advised that it could not be done that way within the budget, and that in any case advertising was the wrong route. The issues involved – consumer interests, protection and opportunities – were of public concern and needed to be discussed and debated in an informed context. The Worldcom Group, whose British partner is Kestrel Communications, won the tender. How they set about their gigantic task is described in Case 6.4, Chapter 6.

■ Managing Information

Information superhighways will put more and more technology at the service of PR managers and practitioners. Digitised text, audio and video networks – local, national and international – will allow very narrow targeting and on-line access. The provision of 500 channels by the end of the century is perfectly feasible. PR material will be originated, processed and accessed in digital form. Alongside this forthcoming potential for information overload, not to say overkill, more attention needs to be paid to better use of what is already available.

Electronic mailboxing is now in fairly general use but there is much more to e-mail than that. For example, through Telecom Gold, Infopress get at information retrieval systems which they use for independent research into media coverage of clients, actual or potential. They also employ the system to check basic information of the company register type (turnover, profitability, board of directors and so on). This may not seem very revolutionary, but it's surprising how many consultancies don't do it.

■ Policy and Operations

Public relations should be treated as central to the business, department, charity or other organisation. The remaining chapters in this book are about the effect of PR on policies and operations, and the effect of policies and operations on PR. We start with an examination of the relationship between marketing and PR, in terms of what happens in practice.

CHAPTER 3

Public Relations and Marketing

There is no such thing as a general marketing theory.

Gilles Marion[1]

■ A Difference in Perception

At the IPR Sword of Excellence Award 1994 ceremonies in London, Peter Preston, editor of the *Guardian*, confessed to being baffled by the difference between PR and marketing.[2] I know the feeling. If he asked you to enlighten him, what would you tell him?

The answer you would give is bound to depend, to some extent, on what job you do or want to do. One widely accepted view, especially among marketing directors and managers, positions PR as a specialism within marketing. Less commonly, marketing is seen as a sub-section of public relations, and not only by PR practitioners. Both perceptions are valid.

Maybe the simplest distinction is this: marketing focuses on identifying and meeting the needs, interests and aspirations of customers, whereas public relations embraces the concerns of a much wider range of stakeholders, including customers.

The industry itself is in two minds. In 1993 and 1994, 20 per cent of in-house PR departments reported to the marketing director or marketing manager, while 30 per cent drew their budgets from marketing.[3]

Even though the budgeting procedures in a substantial number of firms did not necessarily reflect reporting procedures, it is clear that there is strong support for the belief that PR is part of the marketing resource.

When PR is directed solely or mainly to meeting the needs and expectations of customers, then it is being used as a marketing tool and can be very powerful. Most of this chapter is about that, because that is where much of the practice of PR is carried out. But it is by no means the whole story, as this book abundantly documents.

■ Topicality, Credibility, Involvement

At the 1994 London Conference on Building Brands through Public Relations, Peter Gummer, Chairman of Shandwick, highlighted three principal ways in which PR can contribute to brand strategy: topicality, credibility and involvement.

1. *Topicality*: linking the product with real-time news events.
   Example: The House of Commons cancelled their order for Perrier after the French market leader in bottled water hit a contamination crisis. Highland Spring reacted quickly and delivered their product to No. 10 Downing Street. The photocall made the newspapers and television. The full story of the Infopress Highland Spring campaign is told later in this chapter.
2. *Credibility*: the implied endorsement of a third-party commentator. This generates a degree of trust in consumers which purchased messages never can.
   Example: When Welbeck Golin/Harris launched a salad dressing that required you, the customer, to add the oil, there was great emphasis on getting cookery writers to try it and write about it, outside the context of advertising and advertorials, and all the more effective for that.
3. *Involvement*: creating interactive opportunities.
   Example: Taunton Cider chose to launch their new, light cider, Fres, to a target market of 25–40 year old women. PR consultancy Handel Communications devised a £100 000 programme of regional events, promoted on local radio, and samplings at shopping centres, clubs and pubs, promoted in and with local newspapers.

■ The Business Market

People who know the business press state quite flatly that unless you are selling executive diaries, you are unlikely to need to reach all businessmen.[4] That is just as well, because the cost of getting to all of them would be considerable, and very considerable indeed if you decided to do it through advertising. It is far better to define your market by type of industry, job function, company size, location and anything else that enables you to identify your prime customers in your key markets. Be particularly sceptical of general descriptions such as 'innovators' and 'opinion formers'. There *are* such people, and if you can pinpoint them precisely, well and good. If not, strike them off your brief, along with all others who do not meet your criteria of actual or potential customers.

What of those who may not make the actual purchasing decision but have some effect on it, and those who are affected by it? A particular strength of PR is the ability to reach, cost-effectively, those who may not be customers, nor part of the decision making unit, but are assuredly stakeholders.

Suppose you were responsible for the PR programme of a medium-sized electronic engineering company; you might:

- advertise the availability of the firm's products, in the appropriate trade or technical magazine
- demonstrate the products' capabilities, at a trade exhibition
- mail to likely users a detailed brochure about applications
- catch the eye of potential backers with a well captioned picture story in the financial press
- alert information technology managers through electronic bulletin boards
- attract potential recruits to a company Open Day

You would talk to your marketing people, with a view to developing an integrated approach to products and markets.

Here are some practical examples of that approach, from a variety of firms, in a variety of markets.

■ Existing Products, Existing Markets

Abbey National, well known for its mortgage and banking services, also had a range of products – travel insurance, buildings and contents insurance, personal pensions – that the existing market was hardly aware of. Case 9.1, Chapter 9, describes what Abbey National and Cohn & Wolfe did to improve market penetration (there is a detailed breakdown of results in Table 14.2, Chapter 14).

■ New Products, Existing Markets

Real life is not always tidy and distinctions become blurred. Apple Computer's £250 000 a year PR account with Firefly Communications covered the core business of personal computers (existing products) and multimedia innovations in the information highway sector (new products). The PR consultancy was chosen for its intimate knowledge of Apple's technologies and existing market position and for its broad skills in the business and consumer sectors.[5]

■ Existing Products, New Markets

The main marketing effort on Royal Mail Stamps was traditionally concentrated on collectors. The PR budget was £100 000, more or less. In

1994 a new marketing manager, Yvette Turner, introduced a shift in strategy: to raise the volume of stamp sales and awareness of stamps generally by targeting stamp users as well as collectors. This development of the market was accompanied by a welcome, though not necessarily commensurate, increase in the PR budget.[6]

Visionware's products provide reciprocal links between two massive software systems: Windows, for individual users of personal computers, and Unix, for multi-users. Initially, the main market for Visionware was the USA, but Europe beckoned and the company responded. A PR programme by Good Relations, valued at about £100 000, went for editorial endorsement in France and Germany to support Visionware's objective of bridging and integrating two separate segments of the computer market.[7]

■ New Products, New Markets

For many years the Royal Tournament had been marketed as a military style event appealing to Service and ex-Service personnel. In 1993 two decisions were taken, in consultation with Kestrel Communications. First, the Tournament would be marketed as a new, showbiz-type event; second, that the real market was ordinary families wanting good quality entertainment. Case 3.5, later in this chapter, tells all.

■ A Target of Three

Sometimes only a handful of people are needed to fulfil all your marketing requirements. If you have a castle to sell, only a few people will be in the market. You have to isolate them from the general property market, sell them the benefits of your particular castle and then sell them the actual castle.

Here is a case, a long way from any castles and the sort of money they command, where something of the same considerations applied.

PORTFOLIO
Case 3.1 – Selling the benefits

1. Lambeth Children's Theatre Company (LCTC) Limited are an educational charity with clear objectives:

    (a) to promote, maintain, improve and enhance education, particularly by encouragement of the Arts
    (b) to introduce children to the power of their own imagination
    (c) to present plays that help children form their own views about the world

(d) to discover ways of reaching new audiences.

2. The company took professional advice on marketing strategy and produced attractive, persuasive, informative materials in pursuit of their objectives.

3. About 60 per cent of the company's performances are in schools, at a cost of £350 per performance. This is about twice what many schools can pay. However, LCTC refused to compromise on quality and made a well targeted drive to find up to three sponsors to fund the difference for 200 performances, at a total sponsorship cost of £35 000.

4. The sponsorship pack, an excellent presentation of a well argued and fully budgeted proposition, had a nicely theatrical look to it, and included a very practical summary of the benefits (see Figure 3.1) to a sponsor.[8]

Our project can offer you sponsorship benefits as follows.

1. We will give the project a press launch, inviting all the local press in the areas involved as well as the national and London-wide papers, magazines, radio, television, specialist educational journals and other relevant journalists from the Arts Council's Press Contacts List. Invitations and press releases would carry a credit for your involvement.

2. Your sponsorship will be credited by your logo on at least 5000 A3 posters and 50 000 full colour leaflets. These will be used and distributed by all our venues, not only schools. Each child will have a programme to take home.

3. We will publicise the project by a personal letter addressed to named Head Teachers in target areas agreed with you. We'll mail 2500 schools and follow up with telephone calls. Your contribution to the discounted price will be explained in both letter and call, taking your message into the heart of the school. We expect a response rate of 8% (our usual response rate). This means that 200 schools will respond and you would help us to reach 40 000 children with our work in schools alone. This would be in addition to our work in theatres.

4. We have budgeted to advertise the project via the Education Press, e.g., *The Times Educational Supplement, Education Guardian.* Your sponsorship will be credited in these adverts.

5. We will include your credits in our job adverts in the Trade Press.

6. Our Teachers' Notes will include a credit for your sponsorship or even contact information. A copy of these will go to each school we visit.

7. We would be happy to discuss other benefits (such as hand-outs or hospitality) to fit your individual requirements.

Finally, the production will, of course, go ahead whether or not sponsorship is agreed. However, your sponsorship would greatly enhance the quality of the production. Not only would it offer the children a more valuable experience, it would also allow more schools to participate.

So, as you can see, your involvement would be very precious to us and would help to keep our work accessible to schools. Please contact us on 0171 733 5270 to discuss how the benefits could be attuned to your needs.

Source: Reproduced by permission of Lambeth Children's Theatre Company.

Figure 3.1 Summary of benefits

■ Changing Markets, New Techniques

When the main market for Guy's Hospital's cosmetic surgery service was women from their mid-20s upwards, the technique used to generate clients was advertising in women's magazines. As more men chose to have cosmetic surgery – 15 per cent of the business and growing – Guy's turned to media relations. Their own in-house PR people were augmented by a consultancy on £30 000 fees.[9]

■ Re-organised Products, Re-organised Markets

Leading international software company Microsoft re-organised its products into seven groups and identified three main markets: end-users, corporate customers and equipment manufacturers. In each of these markets the company set up a sales and marketing unit, with its own budgets, which included provision for PR assistance with product promotion.

In addition, PR was overseen and coordinated from the centre so that there was communication with the whole of Microsoft's market.

■ New Products, New Methods

Loudspeaker manufacturing giant, Bose, used Hill & Knowlton's Amsterdam office to provide PR support for trials of two new products through its new direct marketing organisation in Germany, France and the Benelux countries. The account, worth £100 000, was described as principally a media relations job. Direct marketing was chosen because, although the total market was potentially the whole of Europe, the products would appeal to only a narrow segment in each country. If the trials proved successful, the direct sales effort would spread to the other European countries, with a corresponding increase in PR support.

■ Own Products, Market Awareness

Tesco commissioned Beechey Morgan Associates and The Public Relations Business to raise awareness of the store's own-brand health and beauty products. They had in their sights the kind of profile levels enjoyed by market leaders such as Boots. The PR programme of media relations, in-store promotions, sponsorship and brand reinforcement was intended to help Tesco towards its ultimate objective of taking a hefty slice of the market away from the high street pharmacies.

■ Refreshing the Brand

You have recently joined a top consultancy. You enjoyed your induction training. Now, your very first case is about to begin. You are charged with helping to revive the popularity of a personality once seen as intelligent, offbeat, humorous, witty; but now, alas, boring and stale.

'Great', you enthuse, 'who can it be? Some chat-show host losing his sparkle? A fashion designer out of touch with her clients? Maybe a minor Royal with several indiscretions too many?'

No, your problem personality is none of these. What you have got is a well-known brand of confectionery: specifically, a mint. To the manufacturers, their product has – indeed, is – just such a personality.

They cannot be serious.

Oh, yes, they are: and rightly so. In fiercely competitive markets, where a plethora of new products all offer added value to the consumer, it makes very good sense to identify, or invent, a new personality for a product that has become unexciting. Competing products are *strong*, or *soft*, or *chewy*, and all this has led to a certain lack of credibility for your problem product. You'll enjoy playing your part in its rehabilitation. How do I know? Because it's a real case.

The brand is Polo and the consultancy Welbeck Golin/Harris. This is what was done.

PORTFOLIO
Case 3.2 – One to get your teeth into

Analysis
Polo had a great heritage as the original 'mint with the hole'. Now Polo was losing ground to the competition. Penetration was declining most among 16–24 year olds. The area of greatest media weakness for Polo was London.

Objectives
1. Target 16–24-year old Londoners
2. Address the 'boredom factor'
3. Communicate Polo's unique wit and personality.

Strategy
'Make Polo Fun Again' through association with alternative comedy.

Budget
£100 000.

Consultancy
Welbeck Golin/Harris.

Programme

1. Welbeck identified a niche for an industry award on the London comedy circuit
2. This became the Polo Mint Comedy Award, entries to be nominated by fellow comedians
3. Kiss 100 FM was selected as the leading London radio station targeting the youth market
4. A campaign logo was designed and used on all publicity material
5. Two weeks of trailers announced the award and its seven alternative comedy events, followed by seven weeks of daily 'alternative news and views' broadcast live by 21 different nominees for the awards, shortlisted from a field of 150
6. Daily competitions offered tickets to the various events, supported by *Polo Mint Comedy Gig Guides*
7. Welbeck negotiated editorial in key London publications such as *Time Out*, *What's On* and *Girl About Town*, including previews, listings, reviews, competitions, free tickets, T-shirts and other media offers
8. Local press was brought in through 11 competitions and a series of targeted press notice mailings.

Results

1. 5 hours 24 minutes of branded coverage for Polo on Kiss 100 FM
2. 47 per cent of target audience reached, with Opportunities To Hear of 30.3, and 28 041 000 impacts
3. 1000 people attended the seven events
4. In addition to the extensive coverage in *Time Out*, a further 10 631 586 impressions were achieved for the national and regional press
5. Total consumer impressions/impacts exceeded 38.6 million
6. The campaign won a PRCA Award for outstanding consultancy practice.
7. Polo once again seen as a fun product.[10]

■ Brand Positioning

Vidal Sassoon, a Procter & Gamble brand, was promoted through a £250 000, six-month campaign which included sponsorship of the London Fashion Show:

- 3-day trade show
- 1-day public show
- fashion roadshow

The Department of Trade and Industry contributed £30,000. The consultancy was Lynne Franks. In addition, there was a core media programme by Penny Ryder PR. Both these PR efforts supported the total Vidal Sassoon marketing strategy to position the brand as a fashionable range for young achievers.[11]

■ The Dinosaur Effect

The films *Jurassic Park* and *The Flintstones* were part of massive, worldwide merchandising programmes, built on the seemingly universal and continuing appeal of dinosaurs.

In a lower key, three Scottish companies got together and exploited the dinosaur effect. This is the story of Academy Computers, SMARTS Advertising and Design, Flora Martin PR and the *Designosaurs*.

PORTFOLIO
Case 3.3 – Academy wins awards

Analysis
Although computers are being used increasingly in design offices, potential and actual users of Computer Aided Design (CAD) systems were still ill-informed about what CAD is, which professions can apply CAD, and what can be achieved. Academy Computers, information technology specialists and dealers in CAD packages, recognised the need to raise general awareness of CAD in a range of mainstream businesses. With their advisers they identified opportunities to promote the quality of the firm's services.

Objectives
To raise awareness of:

(a) Academy Computers in:
- the general business community
- specific user-sectors
(b) CAD and its various applications throughout industry.

Strategy
An integrated marketing and education drive to marketing consultants, designers (graphic and interior), architects, and engineers (design and consulting).

Consultancies
SMARTS Advertising and Design.
Flora Martin Public Relations.

Budget
£100 000, of which £13 000 on public relations.

Programme

1. Origination and design of four cartoon *Designosaurs*, each character representing one of the four target audience segments
2. Large scale cut-outs, display boards and other items developing the *Designosaurs* theme
3. Targeted press notice campaign to each audience segment
4. Face-to-face briefings
5. Photocalls
6. 'Local boy' press notices about staff appointments
7. 5000 corporate brochures (A4); 2000 brochures for architects (A4); 10 000 brochures with reply-cards (A5)
8. 2000 enamel badges and 200 metal
9. 1500 target mailings a week for three months
10. No-fee seminars to targeted audiences
11. Sponsorship of Building Procurement Conference
12. Liaison with trade and professional bodies.

Results

1. Turnover of Academy Computers up by 25 per cent, from £3.6m to £4.5m
2. Sales up 33 per cent by volume
3. Substantial coverage in all target media, including a 1500–word *Herald* feature
4. 6.6 per cent response to mailers, which was 350 per cent up on pre-campaign returns
5. On average 45 delegates per week attended Academy's Training Centre
6. Lesley Fleming of Flora Martin PR won the Hamp Hamilton Award for Excellence from IPR Scottish Group
7. British Association of Industrial Editors Award for best corporate brochure
8. Trailblazer Award to Academy Computers.[12]

■ Cause-Related Marketing

In Chapters 7 and 8 we look at some examples of the interesting and relatively recent trend towards identifying commercial activities with altruistic causes.

The Amex *Charge Against Hunger* programme and Time Warner's *Time to Read* are important, successful activities, though they could hardly be called mainstream.

This kind of cause-related marketing relies largely on PR to reconcile potential conflicts of interest, so that companies that do good also do well, and vice versa. A prime motivator is that all concerned should feel good. Charities do this all the time.

Just now and then a thoroughly successful commercial enterprise emerges where the entire operation is perceived to be cause-related. Perhaps the best known example is Bodyshop. The risk is that, should such a company's moral stance fail to stand up to scrutiny, the market could contract or even collapse, though the products themselves may be just the same as before.

■ Marketing Support for Intermediaries

Marketing support programmes can be specifically designed to generate, maintain and improve the end-users' perception of your company through their contact with intermediaries. There are consultancies that specialise in this. Alternatively, the company can do it as an in-house activity.

Either way, you are concentrating on the 'once-removed' network that links you to the customers in your end-market. This network includes:

- agents
- dealers
- distributors
- franchisees
- third-party sellers
- value-added re-sellers
- wholesalers

It is worth putting considerable effort into persuading this network at the very least to be interested in increasing their volume sales of your products, and, if possible, committed to doing so. This will affect their commission of course, but that in itself may not be enough to motivate them fully. You need to build real relationships with them.

Such an approach ought to be cost-effective because you are not putting any real financial investment into the operation. The staff are not on your payroll or subject to your manpower ceilings. You therefore have great flexibility. Disadvantages are that, because the product is not actually the intermediaries' own, they are not likely to have as much commitment as you, however hard they and you may try. Yet the satisfaction of your customers is in their hands.

This intermediate network of the once-removed is a market in its own right. You have to make sure that an adequate system of incentives and rewards is in place. But there is another dimension – PR – which can help to forge successful partnerships.

■ Product Placement

In popular fiction, the lifestyle of a protagonist is often expressed through the brands he or she drives, smokes, wears, drinks and so on. No doubt this has its effect on readers, who may be expected to be favourably disposed towards the same brands and may even buy them. You don't, of course, actually see the products in use, except in your imagination and occasionally on the dust-wrapper, and you probably don't care much what deals, if any, might have been struck between writer and manufacturer.

It is different when a brand is used in a television programme or feature film. There are no restrictions on the free supply of goods to television and film companies – including the BBC – and as production budgets shrink so product placement flourishes. The impact on the viewer can be of significant, if unquantified, commercial value. So it is hardly surprising that some PR companies offer product placement among the services they provide. Some specialists do nothing else. Many of the brands deal direct with the programme makers. However, product placement strategy, whether seen as PR or as marketing, is pretty hit and miss. There is no guarantee that the goods will appear on screen in a helpful context, for an effective length of time, or at all.

You see, editorial integrity has to be safeguarded, so there can be no inducements of any kind. No money ever changes hands.

That's the theory, anyway.

Whatever you believe, it is one of those issues, like advertorials and infomercials, with which sooner or later you are going to be confronted and on which you will have to take a position. It is not too soon to start thinking about it now.

■ Quality Upgrade

Relaunching Highland Spring mineral water involved moving it up market. This is how it was done.

PORTFOLIO
Case 3.4 – From 2 per cent to market leader

1. Highland Spring mineral water had around 20 per cent of the UK market – second behind Perrier's 50 per cent – but nearly all of this was accounted for by own label production for supermarkets. Highland Spring's brand share was 2 per cent and falling. A major relaunch was called for.

2. Using the combined resources of Michael Peters (design consultants), Cope Matthews (advertising agents), and Infopress (PR consultants), the objective was to increase the market share of the Highland Spring branded product, repositioning it at the quality end of the market.
3. The contribution of the design consultancy was essentially a new, up-market label and point of sale material, and a quality upgrade to glass containers from PVC.
4. The advertising agents provided television advertising during the crucial pre-Christmas sales period.
5. Another vital repositioning decision was to part company with the brokers who had been responsible for sales to retailers and wholesalers, and replace them with new ones.
6. The PR programme began nine months ahead of the relaunch, building credibility with the media and especially with trade journalists.
7. An embargoed programme of site visits and interviews for trade and local press was followed by a national press conference and a consumer campaign.
8. A lucky break – Perrier was banned from the House of Commons during launch week – was exploited with broadcasting and press coverage of bottles of Highland Spring being delivered to No. 10 Downing Street.
9. Alongside the pre-Christmas advertising campaign, a consumer awareness programme used the results of a specially commissioned survey on the dining habits of the nation to secure major radio and press coverage.
10. The result of all this was that Highland Spring brand mineral water became undisputed market leader among UK brands, and third in the overall market after Perrier and Evian.[13]

■ One for the Money, Two for the Show

Yesterday's attractions of stage and arena can become today's problems. If decline is to be arrested and reversed, audiences have to be redefined and events re-invented. That is how the Royal Tournament coped with change: this is the story.

PORTFOLIO
Case 3.5 – The Royal Tournament

The brief

The brief was simple: increase the number of people attending the 1993 Royal Tournament. The main challenge was to educate and inform potential audiences who had few Service connections that the Royal Tournament was good family entertainment. The campaign concentrated mainly on press relations and promoted the showbiz element of the Tournament rather than the military. PR was expected to reinforce existing marketing efforts and open new opportunities.

Objectives

1.   Achieve an occupancy of at least 80 per cent (that is, 10 000 people per performance on average)
2.   Generate minimum revenue of £1 680 000.

Consultancies
Marketing: P & O Events.
Public Relations: Kestrel Communications.

Budget
£550 000 for total marketing, including the new budget for public relations.

Programme (November 1992–July 1993)

1.   Media liaison (approximate cost £20 000):
      (a)   Royal Tournament Press Office run by Kestrel at own premises on dedicated phone lines
      (b)   news items, demonstrations and interviews tailored to national, regional and satellite television; local radio; national and regional newspapers and magazines; local press
      (c)   competitions backed by editorial for television and radio stations; weekend and leisure press
      (d)   ticket offers through selected media
      (e)   editorial in Services magazines.
2.   Inserts (cost £33 500):
      1 700 000 inserts in six different titles.
3.   Mailings (cost £75 000):
      (a)   three major mailings
      (b)   lists included individual bookings; tourist information centres; coach operators; military and other uniformed forces and associations; ticket brokers.
4.   Advertising:
      (a)   Television commercials (cost £100 000)
      (b)   Press (cost £25,000).
5.   Others (approximate cost £20 000):
      (a)   posters
      (b)   fax shots
      (c)   media testing (for example, QTV advertising in London post offices)
      (d)   general administration.

Results

1. Seat occupancy 85 per cent in 1993, compared with objective of 80 per cent (occupancy was 74 per cent in 1992)
2. 216 186 seats sold, against 210 000 objective
3. £1 711 416 net revenue against £1 680 000 objective
4. Nine separate Tournament items featured on four television stations
5. Substantial editorial in more than 40 national media and nearly 70 local and regional media
6. Reports, interviews and competitions on four radio stations
7. Editorial plus ticket offers in 16 national newspapers and trade magazines; four radio stations; 37 local and regional papers with over 100 editions between them.[14]

A breakdown of cost per visitor is shown in Table 14.3, Chapter 14.

■ The Overall View

In the 1994 IPR Membership Survey, 38.2 per cent of members reported direct to their chairman, managing director or chief executive.

Although the customer is a major stakeholder in the business, there are others. Members identified their main PR publics as media (52.9 per cent), corporate (38.3 per cent), employees (34.3 per cent), consumers (33.2 per cent), community (26.9 per cent), government (20.9 per cent) and special interest groups (16.3 per cent).[15]

It is the job of PR to reconcile and satisfy the needs of all the stakeholders, and in that sense marketing can be viewed as a sub-division of public relations. Marketing makes by far the biggest contribution towards meeting the needs of customers, at home and abroad (most notably in Europe). According to the Confederation of British Industry (CBI):

The changes in the circumstances for trading in Europe are so fundamental and widespread that they will affect every firm, either directly or indirectly . . . There will be no change in the fundamental principles of marketing. You will still have to identify what your customer wants and how you can best satisfy those requirements . . . The key to the formulation and implementation of strategy is to 'think local, plan global and act focal.'[16]

At the 1994 IPR Conference, the political journalist and communication consultant, Vincent Hanna, said: 'You've got to convince people like the CBI that there isn't a conflict between PR and marketing.' Your own company may be global in its organisation, and its products may be available globally, but its customers, and the consumers of its products or services, may not be global at all. The way forward is to identify all stakeholders in all segments and customise them through public relations.

CHAPTER 4

Research and Public Relations

Every source of information is useful.

Roger Corbin[1]

■ The Purpose of Research

Although Roger Corbin was actually talking about how to choose an advertising agency, his assertion that every source of information is useful should be displayed in letters of gold above every PR desk in the land. It is not that every *piece* of information is necessarily as useful as every other – data overload can be bad for your health – but you cannot afford to discard any *source* without first extracting from it all you can use.

The key word is 'useful' because the purpose of all research is, or should be, to provide information to help us make decisions.

There are different kinds of research, different types of data and different techniques; this chapter will have something to say about all of that. There are also different reasons for needing to make the decision, and some of these are examined in various places throughout the book.

■ Research Planning

Before any research is started, there should be a clear understanding of how the results will be used. This should be built into the planning process for information collection, which involves the following key steps:

- defining what information is needed to aid decision taking, and specifying the level of detail and accuracy that is required
- determining what data already exists in-house and that which can be easily acquired
- ensuring that it is feasible to collect the information
- checking what in-house resources are available to collect information
- deciding the outside limits of the budget that would be acceptable, which must bear a relationship to the value of the decision being taken

51

- determining the timescale within which the data must be available in order to be useful

The results of this analysis will set the basic parameters for research and determine the techniques that will be required and what, if any, external assistance is needed.[2]

■ Kinds of Research

Broadly speaking, there are four main divisions.

■ Secondary Data

Often known as desk research, this is what somebody, somewhere, already knows. This information may be obtainable from internal or external sources. For example, local authorities have an abundance of secondary data within their own records or services, such as housing, library lending, leisure centre admissions and planning applications. External secondary data is available from census data, trade and professional journals, government statistics, professional institutions and so on.[3]

Re-examination of secondary data can produce surprising results. The award-winning Bail Bandits campaign was sparked off by research. A detailed three-part survey involving records from detectives, custody officers and magistrates' courts revealed that not only was there a substantial level of re-offending on bail in Avon and Somerset, but it was possible to identify those most likely to re-offend if granted bail.

The study added scientific support to the gut feeling of many officers that a significant number of offences – particularly burglary and car crime – was committed by people released on bail and awaiting trial for other alleged offences. The new evidence was used to power a campaign that led to a change in the law (see Case 14.1, Chapter 14).

■ Primary Data

This is obtained when research is commissioned by you for your own specific purpose and carried out according to your brief. Here is an example.

General Accident Life (GA Life) carried out two studies with disturbing results. The first showed that although General Accident was very well known as a provider of general insurance, GA Life was not very visible to consumers of life and investment products. The second survey showed that even financial journalists didn't know much about GA Life.

Yorkshire-based PR consultancy Northern Lights got the job of increasing awareness of GA Life and its products through the consumer media. The first action they took was to carry out their own research amongst journalists writing in the consumer media on personal finance. The consultancy also did its own analysis of GA Life products.

What the Northern Lights research revealed, and how an award-winning campaign (including further research) was developed from this new knowledge, are described in the next chapter, Case 5.2.

■ Syndication

This is a way of making use of research, usually ongoing, that is carried out by or with some other organisation, specialist or general. You could piggyback on a National Opinion Poll (NOP) questionnaire, for instance. This can be particularly cost-effective if you only have a few questions, because the main costs of setting up and running a big sample survey have already been covered by somebody else. It is a common way of tracking shifts in popular awareness, much used by political and government organisations and by quangos.

Like Wycombe District Council (WDC), you could give yourself a piggyback. It is good practice to measure your baseline before you start an awareness campaign so that results may be quantified. Sometimes this is not practicable, as in the case of WDC. There were no funds for a special survey, but the Council's regular biennial survey was already scheduled to be carried out a few months after the start date of the campaign. That is when baseline measurements were taken. From then on, changes were to be measured regularly and targets set and re-set accordingly.

■ Combination

This implies two or more of the other three kinds. It is quite common to start with secondary data, if only to find out from desk research what relevant information is and is not available to help in decision making. You then have some indication as to what else you should do in the way of syndicated or originated research.

When Counsellor, on behalf of Stafford-Miller Ltd, launched the Sensodyne Advice Centre, they had two strands of information as justification: the findings of a specially commissioned survey on how many people suffered from tooth sensitivity, how much they understood, and what they did (or didn't do) about it; and Stafford-Miller's substantial practical experience of consumers' problems. The full story is told in Case 9.4, Chapter 9.

Three separate sets of research results underpinned the Bananergy Campaign. Two were from existing research: a study by Newcastle University showing that the diet of 11- and 12-year-old children was high in fat and sugar; and a survey of schoolchildren and office workers showing that those who eat breakfast tend to perform better during the morning than those who don't. Independent research specifically commissioned from Audience Selection suggested that three out of ten schoolchildren and one in three mothers started most days on too little food. All this information, from primary and secondary sources, helped shape Beechey Morgan Associates' campaign for the Banana Group (see Case 9.5, Chapter 9).

■ Types of Data

Information comes in all manner of guises. It can be analytical or anecdotal, descriptive or numerical, but essentially it is either quantitative or qualitative. Each can provide a sound basis for making a particular decision: quantitative information when you need statistical authenticity, qualitative when you are concerned with tone, style and value-judgements. For many decisions you need both kinds.

■ Research Techniques

1. When you want qualitative information, and time is not desperately short, *group discussions* with hand-picked and quite small samples can test the personality of a company, or the class image of a service. If you want to be sure that a speech, a leaflet or press notice is not racist, sexist or ageist, expose it to group discussions and let them tease out the hidden meanings of everyday phrases or the resonance of even a single word. Take your time when drawing conclusions from the results of group discussions.
2. If you have abstract ideas or propositions that need exploring in depth, or if you want to know what individuals really think and really feel about sensitive or confidential issues, you'll chose the *face-to-face* or one-to-one technique, taking as long as it takes to get the depth of information you are after. The other main example of face-to-face research is when you use a large random sample survey of the Gallup type to provide good, if rather general, quantitative data from people stopped in the street.
3. For a fast response from a reasonably large sample and a relatively small number of questions, the *telephone questionnaire* is becoming increasingly popular. It is quick to set up and carry out, and not particularly expensive, but you would not expect to get much in the way of qualitative information, and you have to be prepared to accept highish refusal rates.
4. The three research techniques discussed so far have been dialogues between questioner and respondent. In the case of *postal surveys*, that is hardly practicable, given that very large samples and wide geographic spreads are usually involved. On the other hand, properly constructed and administered, postal surveys give information that is statistically respected, valid and consistent. Response rates can be modest, but unit costs are low.

■ Telephone Research with a Difference

Using the telephone as a research technique works best when those making the calls have been trained in PR techniques. Here is how you could do some research on that.

When you last made a phone call to a stakeholder, how long did they take to respond? Did they get your name right? Did the person answering the phone seem knowledgeable? Was the voice welcoming and confidence-inspiring? How long were you kept hanging on? Were you able to hear any extraneous conversations? If you couldn't be put through, how helpful were they? How important did they make you feel? If you had a complaint to make, did they listen? Did they seem to care? What did they do about it?

Now think about your own company's performance. How does it compare? Why not find out? Telephone in as if you were an outsider and ask a few awkward questions. Keep score, and arrive at a rating.

You could incorporate this research into a PR audit, or you could handle it as a one-off, and do it today.

PORTFOLIO
Guideline 4.1 – Ringing the bell

This is the way BT recommends rating telephone performance.

A. Response time:

1–5 seconds	5
6–10 seconds	4
11–20 seconds	3
21–30 seconds	2
Over 30 seconds	0

B. Remembering your name:
0 (very poor) to 5 (excellent), depending on how accurately it is remembered and pronounced.

C. Extent of company knowledge:
Score 1 for each correct answer to the questions you ask. Deduct 1 for each incorrect answer.

D. Manner:
Does the voice inspire confidence and make you feel welcome? First impressions 0 (very poor) to 5 (excellent).

E. Kept hanging on:
Deduct 5 if you're left for more than 10 seconds without any explanation or apology.

F. Not paying attention:
Deduct 10 if you overhear any background conversation that isn't directly relevant to your inquiry.

G. Couldn't be put through:
0 (no help at all) to 5 (couldn't have been more helpful).
H. Status:
How important were you made to feel?
0 (totally insignificant) to 5 (vital prospect or customer).
J. Complaints:
Did they listen?
Did they care?
Did they take action?
0 (couldn't care less) to 5 (really made an effort).

Your company's score

Over 20   Excellent. You look very good on the phone.
16–20   Good. But try to get rid of the few weaknesses you have.
10–15   Not bad. But there is a lot of room for improvement.
Under 10   Terrible. It'll take a lot to turn things around, but if you start now you could soon be doing a lot better.[4]

Now get someone to ring your own office and report on how *you* shape up. Bound to score at least 20, yes? Go on then, prove it.

■ W. A. Muzack

Atmosphere can count for a lot. One of the things that really irritates me is when they keep me hanging on and play synthesised music at me: Handel, Vivaldi, Mozart, but only the bits you hear everywhere. You might call it Wolfgang Amadeus Muzack.

It could be worse. Would you believe that some companies use the time when you are hanging on to play you a sales tape? Yes – they keep you waiting, at your expense, and then try to sell you something into the bargain. Mind you, I've never come across anybody who does it, but there was a firm that tried to make a living producing and marketing such tapes. I can't believe they researched the idea first, or they would never have decided to go ahead . . . I hope.

■ No Material Risk

Sometimes researchers seem to live in another world from ours. They can explain and interpret results in a way that no doubt makes perfect sense to them, but leaves ordinary mortals doing a double-take. For instance, a long term study of contraceptives came out highly favourable to the diaphragm method. The researchers found that using it had 'no material risk', *other than pregnancy*.

■ Using Research Results

We have already noted a number of organisations' uses of research – Avon and Somerset Constabulary, WDC, GA Life and Northern Lights, The Banana Group and Beechey Morgan Associates. Now let's look at some more examples, this time in a bit of depth. First British Aerospace, then Shell Select and Paragon, followed by Computer Associates and Infopress.

■ An Attitude Survey

Mainly as a result of the end of the Cold War, but also because the nature of the business itself was changing, the Military Aircraft Division of British Aerospace was undergoing radical upheaval. Sites would have to be closed, leading to 5000 redundancies. It was essential to inform and motivate the 20000-strong workforce so that they understood and supported the process of change.

An employee attitude survey showed that managers were seen as secretive, remote and uncaring, and that the information priority for staff was details of Military Aircraft's current performance and future business plans. Four out of five respondents said that the company must change to survive. The company's response was a 'major strategy rethink for internal communications' and an award winning campaign described by the *Financial Times* as 'one of the UK models for two-way communication'.

■ Probing, Tracking, Evaluating

For the launch of Shell's forecourt shops, Paragon used secondary sources to establish PR objectives and strategy, commissioned attitudinal research as the springboard for the programme, collected feedback through a consumer questionnaire, measured changes in awareness by tracking research and carried out a thorough evaluation of media coverage. Case 4.1 tells the whole story.

PORTFOLIO
Case 4.1 – Launching Shell Select

Initial desk research

1. Analysis of media and client briefings showed that no natural news platform or differential existed which could be used to launch Shell Select forecourt shops
2. Analysis of existing research data indicated a number of social and economic trends pointing to a set of new consumer needs – for frequent, car based shopping visits
3. Studies of the retail sector confirmed that no single retailer had yet met these newly identified needs
4. Further media study revealed that the new social phenomenon had not been branded.

Objectives

1. New lifestyle development to be branded 'The Top Up Society'
2. High profile national consumer media launch of Shell Select
3. Educate and raise awareness of Select amongst Shell customers
4. Create opportunities for customer feedback.

Strategy

1. Research and define The Top Up Society
2. Publish research report and use it as media peg
3. Demonstrate Shell's commitment to better forecourt services through Select Customer Pledge.

Budget
£70 000 total spend, including fees and expenses.

Consultancy
Paragon.

Programme

1. Commission attitudinal research from Gallup
2. Publish Top Up Society Report based on Gallup findings
3. Commission leading sociologist (Professor Laurie Taylor) to review findings and present them at media launch
4. National launch of *Top Up Society* at London Shell Select site
5. Negotiate press competitions with key regional media in Select Shop areas
6. Produce and distribute Video News Release (VNR)
7. Produce, distribute and syndicate radio tape featuring Professor Taylor

8. Negotiate live radio interviews with Professor Taylor
9. Write and produce Select Customer Pledge and display it in 300 + Select Shops
10. Write and produce 200 000 consumer leaflets, including a consumer questionnaire and £1000 prize draw.

Measured results

1. Shell tracking research revealed greater awareness of Select
2. 13 000 + consumers responded to leaflet
3. 91 per cent of respondents ranked Select Shops above rivals
4. 99 per cent of respondents confirmed that Shell's Customer Pledge was fully honoured
5. Over 33 million Opportunities to See (OTS) in target media during launch month
6. Coverage delivered an average 2.5 messages from possible four.[5]

■ Multi-Dimensional Perception

When Infopress was appointed to handle corporate and product PR for Computer Associates, the consultancy recommended starting with an internal communications audit, to assess how managers thought the company was perceived by staff and customers, and how they would wish it to be perceived. The results would enable Infopress to plan a programme of activities to meet the company's communications needs, and also to agree how the success of that programme could best be evaluated.

It took a fortnight of in-depth interviews with senior directors and managers to cover actual and desired perceptions of the company, its stature in the UK, USA and internationally, the target audiences and product range, and current communications activities. The following key points emerged:

● main individual brand names of Computer Associates' products were strongly recognised
● awareness of the company and its integrated product range needed to be improved
● senior management wanted the company to be more proactive, balancing a sales oriented approach with a caring image
● the company needed to promote its international strengths

These and other points identified from the communications audit were the basis of a 12-month programme of PR activities developed and carried out by Infopress.

■ Presenting Information

Research data is normally produced in the form of a computer print-out, and this has to be turned into usable information. One way of doing this is by using charts which clarify facts that might otherwise be hard to take in, or make visible those which are submerged.

To break the ice at the start of the Computer Associates audit, Infopress devised a multi-dimensional perception analysis chart (Figure 4.1) to map where the company stood and in which direction it should go.

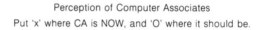

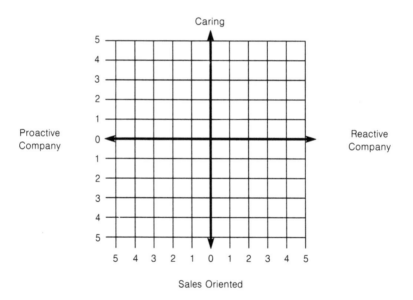

Source: Reproduced by permission of Infopress.

Figure 4.1   Perception analysis chart

The type of chart you choose should enlighten by drawing attention to the facts, not to itself. You want to plant the notion that the method you have chosen is the natural way to convey the information.

PORTFOLIO
Guideline 4.2 – Choosing a chart

Whether you are simply reporting the facts, or presenting them so that they convey a message, you have only four basic types of chart to choose from.

1. *Line graph, or fever chart*
    Visualisation of quantities, plotted over a time period, by means of a rising and falling line.
    Example – sales graph.
2. *Bar chart*
    Visualisation of quantities, each one represented by an individual column or bar corresponding in height or length to the amount being counted.
    Example – comparison of GDPs of several different countries at a single point in time. Gantt charts and histograms are both bar charts.
3. *Pie chart*
    Division of a whole into its components, usually in percentages.
    Example – market share analysis.
4. *Table*
    A display of numbers or words arranged into columns or boxes. A matrix is a table.

Of course, charts are used for many other purposes besides displaying and presenting research data. Variations on the basic types include multi-charting, three-dimensional presentations and combination charts.

Bar/line charts can be particularly useful for presenting two or more data sets together, such as monthly sales figures (bar) and percentage changes on the previous year (line).[6]

Each basic type of chart is used at least once in this book.

■ Change Means Opportunity

Any salesman knows that one of the best times to sell somebody a product or service is when a major change is taking place. Newlyweds have a new home to furnish; the arrival of the first baby turns people into parents; promotion at work can move a customer up-market; a lump sum on retirement demands to be invested; these occasions of change are also windows of opportunity.

What is true of selling is also true of public relations. If you want to change an individual manager's perception of your firm, or his/her company's attitude towards it, one of your best opportunities is when he/she or the company are undergoing a change of some kind already.

So you need to be aware of what is happening, or about to happen, to people and companies in the sectors of concern to you. Some of what you ought to know can be bought as a package – The Marketing Guild, for instance, runs a subscription service called *Names in the News* – but you will also need to organise your own research. Remember to bone up on the requirements of the Data Protection Act.

■ Cost-Free Research?

In a well managed organisation, information which was never intended to be used for research, and which would have been costly to obtain through formal research techniques, can be available without extra charge. It is a special kind of secondary data and it comes from customers, suppliers, agents, the sales force, the shop floor, and other stakeholders, in the form of complaints, compliments, inquiries, requests and suggestions.

A good organisation makes it easy for people to communicate with it in these ways. Of course, complaints are investigated and errors corrected, compliments are acknowledged and passed on to those directly concerned, while inquiries, requests and suggestions are considered conscientiously and acted on promptly. All this is excellent management practice which must strengthen the reputation of the company in the eyes of the individuals concerned.

That need not be the end of the matter, however. The information gathered should go in to the company's database, which will also include information from other sources such as charge cards, competitions, coupon redemptions, credit cards, guarantee card returns, rebate applications, service call-outs and subscription lists. Treat this mass of data as if it had been generated by specially-commissioned research, and use it to identify gaps in the company's total communication programme.

Once again, the most importance sources are your own additions: the ones you think of yourself. You will probably get some particularly useful ideas during periods of change.

■ PR Auditing

Could there be definitive and widely accepted standards for the format and content of PR audits? Standards that would cover the vast majority of situations, rather like, in the financial world, the Accountancy Standards Board's FRS3?

Fat chance.

PR auditing is still relatively new, and there is too much variation of approach and dilution of quality for standardisation to be a real possibility just yet. But there is another reason, which is that too many of the organisations being audited prefer flattery to realism. Not that they want to be told they're perfect – if they did, why would they risk an audit that might show otherwise? – but because they'd rather blame any reputation shortcomings on the communicators than on the policies.

PR auditing should be carried out at times of crisis or major change, such as:

- acquisitions, mergers or innovative joint ventures
- complete change of strategy
- re-organisation
- loss of key personnel, such as chairman or chief executive
- site closures; redundancies
- change of legislation (for example, deregulation, privatisation, removal or erection of major trade barriers)
- turnaround from lossmaking to break even or profitable
- flotations and public offerings
- crucial market fluctuations
- change of marketing strategy
- human resources problems (for example, succession planning, exceptional needs, identifying new talent)

What all these changes of condition have in common is that they affect, or can affect, reputation.

To ensure independence, the audit team could come from outside the company altogether. There are several consultancies able to carry out the task. Alternatively, the company could appoint its own experienced staff, who should be thoroughly familiar with the nature of PR but not necessarily in the PR department.

Ideas for handling change are most convincing when they come from, or at any rate are agreed with, those affected by it. Ask them.

■ International Research

With the emergence of global markets, local and national business perspectives are no longer enough.

The CBI points out that there are many different ways of conducting international research, and all are on offer within the UK research industry. In terms of choice of supplier, international clients can take their pick from a number of options available:

- international chains of research agencies, with offices in different countries under common ownership
- loosely knit groups of affiliates, separately owned

- independent coordinator companies, selecting local suppliers on a project basis
- individual freelance researchers

Each of these possibilities has potential strengths and weaknesses but all can be, and are being, used effectively and influentially on international projects.

Far from its occasional daunting image, therefore, international research is every bit as useful a tool for the international marketer as local research is for the local business. Like the international marketing context, it is demanding in some respects and is less familiar territory, but, again in parallel with the marketing context, the opportunities are there for those who have the vision and commitment to make it work.[7]

To find out what industry leaders in Europe and North America knew about the changing scene, and especially about the European Single Market, Worldcom carried out research into 250 companies in 1990, measuring awareness, perceptions and attitudes.

To begin with, the survey results were only available to Worldcom member firms and their clients, but it became clear that the information was of wider interest.

A book containing the research conclusions was published in 1991 and was instrumental in an EC decision to launch a consumer information campaign across all 12 member states with their nine official languages. In a competitive pitch involving 28 communications companies, Worldcom got the job of devising and carrying out the programme (full details in Case 6.4, Chapter 6).

■ Pseudo-Research

Steer clear of all that pseudo-research which is simply a hook for a sales pitch, or an unwarranted intrusion. You know the kind of thing; it's what Colin Morris describes as 'those dollybirds who simper up to one in airports and ask all kinds of impertinent questions, claiming that it will enable some airline to provide a more efficient service'. Morris is highly sceptical. 'They mean maximise its profits at the expense of my right to keep to myself the reason for any journey, the size of my salary and the number of grandchildren I have. If I've got to choose, give me privacy over efficiency, any day.'[8]

You don't have to choose. Privacy and efficiency are not in the least incompatible.

■ One More Questionnaire

For all those occasions when research is being considered, here is a handy checklist. It can help to focus thinking, especially your own. Perhaps it will be of greatest value whenever somebody is stuck for an idea and says 'I know, we'll do some research about it.'

PORTFOLIO
Checklist 4.1 – Key questions about research

1. What decision do you need to make?
2. What quantitative information will help you make the decision?
3. What qualitative information will help you make the decision?
4. What do you know already?
5. What kind of research should be undertaken?
   Secondary?
   Primary?
   Syndicated?
   Combined?
6. What techniques will be used?
   Postal?
   Phone?
   Face-to-face?
   Group?
7. Who will undertake it?
8. How long will it take? What will it cost
9. How will the results be presented?
10. What specific use will be made of the re
11. How will the cost-effectiveness of the re   measured?
12. Will it matter if the research is not unde   all?

CHAPTER 5

Corporate and Financial Relations

Identity, n – Absolute sameness; personality.
Image, n – Artificial imitation; semblance.
Semblance, n – What looks like something.

Dictionary definitions[1]

■ Image or Identity?

Every firm, every government department, every school and college, every charity, has an image (what it looks like from the outside). Most of these images are unplanned, made up of the style of doing business, the attitude of the staff, the way customers and suppliers are treated, or even the appearance of the buildings. Image is the result of a host of such impressions, major and minor.

Even when a house-style exists, so that at least somebody has thought about some of the visual aspects, the effect on the total image may be pretty haphazard. That is no way to carry on, but it is difficult to do anything about it unless there is a reason powerful enough to make people want to. What sort of reason would that be?

Inevitably, businesses find themselves faced with a change in circumstances, and this can be used to trigger a fresh look at how to turn an image into an identity. The occasion could be when a new company is founded, or there is an acquisition or merger, or new ownership. It might be a change of function, or a bid to correct market perception when it is not commensurate with market share. Perhaps there is a need to motivate staff who have been through a morale-sapping experience. Maybe the competitive position needs to be improved. Repositioning in the market can be a pressing need. So can streamlining/rationalising a variety of brands. Possibly there is a problem in recruiting the right calibre of senior staff.

■ Who Takes Charge of Identity?

For any of these reasons, and often more than one, a top-level decision is taken to do something about corporate identity. The question is, who should be in charge of the exercise?

Some would say design consultants, and it is true that the visual element is very important. This is because it is the visible expression of the identity; but it is not, in itself, that identity. Indeed, a purely design-led identity can generate an image that is out of line with corporate performance, and therefore unconvincing. We will come back to the question of corporate design a little later in this chapter.

Should we expect the company's advertising agency to take the lead in establishing corporate identity? After all, advertisements are a very prominent aspect of the company's communication with its publics. Agencies have design directors and all kinds of expertise. Without doubt, corporate advertising can play an important part in projecting identity. Indeed, every advertisement for the company, from product to recruitment, says something about the company, whether intended or not. But the functions of advertising and the nature of advertising agencies are too limited for the lead role in establishing corporate identity.

The marketing department? That's getting nearer. Marketers have much to contribute on corporate identity because they see the firm from the customer's point of view. To some of those customers the brands are the company, to others the company is the brand. Either way, the brand image is a kind of company representative by proxy and plays a decisive part in expressing identity. We will explore that too, later in this chapter.

What about mission statements? Do they help to establish corporate identity? I have to agree with Wally Olins when he says that, like the Boy Scout promise to be clean in mind and body, mission statements reflect the wish rather than the reality.[2]

Identity is actually the personality of the organisation, and therefore the responsibility of everybody in it. But a broad coordinating view has to be taken and you will not be surprised when I say that it can only come from PR. Think of the range of skills and knowledge that needs to be marshalled and applied: research into how the firm is perceived; analysis as to why; planning what to do about closing any gap between image and reality; internal communication at all stages; coordination of design, advertising, print, media liaison, production and marketing; project management; external communication; financial control; evaluation and feedback; where else would you find all that except in a PR consultancy or in-house PR department?

Let's look at four of the best-known ways of establishing corporate identity:

- corporate values – reflecting the business approach
- design – for the coherent look

- brands – for reputation by proxy
- sponsorship – for that 'do good, do well' factor

■ Corporate Values

Toyota's corporate image is a reflection of the company's business approach based on a number of corporate values:

- to be a good corporate citizen
- the customer always comes first
- quality applies to everything Toyota does
- respect for the value of people
- Toyota responds to local needs and is sensitive to local traditions in every market in which it operates
- Toyota seeks success through competition and collaboration

Working with Scope: Communications, the company presents itself to the *City* as an investor to be welcomed; to the *communities* of Derby, Deeside and Redhill as responsive to local needs and concerns; to the *motor industry* as a good partner and fair competitor; to the *government* as a good corporate citizen; to the *media* as an open and honest communicator; and to the *customer* as a manufacturer of reliable, value-for-money products.

To build understanding and support in the *business and financial community* Toyota Motor Corporation (TMC) decided to participate more – meet business leaders, speak at business meetings and events, become involved with business organisations – and to develop comprehensive investor relations, such as European listings, on-site meetings with analysts, regular dialogue with the financial media and information exchange with the City.

A regular City Information Meeting brings together very senior board members from TMC London, industry analysts, senior opinion formers and senior journalists to discuss the state of Toyota across the world, and in particular as it relates to Europe. This is a key meeting for the UK organisations as it sets the context for business over the next 12 months. It is also intended to reinforce Toyota's position as a global company. The meeting manages to attract senior analysts even though the company has no listing on the UK market.

■ Corporate Design

Corporate identity does need visual expression through corporate design. Your firm may be able to manage that from its own resources, but it may do better with a design consultancy. What is the best way to choose one?

Getting a long list together is not too difficult. Some consultancies are well known for doing just the sort of work your firm has in mind. Others can be located with the help of trade and professional bodies, such as the Design Council or the Chartered Society of Designers. Quite a good way is just to ask around.

It may be more difficult to narrow the long list down to the much smaller number who will be asked to make a credentials pitch. If you were to become involved at this stage yourself here is a simple six-point plan to help you.

- look at their work
- talk to their people
- question their experience
- talk to their clients
- visit their premises and facilities
- look at their work again

Out of the handful of hopefuls who made a credentials pitch, it should be possible to pick two or three who are real contenders.

Visualisation of corporate identity can involve products, brands, trademarks, symbols, logos, buildings (inside and out), literature and other communication material, stationery, vehicles, uniforms, and a system or manual to ensure compliance and consistency. Due account needs to be taken of the effectiveness or otherwise of what exists already.

Choosing the design consultancy to do all that is a painstaking process, much like the procedures for choosing a PR consultancy, as set out in Chapter 2.

Of course, it may not always be necessary. Perhaps what your company really needs is a house-style face lift. That's fine, but no one should be misled into confusing that with a proper review of company identity.

■ Brands

In 1993, the top brand in the world was Coca-Cola, valued by *Financial World* at $35.95bn. According to *Checkout*, Coca-Cola was also the top selling grocery brand in the UK, with sales of $427m, while *Marketing* made it top of the fmcg brands and, it hardly needs saying, top carbonated drinks brand.

You might expect the product that dominated the sales and valuation league tables to be the top spender on advertising. You would be wrong. In the UK, for instance, seven of the top 50 fmcg brands spent at least as much on advertising as Coca-Cola did, and some considerably more. Clearly adspend was not the only factor in the marketing mix, or necessarily the most important.

A few years earlier, a survey of 10 000 consumers compared world rankings of leading brands with UK rankings. The criteria were familiarity and esteem: how well they were known, and how well thought of.

World Brand number 1 was – yes – Coca-Cola, but UK Brand number 1 was Marks & Spencer (M&S). Only one name occurred in both the World Top 10 and the UK Top 10. In the UK, Nescafé was ranked number 5, compared with Nestlé's World ranking of number 6. That's pretty close to being equal, but of course Nescafé is only one brand under the Nestlé brand umbrella.

Although the pecking order might be different from year to year, I would be surprised if the majority of today's top 10 brands, World and UK, did not appear in at least the top 15 or 20 for a decade or so.

These were the brand rankings.

	WORLD	UK
1.	Coca-Cola	Marks & Spencer
2.	Sony	Kelloggs
3.	Mercedes Benz	Cadburys
4.	Kodak	BBC
5.	Disney	Nescafé
6.	Nestlé	Heinz
7.	Toyota	Boots
8.	McDonalds	McVities
9.	IBM	Yellow Pages
10.	Pepsi Cola	W. H. Smith

In 1994, a study by Loughborough University Business School for *Management Today* asked the chairmen, managing directors and selected main board directors of Britain's ten largest companies, in each of 26 industrial sectors, to evaluate their peers. Analysts in ten leading investment companies were also polled. Nine criteria of performance were applied to all 260 companies. M&S ranked third in the 'most admired' category and also appeared in the top ten for each of the following: management quality; financial soundness; goods and services; recruit/retain staff; long-term value; capacity to innovate; community/environment; use of corporate assets.

The only criterion of performance where M&S did not make it into the top ten was quality of marketing. How, then, did they scoop the number one position – by a huge margin – when respondents were asked to step out of the role of industry expert, assume the guise of generalist, and vote for the company they most admired?

It is because M&S is 'the beneficiary of the ultimate virtuous circle, caught in an upward spiral of admiration in which reputation, presentation, and perception act only to enhance each other'.[3]

In all this, the company's PR is identical to the brand's. But what brand? Strictly speaking, the brand is St Michael, and that is what appears on the labels in the food department. In the clothing department it also appears, above the company name. Yet nobody I know buys St Michael shirts or knickers. They may recognise that brand, but what they call the goods is always Marks & Spencer's, often shortened to M&S. To perpetuate the St Michael notional brand, when the real brand is the company, does not seem logical.

Still, it must seem reasonable to M&S, and the customers don't appear to mind. They know what quality of goods and service to expect and what value. They know what kind of company they are dealing with. They know that shopping will be a pleasant, no-nonsense experience, with hassle-free returns for replacement or refund. What is more, they know that all this will be the same in any M&S store, anywhere. That is corporate identity, carefully created, carefully expressed, carefully maintained and branded.

■ Brand versus Price

Try this little four-part test on yourself and your colleagues.

1. Which of your frequent purchases – breakfast cereal, instant coffee, petrol, toilet paper and so on – do you buy solely or mainly on price?
2. What about less frequent purchases, like carpets, lawn mowers, spectacles, watches?
3. When you give to a charity, are you absolutely certain you know what they'll spend your money on?
4. Which airline would you rather fly? What would your second choice be?

Your answers are an illustration of the never-ending battle between brands and prices.

Conventional economic theory has it that most people will buy more of something if the price goes down, and less of it if the price goes up. But some purchases are more price controlled than others and, when price is the dominant factor, competitive pricing can soon get out of hand, such that one competitor eventually adopts a predatory pricing policy. This leads rapidly to a position where prices are cut to an uneconomically low level, until rivals are forced out of that market sector, or even out of business altogether.

Very low prices have obvious advantages to customers in the short term but, over a longer timescale, as rivals are seen off, the surviving company can – and usually does – raise prices again to at least the level they were before predatory pricing took effect.

What else could matter as well as price? What could matter more than price? Well, quality for one. When *The Times* newspaper cut its price, many other newspapers felt threatened. *The Independent* saw it as predatory pricing and complained. Immediately afterwards the price of the newspaper went up: no, not *The Times* but *The Independent*. It is difficult to believe that people buy newspapers because of the price. What they are buying, surely, is justification and support for their own prejudices: a kind of brand endorsement. You need to know what you're buying and tend to resist any changes. A *Guardian* reader would not become a *Daily Mail* reader just because the price was lower, yet the price of *The Independent* did come down before very long. What effect, if any, do you think this price manoeuvring had on the reputations of the newspapers concerned?

■ Brand as Strategic Image Statement

When Gaymers relaunched Babycham as a fruitier-tasting, higher alcohol drink in a big blue bottle, they launched at the same time a brand extension, Babycham Xtra Dry: 25cl of 8 per cent alcohol, in a green and red livery. Xtra Dry was also, according to Gaymers, a 'strategic image statement intended to directly confront prejudices about the brand' with a 'demonstration of an even greater sense of change for the relaunch as a whole'.[4]

What this seems to imply is that all the characteristics that sold four billion bottles of the original Babycham – baby-size servings, champagne-style bottle, sweet taste, Bambi look-alike brand animal – have gone. Retooling cost £2m, and marketing cost £5m in relaunch year alone. Time will tell whether the new identity pays off. How would you help that to happen, given the opportunity?

■ Other Factors

Performance is another reason for preferring a brand, while in some industries, service back-up counts for a great deal. Less tangible, but no less important to some purchasers, are factors such as lifestyle styling, novelty and conferred status. In all these, the personality of the brand can be decisive.

■ Corporation as Brand

Some cities have deliberately tried to make themselves into brands. Usually led by the city corporation, a coalition of public and private resources is put together to position and market the city: Birmingham as Britain's Second City, Barcelona as Spain's. The brand character of each is distinctive. Glasgow, Düsseldorf and Milan are all developing their corporate, corporation identities. They have the logos, trademarks, slogans, mission statements and so on. Perhaps none of the city brands is totally convincing yet, but ask me again in five or ten years' time.

■ What is a Brand Anyway?

A brand can be a stand-in for experience, a promise you expect to be fulfilled, a strategic image statement, a proxy for reputation. In other words, PR.

■ Sponsorship

In the UK, about £350m is spent on sponsorship each year, though the figure goes up and down depending on the general health of the economy. Most of it is corporate sponsorship.

Sport takes the biggest share, at around £240m. Next in order of importance comes the arts, at about £60m. It is interesting to see the variety and type of business that goes in for arts sponsorship, often combined with television or radio sponsorship, on which a further £30–50m is spent. They have their reasons.

Lloyds Bank's £2m cultural sponsorship programme included the BBC television *Clothes Show Live* six-day event at Birmingham National Exhibition Centre. This ensured that the bank's Black Horse logo was beamed to 8 million viewers, mostly the young, fashion-conscious generation they want to recruit as customers. 'Our sponsorship is giving us a dialogue with the punter', commented David Goldesgeyme, Lloyds' sponsorship manager.[5]

Even more direct was Geoff Shingles, chairman of Digital, the electronics manufacturer that sponsors performances by dance teams to which it takes potential clients such as board-level decision makers. 'If it stops being good for business', he said, 'we'll stop doing it.'[6] So far they haven't.

Although there may sometimes appear to be a correlation between the amount of media criticism an organisation gets and the subsequent size of its sponsorship budgets, there may be no obvious correlation between its own business interests and the projects it sponsors.

■ A Short Quiz

Here are three questions for you to try.

Question A Which company sponsors
- a university chair in mineral processing?
- a readership in environmental engineering?
- a lectureship in mineral law?
- schools information packs on mining and geology?
- geographical expeditions for young people?

Question B Which company sponsors
- holiday courses and classes for young musicians?
- bursaries to prepare postgraduate students for professional careers in music and drama?
- performances by a young dance company?
- postgraduate scholarships in painting and sculpture?

Question C Which company sponsors
- inner city trusts for disadvantaged youngsters?
- youth enterprise schemes?
- science conventions for young people?
- first-aid teaching in schools?

The answer to question A is not surprising. It is the RTZ Corporation, the international mining company and biggest in the industry.

However, the answer to Question B is also RTZ. So is the answer to Question C. Altogether, RTZ spends £9m a year on sponsorship worldwide, £4.2m of it in the UK. Why? The company says that it is in the business of developing resources and people. I expect you could think of some more convincing reasons.

■ Educational Sponsorship

The examples of RTZ sponsorship are largely educational, and corporate sponsorship of educational material is becoming increasingly popular in the battle of corporate identities. The problem is to reconcile self-interest with educational integrity.

The National Consumer Council's (NCC's) business sponsorship working party developed some guidelines, pointing out that bad practice lowers the confidence of teachers, parents and pupils, and blocks the effective use of good material. The NCC working party was representative of business, consumer interests, teaching associations and local education authorities. Their guidelines are summarised in Guideline 7.2 in Chapter 7, and are available in full from the NCC.

■ Some Principles of Sponsorship

Sponsorship is not in itself news, and work has to be done to make it so. Even then, media coverage of the sponsorship does not always credit the sponsor, because journalists might regard that as free publicity that ought to be paid for. For advice on how to manage the media aspects of sponsorship, turn to Chapter 10.

Both sponsors and the sponsored need to look after each other's interests as well as their own, and understand each other's motives, aims and expectations. They need to agree on who the principal negotiators will be and be clear on exactly what part any intermediary will play. All concerned must recognise and accept the financial and other constraints which apply, defining precisely who has the power of veto and over what. Sponsors and sponsored have to be prepared to do all they can to reconcile conflicts of interest and maximise benefits for everybody. These principles apply to any type of sponsorship – sports, television, radio, education, arts – whatever it may be.

Not all sponsorship needs to involve millions of pounds. Here are a few examples of sponsorship opportunities that were all available during one month in 1994:

- a West End theatre entertainment venue for corporate hospitality and events – from £250
- Hippo Club childcare crèches – newsletter at £5000
- 200 performances in schools of a specially devised theatrical show for children – £35 000 split between three sponsors: (see Case 3.1, Chapter 3)

- British Grand Prix: VIP hospitality, company name on two Rover *Tomcat* 150m.p.h. racing cars, entries in ten televised *Best of Britain* championship races – £35 000 inclusive.

Each area of sponsorship has its own specific opportunities and problems. The Association for Business Sponsorship of the Arts (ABSA) issues a range of helpful publications. The following guidelines, which can be adapted to any area of sponsorship are reproduced with ABSA's permission.

PORTFOLIO
Guideline 5.1 – Good sponsorship

Aims and objectives
- Establish a policy and the method of carrying it out
- Communicate the policy and any limits on it
- Research sponsors or arts organisations
- Target your approach
- Try to understand the other's needs and expectations.

Intermediaries
- Intermediaries must be open in their method of operation
- Any relevant personal or commercial interest must be disclosed
- References should be provided and taken up
- Non-specialist intermediaries should seek specialist advice to research the art world.

Negotiations
- Put all agreements in writing
- Open communication is essential
- A timetable, chain of command and named principal negotiators should be established early
- Be aware of conflicts of interest in multiple sponsorships.

Programming
- Recognise each other's time constraints
- Budget ahead
- Build up continuing relationships between arts organisations and businesses, independent of sponsorship
- Sponsorships tailored to a sponsor must recognise arts constraints
- Establish notice periods, options to review and length of sponsorship in advance
- Long term sponsorships have advantages for forward planning.

Artistic content
- Artistic interference by sponsors is not acceptable
- Discussion of artistic content is necessary, and is not equivalent to censorship
- Sponsors have no obligation to support art forms they find unattractive

- While most sponsorship goes to the 'safe' arts, unconventional or experimental art can enhance a sponsorship, and is the seed-bed for the future.

Making the most of the sponsorship

- Corporate entertainment is important and requires courtesy and consideration on both sides
- 'Dos and don'ts' of corporate hospitality should be thought through and communicated early on
- Arts organisations must know what they can and cannot offer, and then stick to it and back it up
- An excessive presence by the sponsor can run counter to the aims of the sponsorship
- The arts, as well as business, would benefit from media credits to sponsors; both sides should encourage, rather than coerce, the media
- Evaluate the success of the sponsorship and communicate the results to all parties.[7]

■ The Financial Arena

Corporate PR is about building a solid reputation that inspires confidence; so is financial PR.

It is a complex and tricky area with rules, guidelines and conventions ready to trip the unskilled and inexperienced. Every in-house PR practitioner needs to learn enough about it to know when a specialist consultancy needs to be called in.

The City and Financial Group of the IPR points out that:

> What is inexcusable for a financial communications practitioner employed or retained by a company is ignorance of the regulations pertaining to the case or failure to advise his client or employer of their import and of the consequences of any breach, bearing in mind that in the first instance these consequences, whether in the form of disciplinary action or sanctions or even possibly criminal proceedings, will fall upon the employer and indeed in certain circumstances on himself.[8]

Be warned.

■ Privatisation and Flotation

There are many reasons for going public, quite apart from the obvious ones of raising debt-free cash and getting access to the market: better opportunities for

acquisitions and mergers for one. Then there is the matter of status and
reputation. This is what Price Waterhouse, chartered accountants and financial
advisers, have to say about that, when they address the Board of Directors of
clients or potential clients.

> Going public is generally seen as an enviable mark of great prestige,
> contributing to a company's continued or ultimate success . . . your
> company's profile will be raised both during and after the flotation
> process. Press comment and analysis of your results, and a higher public
> profile of your management team, will result. Your company's standing
> can be enhanced amongst the public, investors, customers, suppliers and
> your employees. Commercial benefits should arise for your company and
> its products and services . . . and consider . . . the potential beneficial
> effect on the people who work in your business.'

However, Price Waterhouse also warn of the downside:

> Information must be disclosed . . . all press releases concerning your
> company's results and activities will be subject to public scrutiny and
> analysis. After the flotation you will be spending more time as well as
> money on the additional obligations of reporting and publicity. Costs of
> professional advisers . . . and other costs involved in publicising the
> flotation, will be incurred, regardless of whether the flotation is successful
> . . . and there will be ongoing costs in respect of more detailed reporting
> regulations and further publicity.

The overall costs of going public may amount to approximately 4–8 per cent of
the funds raised from the flotation.

Price Waterhouse have a clear message to company directors, investors,
employees and others concerned: the flotation process is just the start of a much
longer process; it is not an end in itself. The best way to manage your PR is to
plan early.

> Consider hiring a financial PR firm that is experienced in handling the
> financial press and the investment community. They will develop a mailing
> list and enhance the general awareness of your products and services within
> the market, which should result in greater benefits to the company . . . well
> beyond the eventual flotation. Bringing your products into the public eye
> will enable people to differentiate your company . . . giving it its own
> identity and . . . easy recognition by potential investors. A cogent and well-
> argued business plan will be an invaluable aid.

Finally, Price Waterhouse offer some practical advice on PR programmes.
'The PR people will be responsible for developing public awareness . . . arrange
for publication of articles about your company, or its impending flotation, in
the national, financial and trade press. They will also be involved in the

presentations to be made by you to potential investors, providing you with valuable advice on how best to approach the Roadshows.' The company's securities are marketed at Roadshows to prospective major institutional buyers and to analysts, in the two weeks or so before publication of the final listing particulars.

The more interest in your company that you can generate amongst major investors and analysts, both before and after the initial offer, the higher the pricing or market value. 'Start rehearsing your presentation early', is the advice of the accountancy firm, 'and gradually refine it to a style that suits you. Use slide shows if that works for your team – but don't be afraid to keep to a more conversational question-and-answer style.' Up to five presentations a day are not uncommon for ten to a dozen working days. The most difficult questions are the 'unexpectedly personal . . . and the open-ended "why?"'

On Impact Day the Stock Exchange finally approves entry of the issue to the Official List. The terms of the issue are first released, and the underwriting of the issue takes place. A press conference is held to announce the flotation, but that is by no means the end of it. Price Waterhouse counsel:

> As you look ahead, continue your company's PR with the City . . . nurture your public image . . . provide timely and reliable information . . . develop good relations with the financial community . . . disclose material information, good or bad, as promptly as possible . . . Virtually all companies will have bad news to convey at some point . . . Present that information timely, effectively, and honestly . . . Keep in touch with your stockbroker, particularly if you become aware of difficult issues approaching. Use your PR firm to ensure that you are sending the right noises to the press . . . Commission 'no-names' surveys of analysts' views on your previous presentations and company prospects . . . get feedback.[9]

Table 5.1 shows a typical timetable for a flotation, the principal advisers and their responsibility at each stage of the process.

Table 5.1   Timetable for flotation

	Company	Sponsor/ Broker	Reporting Accountants	Lawyers	PR
Detailed planning *4–8 months before flotation*					
Appoint advisers	✓				
Overall timetable agreed, detailed instructions to all advisers		✓			
Detailed timetable and list of documents prepared		✓			
Any problem areas reviewed	✓	✓	✓		✓

	Company	Sponsor/ Broker	Reporting Accountants	Lawyers	PR
Accountants' long form report begun			✓		
Drafting of documentation *2–3 months before flotation*					
Draft prospectus/listing particulars	✓	✓		✓	
Draft short form report			✓		
Draft other documents (e.g. profit/working capital forecasts)		✓			
Begin legal work				✓	
Submit draft documents to the Exchange		✓			
Begin PR/press meetings	✓	✓			✓
Submission of finalised documents and *marketing 0–2 months before flotation*					
Issue terms finalised	✓	✓			
Verification of listing particulars	✓	✓	✓	✓	
Presentation to investors and analysts	✓	✓			✓
PR/press meetings	✓	✓			✓
Finalisation and submission of documents to the Exchange		✓			
Company re-registered as PLC				✓	
Impact and offer period Flotation *week/impact day plus 1–2 weeks*					
Approval by the Exchange of all documents		✓	✓	✓	✓
Agree underwriting and sub-underwriting	✓	✓			
Listing particulars registered				✓	
Presentations to investors and press	✓	✓			✓
Announce flotation and publish/ advertise listing particulars	✓	✓			✓
Application lists open and close		✓			
Basis of allocation decided and announced	✓	✓			
Listings granted and dealings in new shares begins		–			

Source: Reproduced by permission of Price Waterhouse.

■ Distinctiveness

Although money – especially your own – is a fascinating subject, there are dry and arid areas. When did you last get excited about factoring (the practice of buying debts at a discount)? If the subject caught your attention at all in 1992/3, it was probably because of the creative and precise use of photography in a campaign to distinguish Lombard Natwest from the rest. This is the story.

PORTFOLIO
Case 5.1 – Putting factoring in the frame

Analysis
The media tend to regard factoring as uninteresting and insignificant, and even the top ten factors have to compete fiercely for very limited editorial coverage. There is a sameness about the products and services offered, and not much scope for new product development. Lombard Natwest was not the biggest in the sector; or the smallest; or the most international. The company's managing director was not chairman of the Association of British Factors and Discounters (ABFD). The company may have been outstanding, but there was apparently nothing that made it stand out.

Objectives

1. Lombard Natwest to dominate existing editorial opportunities
2. Create new opportunities to promote the company's factoring services to the business community
3. Distinguish Lombard Natwest from the factoring crowd.

Budget
Confidential.

Consultancy
LeFevre Williamson, of Oxford.

Strategy
Create a unique media hook for Lombard Natwest through pictures. Make editors who already covered the subject want to feature the company, and persuade those who didn't cover the subject to do so.

Programme

1. Identify the target media: national tabloids, broadsheets, business and management magazines, regional magazines and newspapers, and the sector press
2. Research the photographic requirements of picture and business editors of the target media
3. To meet researched editorial style and preferences, top national news photographers with regional and business press experience were commissioned to compile an imaginative portfolio of photography. Lombard clients and key personnel were the subjects
4. Precise use of different types of print for maximum take-up: 12" × 10" black and white prints, handprinted by the photographer, for the nationals; 10" × 8" machine prints for the regionals; 35mm transparencies for general colour use.

Key business magazines were sent larger format handprinted black and white prints. The impact value whetted their appetites for the colour photography.

Results

1. More coverage for Lombard Natwest than for the entire membership of ABFD for a whole year
2. 58 exclusives in national newspapers and business magazines
3. Dominant share of 65 per cent of scheduled factoring features (an equal share of voice)
4. 15 spokesman opportunities
5. Features in business and management magazines that had never covered factoring before
6. Five general features on factoring using only Lombard Natwest pictures
7. *PR Week* award for Best Use of Photography.

User feedback
'Perfect for us. They really made factoring a *Daily Mirror* story' (*Daily Mirror*).
'So many good shots I gave it a full page' (*European Window on Industry*).
'Have justifiably won our attention and extensive usage' (*Evening Standard*).[10]

■ Management Buy-outs

Financial information has to be convincing, which means that the source of the information has to be credible. Although you should not fall into the trap of believing that presentation is more important than content, it is nevertheless true that good presentation is vital. Nowhere is this more evident than in the area of management buy-outs (MBOs), when the management teams are usually taking a leap in the dark.

PORTFOLIO
Guideline 5.2 – Financing a BIMBO

Every year there are up to 600 MBOs and management buy-ins (MBIs), collectively known as BIMBOs. Some will involve very large sums, but the majority are valued at under £10m.
According to Livingstone Guarantee, an MBO is:

the acquisition of a company or a business by members of the existing management, usually in conjunction with one or more financial institutions as equity investors, as well as some debt finance provided normally by a clearing bank . . . MBIs involve a management team acquiring a business from the owners which they don't currently work in. The financial backers will be the same . . . The position of managing director is crucial. Ideally, the choice would often be the marketing or sales director because the buyout will succeed or fail primarily upon the ability to win profitable business.

Before any new business can be won, the MBO or MBI has to be completed, and that means winning the necessary investment first. To do this, the management team presents a business plan. The content of that plan has to be right, of course, but how it is presented can make the difference between success and failure. Usually, there are no second chances.

Here is the advice of one of the leading experts in the field, Barrie Pearson, of Livingstone Guarantee:

A substantial majority of business plans are rejected by equity investors, before even meeting the management team. Furthermore, most of them deserve this fate. Failure at this first hurdle must be avoided. It is not enough to take the internal business plan as presented to the group board, carry out minor editing, and add a brief profile of each member of the management team. Prospective equity investors do not have the local knowledge and market insight of the group board.

The content of the business plan presented to equity investors needs to include:

- an executive summary which sets out the entire plan, preferably on one side of paper, and certainly on not more than two
- a relevant history and description of the business including products or services, markets served, distribution channels used, location and size
- market place and competition: an assessment of future trends in the market place, together with current and likely competitors
- future strategy for business development: the key changes and innovations which the management team plan to pursue
- a profile of each investing member of the management team
- the organisation chart proposed
- a summary of financial history and projections, giving profit and loss and cash flow for at least three years forward

For most BIMBOs, the plan should be no more than 15 pages long. Waffle and irrelevant detail are counter-productive. Appendices should contain:

- detailed projections for profit and loss, cash flow and balance sheets with a statement of the underlying assumptions
- relevant press articles about the company

- extracts from market research reports supporting the expected market trends
- corporate brochure or product literature

It is important that the prospective equity investors recognise that the business plan has been written by the management team, and not the financial advisers. Nonetheless, the financial advisers should edit the final draft because they will be able to read it from the perspective of the equity investor. Most importantly, the credibility of the business plan is enhanced when it is delivered by a respected financial adviser on behalf of the management team.[11]

■ Writing Reports

Annual reports, client reports, feasibility studies, programme proposals, business plans: these are all reports of one kind or another. Corporate and financial affairs are great generators – and consumers – of reports. Writing them is a fundamental PR skill. Here are some general purpose guidelines which you should be able to adapt to any particular report.

PORTFOLIO
Guideline 5.3 – Reports: arranging your material

The sequence in which you present your report is largely determined by the kind of report it is.

1. Case histories and legal documentation usually benefit from having the material presented in the order of the dates or times when things happened
   Type – chronological.
2. Branch reviews and some comparative analyses lend themselves to arrangement by geographic location
   Type – spatial.
3. Argumentation or criticism usually require the least important points to be made first, building up to the clincher
   Type – ascending order of importance.
4. Selling and promotional reports work best if you start with the most important points, backing them up with subsidiary points
   Type – descending order of importance.
5. Educational, academic and intellectually based reports can start simply and steadily become more elaborate and demanding
   Type – complexity.

6. Advice, reassurance and conciliation are best served by moving carefully and smoothly from the known and comfortable to the unknown and challenging
    Type – familiarity.
7. The most compelling reports are about doing something. Here are two ways of presenting the same material:
    chronologically (A), or action oriented (B).

Example A: chronological

(a) Purpose	–	the objective of the report
	–	the reader's expectations
	–	the background and history
	–	the authority for the report
	–	any limitations or exclusions
(b) Method	–	what materials, equipment or systems were drawn on
	–	what happened, step by step
	–	observations on what happened
	–	any calculations on the material data
(c) Results	–	expressed in words
	–	illuminated by charts, diagrams, tables
(d) Conclusions	–	how results compared with expectations
	–	how results compared with other relevant results
	–	explanation of differences
	–	how the systems, equipment or materials behaved
	–	reliability and repeatability of methods
	–	clear indication of margins of error or tolerances
(e) Recommendations	–	succinctly expressed
	–	logically ordered
	–	persuasively presented
(f) References		

Example B: action oriented

(a) Introduction	–	the objectives of the report
(b) Recommendations	–	succinct
	–	ascending or descending order
	–	persuasive
	–	arising from the body of the report

Recommendations will be the only part of the report that many people read.

| (c) Method | – | chronology |
| | – | observations |

(d)	Results	– words and graphics conceived as one
(e)	Conclusions	– results compared with expectations
(f)	Appendices	– background and history
		– authority
		– limitations and exclusions
		– materials, equipment, systems
		– reliability and repeatability of method
		– calculations and numerical data
		– comparison with other results
		– explanation of differences
		– errors and tolerances
		– other factors
(g)	References	

■ Personal Finance

One of the sectors which has been undergoing far-reaching changes – and they are not over yet – is the personal financial services sector. Among the areas most affected by change are

1. *Suppliers*: Not only are well established suppliers of services and products blossoming, but there is also a new wave of sources within the UK and from overseas.
2. *Legislation*: Old regulations have been swept away by deregulation, in the wake of which have come new regulations.
3. *Markets*: The whole market has been getting bigger, not only by enlargement of the traditional markets, but by segmentation and niche markets. The customer base is now much broader, and there are more middlemen.
4. *Technology*: Everyone is affected by new and better technology, from suppliers through intermediaries to consumers. Cash dispensers, credit points, transactions by post, by telephone and on-line – have all profoundly affected not only the way things are done but what things are done.

■ New Markets

In the 1990s, as personal financial services and products became more accessible and perhaps a bit less expensive, they were bought by people who were entirely new to the market. Reputation and product differentiation became increasingly important, but before either of these could have any effect there had to be awareness and visibility. Here is an example, taken from life (GA Life, in fact).

PORTFOLIO
Case 5.2 – Success is no accident

Analysis
General Accident Life had discovered that although General Accident was a household name for general insurance, the GA Life name was not at all well known amongst consumers for life and investment products nor amongst financial journalists.

Objectives

1.   To increase awareness of GA Life and its products amongst the public through consumer media
2.   To publicise existing GA Life products, with new consumer angles.

Budget
£15 000, including all fees, research, design and printing.

Consultancy
Northern Lights, of Harrogate.

Research

1.   Attitude research amongst journalists covering personal finance in consumer media revealed that they strongly disliked featuring life companies and their products because of the industry's reputation for aggressive sales techniques
2.   Product analysis showed that many people who would not normally think of themselves as being in the inheritance tax bracket could have an estate valuable enough to qualify
3.   A package aimed at families, and their need to plan for the time when parents become incapacitated, or die, could let in other GA Life products (healthcare, pensions, will writing and so on).

Programme
Northern Lights recommended that the PR campaign should centre on human issues, rather than GA Life products. To overcome consumer scepticism, and journalists' resistance to life companies, an independent third party was enlisted. He was Dr Peter Stratton of Leeds University, a leading family psychologist.

The human issue developed with Dr Stratton was that families who avoid talking about practicalities, because of sensitivities about death, can experience considerable grief when parents die without having discussed their wishes.

Campaign elements, with Dr Stratton's advice and help as an independent expert, were as follows.

1. Gallup research amongst parents (most over 45); adult children with parents alive; adult children whose parents had died. All were asked for their views on raising and discussing with parents such financial matters as planning for them if they became unable to look after themselves, or died

2. Advice booklet analysing why families fear discussing the subject, and giving practical advice on how to raise sensitive family issues. The booklet included information researched with Age Concern and Citizens Advice Bureau

3. The booklet and research results were launched to regional and consumer media through press notices and radio interviews. Copies of the booklet and findings also went direct to Agony Aunts

4. The number of inquiries generated from media coverage was targeted at 500. GA Life set up special systems to ensure that such inquiries were not treated as sales leads.

Results

1. Inquiries for the booklet exceeded the target by 100 per cent in the first three months

2. Radio coverage included national BBC and several regional programmes

3. Press coverage included national heavyweights and tabloids, major provincials, and financial and consumer magazines

4. Award of IPR Certificate of Excellence

5. Industry approval: Clear English award in competition organised by *Financial Adviser/IFA Promotion*

6. Client satisfaction. (GA Life staff were among those requesting the booklet.)

Evaluation
A successful format which became a model for further campaigns.[12]

■ Reputation

You cannot sell a financial service or product without also selling performance, security, track record, probity; in a word, reputation. It is the business of PR to help the perception and acceptance of good reputation. This is not done by hype, or by image manipulation, but by knowing what is happening and keeping all concerned informed.

Personal finance products compete in what might be described as a review-driven market. What sells the product is the reputation that arises from favourable editorial coverage. In this sector, informational advertising and direct mail are very heavily used, but they are chiefly effective in making it easy to buy the product. Their influence on the decision to purchase is relatively minor.

Financial advertising agency Elgie Stewart Smith (see Chapter 1) spent £7000 with Paragon. The PR strategy was to identify and brand a new market segment, the so-called Inheritance Generation, and launch a report about it to targeted media. Seminars were held for financial institutions, and the campaign scored 9 400 000 OTS at a unit cost of 0.007p. At least 100 good-quality inquiries were received from financial institutions. These activities enhanced Elgie Stewart Smith's reputation and played a part in winning £10m of advertising business for them. A new acronym was introduced into popular use at the time: PIPPIES, or People Inheriting Parents' Property.[13]

■ Briefings

The guidelines on investor relations say quite clearly that companies should not give advance briefings to selected journalists before making the same information generally available through accepted channels and by official spokespeople. That is not necessarily what happens in practice.

Clare Dobie of *The Independent* was not breaking any confidences when she reported that, 'Analysts talk to companies in the hope of finding out something that will gain them commission; that is, prompt their clients to buy or sell shares. Journalists talk to companies in the hope of writing stories in a paper – informing the public – rather than stimulating share deals.' Published reports by journalists are available to everybody (fund managers, private investors, the general public, those who have no stockbroker), and not just those with access to the Stock Exchange information network. Financial editor Peter Rodgers put it succinctly: 'Telling the weekend papers of a development – and backing it up by informing news agencies – reaches more investors simultaneously than any other form of communication.'

■ Speeches

Talking to analysts and journalists is one thing, making a speech quite another. A talk is essentially conversational, whereas a speech is more of a statement, used to promulgate and promote corporate policy, to convey messages to the financial world, to attract and reassure investors, and to enhance reputation.

To write a speech, even when you are going to deliver it yourself, is not an instinctive skill, but one that has to be learned, polished and tested against experience. It is not enough to be yourself: you have to sound like yourself.

To write a speech for someone else to deliver is one of the most difficult skills of all to acquire because you are not only thinking like somebody else's brain, you are speaking in somebody else's voice. In practice, you are not likely to be entrusted with the whole job unless you are very able and until you are very experienced. What you will probably find is that some of the research chores come your way (anything from checking statistics to digging up an anecdote or quote).

As you progress, you may take on a more important role in speech writing. Here are some guidelines.

PORTFOLIO
Guideline 5.4 – Writing speeches

Audience
Define who the speech is actually for: those who are present, certainly, but are they the only, or even the main, audience? A Chairman's speech, say on publication of a company's annual report, will be delivered to whoever is in the room at the time. This direct audience will certainly include institutional investors and financial journalists. However, not many shareholders will be present, and to reach them the Chairman has to rely on intermediaries such as the media, perhaps backed up by direct mail.

Purpose
Why is the speech being made: to impress the City; attract good investors; boost staff morale; influence the government? Whatever the reason, if you aren't clear about it, neither will the audience be.

Content and structure
No more than three main points can be got across in a speech. Each one needs to be made clearly, and supported/illustrated by credible material. A typical structure for a 20-minute speech would be

Introduction	2 minutes
Main point 1 and supporting material	5 minutes
Main point 2 and supporting material	4 minutes
Main point 3 and supporting material	3 minutes
Summary	3 minutes
Conclusion and call for action	2 minutes

That leaves one minute for interruptions, topical allusions and so on, as appropriate. Always have at least five minutes reserve material, to be used only if absolutely necessary. It often will be.

Style

When someone told the eighteenth-century orator George Fox that his latest speech read damn well, he retorted that it must have been a damn bad speech. You can see what he meant, because above all else a speech, statement that it is, has to be *sayable*, and that is not at all the same thing as *readable*.

Details need to be concrete, not abstract; precise, not vague; believable; and as visual as possible.

Use the words and phrases your audience uses and don't be afraid of repetition.

If you are writing the speech for someone else to deliver, talk it through with them and hear them say it back to you.

Perhaps the most important thing is that audiences tend to remember *what* you say at the beginning and end of the speech, but only *how* you say the middle bit.

Bear in mind the need for quotable quotes for the press notice and soundbites for radio and television (see Chapter 10).

Promotion and distribution

To ensure that the message of the speech reaches its intended wider audience, you will need to promote it, using methods described elsewhere in this book.

An invariable rule

Always check facts at source.

CHAPTER 6
Government Relations

It is true that there is no Russian word for public relations, but the job has always existed.

Vladimir Tsimbalov[1]

■ How it all Began

It is hardly possible to pinpoint the beginning of public relations, but the origins are much farther back in time than you might think. The ancient Egyptians invented corporate images. The triumphal processions of the Romans were a status builder for the Emperor, while bread and circuses kept the common people docile. The purpose of the Bayeux Tapestry was to justify the Norman invasion of England and so glorify the Conqueror.

In the Middle Ages, sophisticated systems of communication took the royal message out to the people. According to contemporary accounts, in fifteenth-century Italy Lorenzo de Medici was accused of securing popular support with what Savonarola described as 'spectacles and festivals'. 'Because the common people are unstable and long for novelty', wrote Giovanni Botero, 'they will seek it out for themselves, changing even their government and their rules if their prince does not provide some kind of diversion for them.'[2]

Tudor and Stuart monarchs employed famous portrait painters as image makers (quite literally), a practice that continues today in the hands of the Court photographers and some television producers. Of course, government PR was not always successful in the past, any more than now.

It could be argued that inept government PR was partly responsible for the English Civil War. It was not a class war. Indeed, other than as soldiers, the common people were not much involved, at least up to the middle stages. The causes of that seventeenth-century revolution were many and complex: economic, financial, religious, political.

One factor was the lifestyle and public attitude of King and Court. Heavy and illegal taxation; royal extravagance and conspicuous consumption; unpopular religious connections; bypassing of Parliament; wordy and unconvincing justification of domestic policies; autocratic and arrogant actions: all this was summed up in the unshakeable and publicly declared belief that 'princes are not bound to give account of their actions but to God alone'. Princes continued to believe that, long after the people did not. The King was perceived as holding his subjects in contempt. Oddly enough, this perception was strongest amongst those who themselves were in positions of privilege and local power.[3]

To suggest that better presentation of royal policies could have prevented the Civil War would be absurd: the policies carried the seeds of their own destruction. But it is surely not fanciful to argue that if public perception had been taken seriously, the policies might have been better and that could have affected the course of history.

■ Putting Pressure on Government

National and local government PR, good, bad or indifferent, made the running in those early stages. Gradually, others (usually representing vested interests) learned PR strategies and techniques and used them to influence governments. Let us examine one such case in depth.

PORTFOLIO
Case 6.1 – The first modern pressure group

Background
In the early years of the nineteenth century, expansion of overseas trade, higher productivity in agriculture and the dominance of the iron and textile industries were followed by economic crisis. Abroad there were trade barriers and embargoes, at home bad harvests and industrial exploitation. Unemployment rose, real wages fell faster than prices and exports were down by 30 per cent. Stimulated by a 16 per cent increase in the population, and by inflationary budgets alongside higher taxes and speculation in gold, reform was in the air.

Many radical groups were formed, with different agendas for change: parliamentary, financial, commercial, legislative. The privileged classes closed ranks, and the interests of land and property owners were protected by repressive government action. Although the Reform Act of 1832 rationalised the electoral system and extended the franchise by 40–80 per cent, vested interests and the old regime were still very powerful. Dissenting newspapers and journals were heavily taxed. There was a lot going on, in public and below the surface.

Objectives
The Anti-Corn Law League was created in Manchester in 1839, with one clear objective: the total and immediate repeal of the Corn Laws of 1815 (and later amendments). This purpose was simple, easily understood and single minded.

The Corn Laws had been deliberately framed to protect producers, at the expense of consumers, by banning imports of corn if the market price fell below a fixed sum. If the price rose above that figure, then trade was free. This probably staved off, for over a decade, discontent among those of the working population who tilled the land; but it was all at a cost. Manipulation by international dealers and speculators led to wild price swings, and although restoration of the gold standard helped overseas trade generally, there was misery and poverty at home.

Strategy

The League's strategy was as straightforward as its objectives. Demands were kept simple, and separate from all other contemporary reform movements such as the Chartists, Benthamites and Spenceans. The League's message was that repealing the Corn Laws would have the multiple benefits of:

- opening markets to manufacturers, so boosting exports
- reducing the price of bread, still the staple diet of the working class, who ate about 5 lb of it per head per week
- stabilising employment, and at a higher level than would otherwise be the case
- stimulating demand for agricultural products in urban and industrial areas
- contributing to international relations through free trade, and economic inter-dependence.

Biblical precedents were quoted against those who became rich on the hunger of the poor. In attacking privilege and monopoly the League appealed to altruistic desires for equality. Simultaneously, in offering cheaper food it appealed to the self-interest of the middle and working classes.

The spin doctors of the day even managed to convey to consumers that repeal would reduce the price of bread and that real wages would increase, while assuring manufacturers that when pressure to keep prices high was relaxed, wages could be held down.

Resources

A centralised organisation was set up, with professional staff and with a series of committees in parallel, on the lines of the anti-slavery and Wesleyan models. Funding was mainly by subscriptions from sympathetic land owners and the professional classes.

Programme

1. *Public platforms*: at a time when public speeches were not at all common, circulating orators like Cobden and Bright stumped the country acting as PR missionaries. They were reinforced and supplemented by paid professional speakers who knew their job. 'People do not attend public meetings to be taught', said Cobden, 'but to be excited, flattered and pleased.'

2. *Demonstrations* and petitions were organised to show the strength of public support for the League.
3. *Events* such as parties and bazaars raised consciousness and also funds.
4. *Merchandising*: a range of artefacts was marketed, including Anti Corn Law breadplates and anti-monopoly pincushions. Some of these items can occasionally be found in country sale rooms, even today.
5. *Leaflets and pamphlets* were produced and distributed in large quantities (up to 3.5 tonnes a week).
6. *Information technology* was used to get messages out quickly and cheaply. The new Penny Post and the rapidly expanding railway network were exploited.
7. *Editorials* were subsidised in papers like the London *Sun* (a form of advertorial).
8. *Own publications*: the League published its own periodicals such as the *Anti Corn Law Newsletter*, and *The Economist*, founded by James Wilson in 1843.
9. *Lobbying* of MPs and candidates was supported by tactical voting and manipulation of registration. The League also fielded its own candidates.
10. *Interest groups* of various kinds were consolidated into effective coalitions. At the same time, opponents were divided and isolated.
11. *Reassurance* was given to an apprehensive public that the League would act constitutionally and never use violence.

All of those techniques are in use today, but not all of that programme would now be acceptable.

Evaluation
The Corn Laws were repealed in their entirety on 25 June 1846. The Anti-Corn Law League's objective was achieved 100 per cent.

The question is, how much did the League have to do with it? To what extent was their PR programme responsible? What other significant influences were there?

Cobden admitted that: 'The League would not have carried the repeal of the Corn Laws when they did, had it not been for the Irish famine and the circumstance that we had a minister [that is, the Prime Minister] who thought more of the lives of the people than he did about his own continuance of power.' It is true that Peel did resign in December 1845, though he was back again after a fortnight, and seems to have made up his mind to repeal before he knew about the failure of the Irish potato crop. The League's campaign may have affected the timing of the decision, but probably not the fact. Peel's second and final resignation took place on 29 June 1846.

As is often the case in dealing with government, the true effects of the pressure group campaign took some time to work through. 'The controversy over the repeal of the Corn Laws is curiously out of proportion to the results obtained by repeal. The real importance of the League lay in its representation and its status as a milestone in the development of English political institutions.'₄

The League's battle for free trade started in Manchester, and it was a Manchester cotton master from Germany who noted that 'the whole Political Economy of today is at an end'. He was Friedrich Engels who, with Karl Marx, drafted the *Communist Manifesto* in London only two years after the Corn Laws were repealed, and six years before Charles Dickens's *Hard Times* portrayed the terrible social and economic consequences of the continuing shift from farming to factories. Nine years after *Hard Times*, Abraham Lincoln made his Gettysburg address on freedom and equality. Within four years *Das Kapital* appeared, but that's another story.

■ The Government and Other Audiences

Avon and Somerset Constabulary brought extensive media coverage and the support of influential third parties to bear on the government. Specific legislative changes were needed to deal with the specific problem of re-offenders on bail (see Case 14.1, Chapter 14). The campaign addressed six distinct publics: the media; opinion leaders in the criminal justice system; chief constables; the Police Authority; the general public; and MPs and Home Office officials.

■ They Ought to Make a Film About it

National government is a main target audience for local government. Here is an example of a low-cost lobbying campaign that teamed a local authority with a pressure group which had been an opponent.

The proposed sale of one of Britain's oldest film studios, Elstree, was strongly opposed by a group of local enthusiasts running the *Save Our Studios* campaign. Nevertheless, Hertsmere Council did agree to the sale, but only on the strict condition that film production would continue on the site. Subsequently the new owners (leisure group Brent Walker) decided to close the film-making facility altogether. Hertsmere Council aimed to 'raise public awareness of Elstree's plight, market the site as a working studio, and force Brent Walker to tell a high Court judge why it had reneged on its agreement'. The Council's planning department brought a civil action against Brent Walker and from July 1993 to January 1994 mounted a PR campaign with *Save Our Studios* as active partners. Faxes and letters were sent to key contacts in the film industry, worldwide, and 'pretty soon they had the support of Spielberg, Stanley Kubrick, David Puttnam and Kenneth Branagh'.

The national press took up the story, the High Court ruled that Hertsmere Council had a case, and Brent Walker undertook 'not to go ahead with the demolition pending a full hearing later in the year'.[5]

Not a bad outcome for a campaign that cost less than £1000.

■ Winning Contracts

What do you do when you are one of only two companies competing for a big government contract and the other contender is perceived as the clear favourite? That was the situation Devonport Management Ltd (DML) faced over the Ministry of Defence Trident nuclear submarine £5bn refitting contract. DML called in The Rowland Company and together they decided on a two-pronged campaign of lobbying and media relations. Here is the story.

PORTFOLIO
Case 6.2 – Devonport versus Rosyth

Analysis
Rowland's research put Devonport behind their competitor Rosyth, based in Fife, Scotland. DML was practically unknown by the national media, while the local media saw the company as closed and uncommunicative. Local backbench MPs were thought to have little interest in, or knowledge of, the issues. After the 1992 General Election, the new Defence Secretary, Malcolm Rifkind (who happened to be a Scot), was under pressure from Scottish MPs of all parties, who were vociferously pro-Rosyth. In any case, Rosyth was generally perceived as being the natural and obvious dockyard to tackle submarine refits.

Objectives

1. To secure the Trident contract for Devonport
2. To change perception of DML from an unknown surface ship refitter that played things close to its chest, to an open, innovative organisation, well able to handle the Trident contract
3. To raise the profile of DML to equal the status of Rosyth.

Strategy

1. Mobilise support from local community, workforce, MPs, the business community and the media

2. Demonstrate to the Ministry of Defence, political advisers, Cabinet Ministers and Parliamentarians the strategic, economic and political case for Trident in Devonport
3. Project DML as 'winners'.

Consultancy
The Rowland Company.

Budget
Not disclosed. Expenditure was closely monitored with the main cost being senior consultants' time. Remember, a £5bn contract was at stake.

Programme
1. Carry out detailed media audit to identify 'friends' and 'enemies'.
2. Define priority audiences.
3. Produce new briefing materials for priority audiences throughout campaign. The main lobbying document was *The Devonport Case.*
4. Conduct a sequence of personal briefings with defence and industry Ministers, correspondents and regional media, MPs, civil servants and political advisers throughout the summer of 1992.
5. Lobby at party political conference, autumn 1992.
6. Organise workforce rally of 500 to lobby Parliament, and arrange for MPs, management and trade unions' representatives to speak at a mass meeting.
7. Organise 20 000 signature petition and hand in to No. 10 Downing Street.
8. Advise DML to promote its own alternative and innovative proposals for the future of Rosyth. Brief all relevant audiences.
9. Conduct a sustained series of individual briefings and have regular contact with defence, industry and lobby correspondents from national media.
10. Use media training and local media opportunities to prepare and warm up for subsequent national broadcasting activities.
11. Increase local media awareness and encourage *Save the Dockyard* campaigns in Plymouth.
12. Special pre-Christmas briefing for media to keep issues live.
13. Create strong advertising campaign in *The Times* and *The House* magazine, April–June 1993.
14. Fight off last minute bid from Rosyth to undercut the tender price.

Results
1. DML won the £5 billion Trident contract
2. DML established reputation as the leading contender and prime source of information and comments for the media
3. The Rowland Company won public affairs awards in the 1993 *PR Week* awards and the 1994 IPR Sword of Excellence Awards, and a PRCA Outstanding Consultancy Practice award in 1994.[6]

■ Lobbying

The specific effort to influence public decision making, either to bring about a change in policy or to prevent such change, is known as lobbying. This chapter, and others in the book, contain examples of lobbying in practice. Conducted by individuals acting on behalf of employers or clients, lobbying consists of representations made to any public office holder on any aspect of policy, or any measures implementing that policy, or any matter being considered – or which is likely to be considered – by a public body.

Professional lobbyists are usually either *consultants* (lawyers, accountants and other professional advisers, but much more often than not PR consultants) or *in-house employees* for whom lobbying is a substantial/frequent/time consuming requirement of their jobs.

To demonstrate its commitment to high professional standards and greater transparency, openness and integrity, the IPR in conjunction with the PRCA runs a Register of Professional Lobbyists. The scheme is described in Appendix C.

■ The Woman on the Clapham Omnibus

Public relations traffic can also flow from government to audience. There is no lack of sophistication on both sides and no lack of scepticism amongst the general public. As the woman on the Clapham omnibus said, 'What kind of understanding of PR can this government have? They spend £2m on a direct mail campaign to parents, telling us what we already know, when what we actually want is more money spent in the schools to help the kids learn what they need to know.' I have this verbatim, because I was sitting next to her at the time.

■ Select Committees

A relatively new element in the parliamentary machine is the Select Committee. By 1995 there were 17 of them, each shadowing and scrutinising a particular area of government responsibility or activity, such as education or defence. Responsible to Parliament, the committees are independent of government, far ranging and not always very predictable; and although Ministers have been known to stonewall them, they cause a certain amount of alarm.

Don't worry, you are not likely to be called by a Select Committee until you are a pretty senior figure in your profession. What you may well be called upon to do is to assist on research, advice and briefing. The essential point is to take the guesswork out of it by anticipating the Committee's interests and line of questioning and preparing for it thoroughly.

As far as possible, your firm or client should submit written evidence: but you want to get it written into the record. The best way is to make sure that it is also said during a personal appearance in front of the Committee. For maximum effectiveness, see that briefing and rehearsal precede a personal appearance, followed by debriefing. And remember, there is no need to go on the defensive, because there is nothing to hide . . . is there?

Paul Barnes, director of leading lobbyists GJW Government Relations, takes a calm and reassuring position on Select Committees. 'You have to remember that most people are only going to give evidence to a select committee once in a lifetime . . . Say who you are, say why you should be believed, give your evidence, then tell them what *you* want . . . If you don't offer recommendations, there will be other people who will.'[7]

■ Local Government Relations

The Local Government Group of the IPR publishes advice and guidelines to its own members concerning PR *by* local government. This chapter draws on these guidelines quite extensively.

First, however, let us look at it from the other end: relations *with* local government. Here are some key points.

1. Local government is big business and usually the largest employer in its area. A typical county council may have 35 000 employees and a budget of £700m a year. What they do is bound to affect your business.
2. Local government is a valuable partner, in terms of community relations, partnership schemes with industry, and, not least, contacts and contracts. What your business does is bound to affect them.
3. Local government is keener than ever to communicate with – and be involved with – its customers (for example, the Citizens Charter, environmental issues, education). Businesses, including yours, are important to local government, whether as customers or suppliers.
4. Local government is going through massive change: constant new legislation, compulsory competitive tendering, privatisation and structural review in Wales, Scotland and most of England. This will produce a host of new authorities with new approaches and responsibilities and offering new opportunities to your business.
5. There is generally low awareness among industry, commerce and the public of what local government does, how it does it, and who does what within it. Get to know your local authorities and keep in regular contact. It could be very useful if you can find a PR consultancy to help you: but the responsibility is yours.[8]

■ Performance Indicators: Opportunity or Threat?

'Local authorities must develop strong and effective communications with the public' asserts the IPR Local Government Group.

Customer care, quality assurance, decentralisation of services, charters, equal opportunities and performance measures all depend on good PR if they are to be seen as more than just empty promises . . . The PR strategy will include creating public understanding and awareness of the policies, procedures and activities of the authority . . . responding where appropriate to criticisms and putting right misconceptions . . . encouraging public participation and interest in the authority's decision and policy-making process . . . helping to create and maintain an awareness of the need to communicate with the public . . . respond rapidly to media inquiries . . . advise and convince officers and politicians of the need to tell people about the council and its work.[9]

Local authorities approach PR in different ways and with varying levels of commitment. The number of professional PR staff employed can range from 0 to 30, while the amount of money spent on PR activities can range from next-to-nothing to £1m or more each year.[10] As an example, Brent Council spent £60 000 over four years in a sustained attempt to make marketing a fact of everyday life for its 8000 workforce. The programme won several awards, but did it achieve the objective? Read Case 11.2, Chapter 11, and judge for yourself.

Local authorities are required to publish audited performance indicators, measuring 60–80 activities such as 'answering the telephone, collecting rubbish and dealing with a case of child abuse'. Councils must publish, in local paid-for newspaper advertisements, 'all the figures, good and bad, for the services they provide. The ad should be comprehensible and not require any other explanatory information.' The question is whether the information is *presented* or merely *reported*. Inter-authority comparisons are published by the Audit Commission.

Opportunity or *threat*? *Opportunity*, certainly, for politicians who are adept at using league tables for the bloodsport of local authority bashing. Indeed, performance indicators might have been devised for that very purpose. *Opportunity*, too, for PR consultancies to develop new business and show what they can do.

Opportunity for local authority PR departments to justify their existence. *Opportunity* for local and national media to comment on and interpret the raw data.

Opportunity for the public sector to improve its performance and give better value for money? A *threat* to those services which really need a fair amount of explanation for proper understanding?[11]

PORTFOLIO
Case 6.3 – Worth every penny

Analysis
As in other parts of the country, most people in the Wycombe District did not know what services their Council provided, nor what they cost.

A district-wide customer panel survey carried out in the early part of 1993 indicated that for a random sample of 22 services provided by WDC, or Bucks County Council, or both, there was frequent misunderstanding and confusion. For example 80 per cent of those questioned thought WDC ran libraries and 63 per cent thought WDC ran schools; they were wrong on both counts. Over 40 per cent of respondents did not know which was the responsible authority for dog wardens, public conveniences and the removal of abandoned cars. Clearly, WDC's commitment to be outward-looking and engage in effective dialogue with the public was not being realised satisfactorily.

Objectives

1. To increase awareness of the services provided by WDC
2. To convey to the public effective messages about the cost of their services
3. To establish quantitative benchmarks against which changes in awareness could be monitored
4. To achieve the above on a 'no new money, no new staff' basis.

Strategy

1. Partnership with Brunel University Department of Advertising
2. Devise a slogan as a rallying point
3. Use low-cost media.

Budget
£10 000, which was 13 per cent of the total PR budget for the year.

Programme

1. Initial briefing of students in November 1992, followed by development work.
2. Final presentation to Council in January 1993.
3. From slogans put forward by the students, 'We make every penny count' was chosen. This was translated into 'cost per week per service' concepts and designs.
4. Implementation started after May 1993 elections.
5. Posters on 20 or so sites, mainly in High Wycombe town centre.
6. Sloganised buses (five daily, on varying routes) throughout the district for a year.

7.   Cinema screen advertising for a year on three screens out of the six available.
8.   WDC's own publications included 60 000 Council Tax information leaflets sent out to taxpayers. In addition, the tax payments book carried the logo and graphic.
9.   The message was also used on an 'as available' basis to fill any advertising spaces left empty in WDC publications.

Results

Wycombe's biennial household survey was due in autumn 1993, only four months after the campaign started. Questions on the impact of the campaign were included in this survey, with the following results.

Awareness of the slogan – 28 per cent. Of these:

- 43 per cent gave the leaflets as the source
- 20 per cent gave posters and information boards
- nearly 30 per cent didn't know where they had seen the slogan
- 12.5 per cent correctly identified, from four options, the weekly cost of Council-provided services for a Band D property
- 45 per cent put the figure too high and 4 per cent too low
- 38 per cent frankly admitted they didn't know

Evaluation

1.   Awareness of the slogan was judged satisfactory so early in the campaign
2.   Awareness of costs was less good
3.   Cinema screen advertising scored badly and was dropped in the second year of the campaign in favour of illuminated posters in the foyer
4.   Quantified objectives for 1994, set by the Chief Officer's Group, were 50 per cent slogan awareness and 25 per cent cost awareness
5.   An underlying aim of the 1994 campaign would be to make the public understand that most of the money collected by WDC must be handed on to Bucks County Council.[12]

■ The European Dimension

Every business of any size has a political agenda which includes Europe. In the case of Toyota, for instance, the company was very aware in 1994 of post-Maastricht conflict between EU members; impending enlargement of the Union by four new member countries; tensions between East and West Europe; and uncertainties about Russia's position. There was a general trend towards protectionism, and growing criticism of Japanese car manufacturers by other car makers; the benefits of the economic recovery were slow to come through; there was also speculation about the leadership of both Government and Opposition; and other factors of political significance.

Toyota and their PR advisers, Scope: Communications, decided to deepen and widen all political relationships. Big events were created to attract the attention – and indeed the attendance – of Government Ministers, including the Premier. On-site visits were arranged for all-Party associations of MPs such as the motor industry and Anglo-Japanese Groups. DTI initiatives, such as supplier missions to Japan, were supported to help the transfer of knowledge to British industry. Meetings were held with local MPs. After the June Europe elections, positive messages were conveyed to the European Parliament. Local government was involved in Toyota's community relations programmes.

This political programme was part of an integrated PR Corporate Plan developed by Scope: Communications with TMC London Office and the Toyota UK Project in Europe, which included relations with the media and other opinion leaders, the business and financial community, Toyota staff ('the members'), local communities, dealers and distributors, the education sector, and existing and prospective customers and consumers.

■ Europe and You

Identify the skills for Europe that you personally will need and haven't already got. Take steps to acquire them and encourage your colleagues to do the same. If necessary, pressurise your company to institute a policy of training in skills for Europe.

We are not talking only about language skills, important though these are. What about other professional skills? How do practices and standards differ from what you have been used to? In Spain, for instance, it is illegal to practise PR unless you are a member of the recognised professional institution.

Look at the use of media in the different countries. How do they compare one with another on accessibility and costs? How will legislation concerning them affect you? Is the law of copyright any different? What about trademarks?

How will you find out about lobbying practice? What do you need to know? Who do you need to know? What interests should you declare? Can you brief Brussels from London? What information technology will help you?

PORTFOLIO
Guideline 6.1 – Decision making in Europe

You cannot hope to have any influence in Europe unless you understand how decisions are made there. Figure 6.1 sets out the procedures in simplified form.

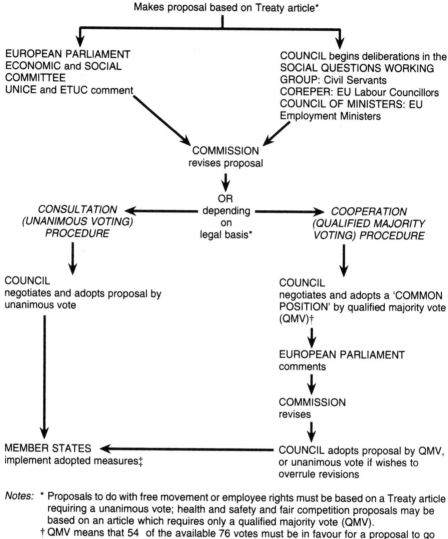

COMMISSION
Makes proposal based on Treaty article*

EUROPEAN PARLIAMENT
ECONOMIC and SOCIAL
COMMITTEE
UNICE and ETUC comment

COUNCIL begins deliberations in the
SOCIAL QUESTIONS WORKING
GROUP: Civil Servants
COREPER: EU Labour Councillors
COUNCIL OF MINISTERS: EU
Employment Ministers

COMMISSION
revises proposal

OR
depending
on
legal basis*

*CONSULTATION
(UNANIMOUS VOTING)
PROCEDURE*

*COOPERATION
(QUALIFIED MAJORITY
VOTING) PROCEDURE*

COUNCIL
negotiates and adopts proposal by
unanimous vote

COUNCIL
negotiates and adopts a 'COMMON
POSITION' by qualified majority vote
(QMV)†

EUROPEAN PARLIAMENT
comments

COMMISSION
revises

MEMBER STATES
implement adopted measures‡

COUNCIL adopts proposal by QMV,
or unanimous vote if wishes to
overrule revisions

Notes: * Proposals to do with free movement or employee rights must be based on a Treaty article
requiring a unanimous vote; health and safety and fair competition proposals may be
based on an article which requires only a qualified majority vote (QMV).
  † QMV means that 54 of the available 76 votes must be in favour for a proposal to go
through. Member states have block votes according to their size of population: UK.
France, Germany, Italy – 10 votes; Spain – 8 votes; Greece, The Netherlands, Portugal –
5 votes; Denmark, Ireland – 3 votes; Luxembourg – 2 votes.
  ‡ DIRECTIVES are implemented through national legislation in each member state by an
agreed deadline.
REGULATIONS and DECISIONS apply in all member states immediately.
RECOMMENDATIONS, COMMUNICATIONS, OPINIONS, etc., have no legal force.
N.B. Proposals may be blocked at any stage due to insufficient support in the Council.

Source: *Pay and Benefits Pocket Book*, NTC Publications/Baron & Woodrow.

Figure 6.1   Schematic of decision making in the European Commission

Specifications, contracts and methods of paying for services may differ from country to country; so may what people expect for their money. Customs are not uniform across Europe; neither are customers.

In the UK, as elsewhere in Europe, a 100 watt bulb is a 100 watt bulb. But what about the method of fixing? What scope is there for harmonisation? In the UK we use bayonet fixings, whereas in some other European countries the screw fixing is normal. Each user country wants its own system to prevail. This probably explains why the attitude of some Britons towards harmonisation is 'Let's bayonet them before they screw us.'

■ Mind Your Language

Language can be a disaster area littered with booby traps. We have all laughed at those extraordinary English versions of foreign notices, brochures and so on. You know the sort of thing: 'If the painters is selected and drawed with oil colories, they can keep it up and give full play of the strokes, and it would be preserved well in a very long time. Artists are welcome to it', or 'For the approval of cherished delegates, French widows may be found in every bedroom'. These stories don't have to be true to be valuable. As long as they remind us of the need for extra care and vigilance with all translation, they can be as apocryphal as they like.

You really do have to be careful with idioms, and be aware of the dangers of literal translation. Baxters of Speyside learned this when they 'decided to introduce the Spanish to the joys of venison soup and such like. To save time . . . the copy for the soup labels was produced in Britain. As a result, the *no preservatives* panel actually tells the expectant reader that the soup contains *no condoms*.'[13]

So when your firm decides to have its sales and promotional literature translated, even into a language you think you're familiar with, persuade them to use a professional translator. When it's done, get it checked locally, by a native of the country who knows something about your type of business. A translation that is even slightly off can badly dent your firm's credibility. Advertising is a particular hazard. Headlines, slogans and straplines do not always translate: extra creativity may be needed.

Finally, introduce one further check. Get someone who knows nothing about your business to translate the translated material back into English. That's to make quite sure that you're saying what you think you are. You could be in for a surprise, like the proud inventors of the universal two-way translating machine used by Moscow during the Cold War. At the first public demonstration of the wonder machine they fed in the English proverb 'Out of sight, out of mind'. In less than a nanosecond, out came the Russian translation. But when they put that into the machine for translation back into English, the printout said 'Invisible idiot'.

Some translation software packages for desktop computers are a bit like that: strong on noun-to-noun equivalents, less good on idioms, and demanding a lot of additional work from the user.

Mobil Europe tackled the problem head-on in its multi-language versions of the staff magazine. Read about *sans frontières* in Chapter 7.

■ Pan-European PR

Global government belongs in the pages of apocalyptic novels or science-fiction paperbacks. Global government relations may not be quite so far-fetched. Pan-European PR is a fact. This is the story of how precise messages from the European Commission were put in front of 340 million consumers, who speak at least nine different languages and live in 12 different countries.

PORTFOLIO

Case 6.4 – A complex, coordinated consumer campaign

Analysis

In the summer of 1990, Worldcom, the world's biggest network of independently owned PR firms, researched 250 companies in Europe and North America to assess the perceptions of industry and business leaders of the world's emerging global markets, with emphasis on the Single Market in Europe. This was an internal exercise for the benefit of Worldcom's own members and their clients, but clearly the potential value of the results went further than that.

When the research conclusions were published in *The Image of Europe '92*, they attracted widespread attention because of their insights into current knowledge – and ignorance – of the EC (as it was then), and the prevailing perceptions and misconceptions.

At about this time the European Parliament voted to finance a major information programme for consumers.

Objectives

1. To develop a set of clear and simple messages about the impact of the Single Market on consumers
2. To convey these messages effectively to specific consumer and media audiences in the 12 member states
3. To raise awareness and the level of public debate about the issues.

Strategy

1. To find partners who could work with the EC's Consumer Policy Service to develop a comprehensive consumer information programme
2. To provide definitive guidance on complex consumer issues, through intermediaries such as consumerists and journalists and to the broad public direct.

Budget
3 000 000 ECUs (European Currency Units: about £2m).

Consultancy
The Worldcom Group network of independent PR consultants. Up to 100 people worked on the project, under the chairmanship of Roger Haywood, Kestrel Communications, and alongside the Commission's own highly professional personnel.

Plans and programmes

1. Over 80 face-to-face briefings across the 12 member states, on key topics of consumer interest. Directed to MEPs, MPs, professional bodies, industry associations, consumer associations and consumer journalists.
2. Information service to reinforce the above. Topics included advertising; banking; consumer credit; contract terms; cosmetics; insurance; labelling; medicines; product safety; travel/tourism.
3. Briefing papers issued to all MEPs and other interested parties on request.
4. Production of VNRs with interviews, comments and supporting filmed material, often in three or more languages.
5. Distribution of VNRs via satellite direct into newsrooms and also through taped copies, on request.
6. Origination by Worldcom writers and editors of core material – definitive documents on each of the selected consumer topics – in the nine official languages, plus background briefers and, in some cases, popular leaflets.
7. Mailings for each topic covered nearly 10 000 journalists, politicians, heads of professional bodies, consumer groups, researchers, academics, advisers and other opinion leaders across the 12 member states.
8. Press and inquiry offices in each of the 12 member states to handle media inquiries and questions from consumer organisations and the public (see Table 6.1).

Table 6.1   EC information programme: material available

	Base document[*]	Back-grounder[*]	Leaflet[*]	VNR[*]
General policy	✓	✓		
Advertising	✓	✓		
Banking	✓	✓		✓
Consumer credit	✓		✓	✓
Contract terms	✓			
Cosmetics	✓	✓		
Insurance	✓	✓		✓
Labelling	✓	✓		✓
Medicines	✓	✓		
Product safety	✓	✓	✓	✓
Travel and tourism	✓	✓	✓	✓
Your rights in the internal market			✓	
Consumer Information Centres			✓	
Second Commission Three-Year Action Plan	✓	✓		

[*]Available in all nine EC languages.

Source: Reproduced by permission of Kestrel Communications.

Results
1. Weekly reviews of programme performance, and monthly de-briefing reports, provided feedback to press and information offices in the member states.
2. Over 2000 media and consumer advisers attended briefing sessions across the EC.
3. 1 000 000 000 OTS were provided.
4. Around 2100 press, radio and television items were generated by the stimulus of programme activity.
5. VNRs were used in at least 86 television programmes in over 60 per cent of the relevant stations.
6. At the start of the campaign, 30 per cent of EC publics felt that consumer affairs were central to the community. By the end of the campaign this figure had almost doubled, rising to 58 per cent.
7. All planned activities were carried out within the 3 000 000 ECUs budget.
8. Client satisfaction with the 'most complex, coordinated public information programme ever run across the EC'. 'Awareness of the relevance of EC consumer legislation has improved in all members states' said Peter Prendergast, Director of Consumer Policy Services in Brussels.[14]

Employee and Community Relations

New recruit:	Why doesn't the firm keep the neighbourhood informed about what's going on?
Old hand (kindly):	Oh, we've never needed to do that.
New recruit:	But why not?
Old hand (baffled):	Don't ask *me*. I only work here.
New recruit:	You mean to say you've been here for years and you don't know the reason why the firm never talks to the community?
Old hand (light dawns):	Oh, there's no *reason*: it's *policy*.

Anon[1]

■ Company and Community

Employee and community relations: why bundle these together in the same chapter? Partly because when employees go home from work, they are members of the local community; partly because their families and friends are, so in a way employees and community are facets of the same audience; but also because employees can be excellent representatives of the company in the community.

If a manager or a machinist or an engineer or a canteen assistant is interested in what he/she does for a living, finds job satisfaction and gets decent pay, why wouldn't they tell the outside world about it? First hand, honest, well communicated enthusiasm can do as much for a company's reputation locally as any of the corporate activities described in Chapter 5 can do on a wider canvas.

■ Communication Styles

In a very structured and professional organisation you would expect the official system of employee communication to be similarly structured and professional, because that's the sort of outfit it is.

A looser knit and more personal system of communication would be more likely in firms that are themselves loose knit and personal in style.

Linear and 'top-to-bottom', or lateral and 'edge-to-edge': which style sounds most like your organisation? Most businesses lie between these two extremes and so do their employee communications.

Much of the real communication is by word of mouth, often bypassing the official channels altogether, but even so the underlying style reflects 'the way things are done around here' in the company.

Community relations are a different matter. Here the characteristic is not that the communication style echoes the management style of the firm, but that it is compatible with the style of the community and in accord with local values. Word of mouth is still the preferred method, but 'the way things are done around here' refers to the community; more about that later.

■ The Toyota Way

The very first entry on Toyota's list of key audiences is not shareholders, or the media, or customers, but members. By this the company does not mean MPs or MEPs but their own employees. These members of Toyota are the key to quality, and every one of them is expected to take responsibility for the success of the organisation. Recruitment standards are high, training is continuous and geared to multi-skilling, management is streamlined and empowering, communication is regular and frequent.

Information, opinions and suggestions are exchanged at start-of-the-day meetings and during the morning break. A Members' Advisory Board (TMAB), composed of elected employee representatives and nominated senior executives, has four main objectives:

- to provide an opportunity for the communication of company plans and performance
- to offer advice, ideas and solutions to resolve difficulties and enhance effectiveness and success
- to provide a forum for the company to obtain and consider members' views when reaching business decisions
- to advise the company on matters of general interest

Concerns and problems that cannot be sorted out at the daily meetings or through TMAB can be determined through Toyota's concern resolution and corrective action committees. There is a single-union agreement with the Amalgamated Engineering and Electrical Union (AEEU) and a strong commitment to flexibility and stability. Adversarial techniques are out.

Anyway, that's how the company sees itself. The philosophy seems to work.

■ Communicating with Staff: Four Principles

First, get the message to everybody who needs to know. Identify your primary audience. Is it all the staff, indiscriminately, or the leaders and opinion formers? Make sure that you reach that primary audience.

Second, talk specifically and directly to each individual in your primary audience. I don't mean literally – though in a small organisation that would be possible – but you should tailor the information you are giving so that it feels to each person that you are addressing him or her personally. Take account of what they already know. For instance, you may need to make sure that they are fully aware that a particular order is vital to the firm's survival. However, if you are certain they have taken this on board already, you can concentrate on showing them how each can make a contribution towards securing the order.

Third, make sure that they know exactly what you want them to do, because you always *do* want them to do something. The more specific you can be, the better. If you want their opinion on something, by all means tell them so. It may be more effective to ask them to tick boxes in answer to multiple-choice questions, though it won't mean a thing unless they are actually able to do what you are asking them to. It has to be within their capability, even if sometimes only just. People can enjoy stretching themselves if they understand why.

Fourth, match the message to the media. Choose the most effective means for reaching your audience. Much of the time, next to word of mouth, it will be through the printed or written word, as in house magazines or staff newsletters.

Here is an award-winning example of how to do it.

■ TSB Goes On-Line

The Trustee Savings Bank (TSB) wanted to project a new attitude to all 25 000 employees and pensioners, aimed at encouraging two-way, open, communication. The existing staff newspaper, *Banknotes*, was replaced with a new, 16-page, all-colour magazine called *On Line*. TSB's own PR department worked with consultants Dewe Rogerson Corporate Publications to develop a magazine based on dialogue between management and employees. In addition to business news and features, human interest stories, social chit-chat and humour – all essential ingredients for any staff periodical – *On Line* had

- a two-way letter page (queries, comments, criticism, with management response alongside)
- dedicated telephone lines for readers to leave comments or questions on work-related topics
- question-and-answer style features, putting top management in the hot seat

The budget was £160 000, which at 10 issues a year works out at 64p per reader per copy.[2]

■ Sound and Pictures

Important though the printed word is in communicating with employees and community, it is by no means the only way. Audio-visual techniques can be particularly useful for staff communication and for community relations. Brent Council's multi-award winning cascaded programme (Case 11.2, Chapter 11) used video as an important medium of information and motivation.

Video equipment ranges from lightweight, portable presenters, which combine videoplayer, screen and minispeaker, to video walls, providing multiple images over a huge area. Between these extremes are a whole series of monitors and single-image projectors.

Programme input – the 'software' – can be via videotape (in any one of a number of different formats), video disc (also in different formats), or computer, which is particularly good for displaying up-to-the-minute information.

Other options include the overhead projector (OHP) and slides, with or without audio tapes. The majority of OHP presentations use prepared transparencies, though a confident presenter can strike up a rapport with an audience by drawing or writing before their very eyes.

You can get advice on selecting and using any of these systems from The Association of Business Communicators (see Appendix A). Here are some questions to ask yourself.

PORTFOLIO
Checklist 7.1 – Choosing and using sound and pictures

1. You need to be clear about

    - your objective
        - training
        - selling
        - motivating
        - informing
    - your audience
        - who
        - how many
        - where
        - what they know already
        - what they expect
    - the required response
        - interest

- knowledge
- understanding
- approval
- action

2. Visual aids where the sound/audio component is provided by a live presenter

- displayed material (including product displays)
- magnetic and other display boards
- write-on aids
  - flipcharts
  - writing boards
  - OHPs
- projected aids
  - slides
  - overhead transparencies
  - computer images
- video display of single images

3. Audio-visual (visual aids using pre-recorded sound)

- still images
  - single slide with sound
  - two or three projector 'dissolve' slides with sound
  - multi-images with sound
- moving (cine) images
  - 16mm film
  - 35mm film
- video images
  - videotape on monitor(s)
  - videotape by projection
  - video disc
- sound and light techniques
- mixed media

4. Asking the right questions should steer you in the direction of a favourite answer, along the lines of Figure 7.1.

VISUAL AID SYSTEMS FOR GROUP MEETINGS

If you need	the favourite is...
1. Informal 'once only' material for an informal audience	flipchart/writing board
2. A teaching session	flipchart
3. A mixture of frequently used and specially prepared material	and/or overhead projector
4. To amend visual(s) during display or presentation	and/or magnetic board

5.	Visuals to have same impact and quality as recorded AV inserts	slides
6.	Material that is easy to prepare 'in-house'	flipchart/overhead projector
7.	On-line computer data to be displayed/LCD overhead panel	video, LCD or data projector
8.	To make presentations in daylight conditions	writing board/flipchart/overhead projector

AUDIO VISUAL MEDIA FOR PRESENTATION TO INDIVIDUALS

If you need / **the favourite is. . .**

9.	Many copies	video/slides
10.	Only a few copies	slides
11.	Easy programme making and amending	slides
12.	'Real time' movement	video
13.	Best image quality	slides
14.	Portability	single slides/video
15.	Low production costs	slides
16.	Interactive programmes	slides/videotape/video disc

AUDIO VISUAL MEDIA FOR PRESENTATION TO A GROUP

If you need / **the favourite is. . .**

17.	Wide (eg worldwide) distribution of programme	16mm/video
18.	Best image quality	slides
19.	Best sound quality	slide with sound/video
20.	Easy programme editing	slides
21.	'Real time' movement	16mm/video
22.	To motivate a larger audience	16mm/multi-image slides
23.	A live presenter to take part	slides
24.	Reasonable production costs	slides

Can I transfer from one medium to another?

Yes – and specialist transfer studios provide these services. But the transfer must be planned from the start, as different media like video, 16mm film and slides have different 'aspect ratios'. This means that information, especially typographic, which fits one medium may be cropped when transferred.

MEDIA TRANSFERS – Ease and Cost

Slides to film	Possible	Expensive
Slides to video	Easy	Reasonable
Film to video	Easy	Reasonable
Video to film	Possible	Expensive

Source: Reproduced by permission of the Association of Business Communicators.

Figure 7.1   Which presentation media?

5. Remember, the medium is *not* the message. What matters is the effectiveness of your presentation, not the techniques employed. Whenever possible, keep the technology simple.[3]

■ Two More Principles of Staff Communication

Fifth, in your regard for the information needs of your primary audience, don't forget secondary and minor audiences. Bring them into the dialogue. Staff have families and friends, some of whom are leaders and influencers in the community. It is commonly accepted that most people know between 10 and 20 others on whom they have some influence, so your secondary audience can be 10–20 times as big as your primary one. And each one in the secondary audience also knows between 10 and 20 people, on whom . . . you get the point. The over-hearing and knock-on effect can produce surprising results, quite apart from the more direct dialogue your firm will have with the community.

Sixth, to improve the chances that the messages you send out will be the same as the ones they receive, strive for clarity. Everybody knows the story of 'Chinese Whispers', the wartime message that started out as 'Send up reinforcements, we're going to advance' and was received as 'Lend us three-and-fourpence, we're going to a dance.' It's a very old story indeed, but Chinese Whispers still happen. Do all you can to eliminate them. This is extremely important when you are dealing with more than one language.

■ Mobil, *sans frontières*

If you were Mobil, Europe, with employees in 20 different countries, how would you structure the company's quarterly magazine, and what would you call it? The answer to the second question is easy: *sans frontières*, what else? As for the magazine itself, the first decision you have to make is about languages. To be effective at reasonable cost, how many language versions do you need? The answer was three: English, French and German. This meant that every reader's copy was in either their mother tongue or their second language. Although the French and German versions needed much longer copy than the English, the design of each edition was kept exactly the same by clever typography. Presentation was very visual, the writing style clear and simple, and the content created a family feeling among the staff, while promoting the value of a united company within a united Europe.

Public relations consultants Paragon did the whole thing – editorial, design, translating, production and distribution, four issues a year of 9000 copies each, in three different languages – for £160 000.[4]

■ The Seventh Principle

Seventh, the tone of voice matters. That's self-evident for the spoken word, and it's equally true of any communication. For instance, video has a tone of voice which is not wholly determined by the sound track but also, perhaps mainly, by the cutting tempo, colour key and other visual characteristics. If instant compliance is required – for legal or safety reasons, say – would you use the same tone as for an invitation to the works outing or for information about staff redundancies?

■ The RAC

The Medium Term Plan of the RAC, involving streamlined and centralised services to customers, also involved several hundred staff redundancies, with the risk of industrial unrest and disruption. Paragon's recommended approach was to show that staff affected were being treated fairly and generously and that customer services would be enhanced through the innovative use of information technology. The tone of voice and key strategy was to communicate honestly, consistently and, wherever possible, face to face. Paragon's four-phase campaign is spelled out in Case 8.1, Chapter 8.

■ Another Three Principles and a Final Thought

Eighth, don't overdo it: and especially don't be wordy. The right number of words for any communication is the exact number it takes, no more and no less. Short copy, short sentences, short paragraphs, short scenes, short sequences can all be highly effective. But some ideas can need more space, more time, more words; if they do, let them.

Ninth, pay attention to timing. The three most common complaints from staff are (1) we weren't told anything, (2) we were told too little, too late: (3) we were over-loaded with bumph long before we could use it. Generally, the smaller the gap between information and action, the better; but, if the time is too short, a feeling of undue pressure takes over, and resentment sets in. People soon learn to recognise spurious urgency, and ignore it. When everything is urgent, what do you do first? If there is a genuine deadline make it very clear what that deadline is and don't extend it, except for equally genuine reasons. The least effective 'deadline' is *a.s.a.p.* What does *as soon as possible* mean? Does it over-ride *urgent*? How does it stand in relation to *immediate*, or to *priority*? Certainly nothing can be done *sooner* than possible: that's not possible.

Tenth, check that the message got through and produced the results you intended. Measuring and evaluating ought to be an integral part of the process. It also needs to be an open process. You won't want people getting the notion that you are surreptitiously checking up on them when what you are doing is openly checking up on your own performance.

Finally – and this is central to all methods of staff communication – don't stop. If staff are only communicated with when there is bad news, or a crisis, or when management wants them to do something they'd much rather not, they will be on their guard and unreceptive; whereas, if there is always a dialogue going on, mutual trust and respect builds up alongside mutual understanding.

Let's put all those principles together into some brief guidelines.

PORTFOLIO
Guideline 7.1 – Staff communication: summary

1. Identify everyone who needs to know – the primary audience
2. Tailor your information to them, allowing for what they know already
3. Make sure they understand what you want them to do, and that they can do it
4. Select the most suitable channels and media
5. Make use of the overhearing effect to reach secondary audiences
6. Be clear

7. Get your tone of voice right
8. Use no more words than you have to, and no fewer
9. 'Too much too soon' is no more use than 'too little too late'
10. Check that your communication has had the effect you want; and keep the dialogue going.

As a matter of fact, those are pretty good guidelines for communicating with *any* audience.

■ The Community

Everything the company does – or does not do – can have a bearing on the local community, and vice versa. Here is an arbitrary, alphabetical list of some potential interfaces. Note once again that the last point – your additions – is the most important.

PORTFOLIO
Checklist 7.2 – Opportunities for community relations

What is your company doing about the following community matters?

1. Animal welfare: people really do care about animals, in the home, on the farm, in the wild. What can your company do to help?
2. Architectural heritage: is there a building in the locality that could be restored and so add to the amenities?
3. Artistic/cultural events: these enrich the quality of life.
4. Children: your firm already runs crèches for children of its own staff, doesn't it? Can the facility be extended in some way?
5. Conservation: be the first to defend what should be defended.
6. Disadvantaged: make contact, find out their needs, help them to help themselves.
7. Education/training: equipment for a school? A series of talks?
8. Elderly: through your Chamber of Commerce and Trade or a local business club, you could arrange shopping trips, and special offers.
9. Emergency/disaster: you may not have a company aircraft to fly, in full livery, to a trouble spot overseas: but can your firm provide manpower, materials and money to help out in a local crisis like flooding or a big fire?
10. Environment: if you can't enhance it, at least do nothing to damage it.
11. Hospitals: a much needed piece of medical equipment? A snack bar for patients and visitors? Visits to the sick?

12. Information: encourage community magazines by offering prizes, with skilled adjudication as a bonus.
13. Local government: run briefings and discussion groups for mutual enlightenment.
14. Medical research: pound-for-pound fundraising schemes.
15. Overseas aid: encourage staff to spend their holiday time on overseas relief projects.
16. Payroll-giving schemes: encourage them, support them, augment them.
17. Sport: why not open up your company's sports facilities to everybody in the community?
18. Young people: support local scouts, guides and other youth organisations.
19. Your additions: your own specific ideas.

■ Social Contribution

In pursuit of good relationships with people and organisations, Toyota established Community Liaison Committees composed of company members, local government and local residents. Community and business leaders visit the plants; employees are encouraged to take part in volunteering initiatives; educational visits are made to and with local schools; local media are kept informed.

Toyota's Social Contributions Committee donates time and resources to local needs, from providing a children's hospital with medical equipment to installing an automated entrance for disabled people at a theatre.

The company aims to make a local, national and international social contribution to education, environment, sport and culture. The Toyota Science and Technology Education Fund, in partnership with Business in the Community, gives grants to help improve the quality of science and technology teaching in the UK. Primary, secondary and special schools become involved with local businesses of all sizes and from all sectors. Over the two years 1992–4, 1331 schools received 614 grants. More than 2750 teachers, 63 000 students and 2500 businesses were involved. Toyota contributed £365 000 and the British government added a further £216 000.

■ Educational Involvement

Firms which truly care about their community should find or devise opportunities for putting something into education, and getting something out.

On a corporate level, your company could:

- run Open Days for schools
- develop joint endeavours with colleges
- get into educational sponsorship

Employees could be encouraged to:

- get involved with all manner of school activities
- become school governors
- raise funds for school equipment

This is how one employer got involved.

PORTFOLIO
Case 7.1 – The business class

For many years the employees of Jones Stroud Insulations (JSI), of Longridge, Preston, have worked with high schools in Longridge and the Hyndburn and Ribble Valley area, helping young people to understand how to set up and run their own businesses.

Involvement
Over a period of six years of deep commitment, the firm guided nine Young Enterprise Companies whose products (chiefly wooden) included toy round-abouts, up-market bird-feeders, a secret keybox, Woody the Friendly Log, marionettes and a Safety in the Home board game. The youngsters learned to raise money through loans and share issues, operate quality control systems, practise language skills and canvass customers and distributors for orders, including exports. They got to grips with health and safety in the workplace, learned the hard way about marketing, appreciated the vital importance of cash flow, and actually showed a profit (not large in real terms, but very respectable as a percentage of turnover).

JSI also ran Training Evenings and French Language Sales Competitions, and helped the students to attend the yearly Jeunes Entreprises Congress in Brussels.

Results
It is clear that the youngsters gained an understanding of entrepreneurial and small-business skills. In addition, they developed an understanding of the value of teamwork, learned to take pride in what they did and acquired confidence in expressing themselves.

JSI was the Small Company Winner of the 1993 Employees in the Community awards, organised by Business in the Community. The company's staff gained experience of cross-discipline working, and at least one former student now works for the company.

But the real reward, according to Gordon Blain, Managing Director of JSI, was the deep satisfaction of teaching young people to understand the real world and helping to make it work for them.[5]

■ Educational Material

As part of the developing relationship between industry and education, many companies sponsor classroom material. There is a distinction between material specifically asked for by individuals, and that provided for general educational purposes or for use within particular areas of the curriculum.

If a pupil or teacher asks for your company's recruitment brochure, or the annual report, why not send it? Your decision will be based on the usual criteria of cost-effectiveness, fitness for purpose and the 'feelgood factor'.

It is a very different matter if you are running a competition for schools, or sending out wall charts for general classroom use, or issuing a video on personal hygiene, or mailing an information pack on engineering. With the best will in the world it is all too easy to get it wrong.

To get it right, follow the *Guidelines for Business Sponsors of Educational Material*, published by the NCC. These are the key points.

PORTFOLIO
Guideline 7.2 – Business sponsors of educational material

1. Sponsored material specifically for educational use should be clearly designated as such.
2. No implied or explicit sales message, exhortation to buy a product or service, merchandising slogan or other attempt to influence the purchasing decisions of children, or their families, should be included.
3. Under no circumstances should promotional material be presented as 'educational'.
4. There should be no attempt in educational material to state, imply or demonstrate that a particular product or service is superior to other similar products or services.

   Where an educational purpose (oral hygiene, for example) is being promoted, it should be clearly stated that the benefits apply to the whole class of goods or services, not to an individual named product.
5. When purporting to give a balanced account of an issue, sponsors should accurately represent the broad range of informed opinion on the subject. It is, therefore, open to sponsors to put forward an argument on behalf of their industry or sector.

6. No unsolicited material should be distributed or direct-mailed to pupils.
7. Under no circumstances should sponsors leave samples of their product without the prior knowledge and express consent of the head teacher.
8. In the preparation of all educational materials, sponsors should obtain advice from those actively involved in education or aware of current curricular needs. Where appropriate, sponsors should ensure that materials are tested by teachers in the classroom prior to their general release.
9. The materials should:
    (a) carry some broad indication (for example, 'primary' or 'secondary') of the age range for which they are intended;
    (b) be available, wherever possible, for local inspection by teachers before they are acquired by schools.
10. Material should:
    (a) be sensitive to the needs and expectations of all groups likely to receive it;
    (b) recognise and project, through both text and illustrations, the broad range of activities and opportunities now open to both sexes, and avoid sexual stereotyping;
    (c) reflect as far as possible the races and cultures among the population of the UK and avoid racial stereotyping;
    (d) recognise the problems and the potential of people with disabilities;
    (e) take account of diverse family types;
    (f) contain no express or implied prejudice in relation to politics, class or religion.
11. Educational material should carry the sponsor's name and the address and telephone number of the department responsible for receiving comments or complaints about it.
12. All material should clearly show the date of publication.[6]

Be realistic. The cable television industry planned to steal a march on British Telecom by connecting all Britain's schools to their network and supplying the set-top boxes which allow standard televisions to receive cable programmes. Free of charge to schools, *Cable in the Classroom* would cost the industry £4–5000 per installation. The proposals, including free programming in consultation with schools, were 'partly to do with community relations' but also realistically acknowledged that 'the children of today will be the consumers the industry needs to target in a few years time'.[7]

■ The American Experience

You can often get a new perspective on your own country when you see it from distant shores. Alastair Bruce, of Bruce Naughton Wade, public affairs management counsellors, made a community relations study tour of the USA in 1993. He found three specific aspects that needed attention there and also here in the UK:

- responding to external social and community developments
- meeting changing internal business needs
- enhancing professionalism and effectiveness

■ Changes in External Environment

Patterns of work and employment are changing. There are more dual-worker families and more women at work. Temporary and part-time jobs are increasing; so are multiple jobs and flexible time schedules. Greater diversity within society, and wider differences of needs and opportunities, coincide with industrial downsizing and net job losses. Careers are becoming more centred on the individual and less on the firm. As the prospect of any sort of employment remains uncertain and the concept of a job for life disappears, so too does the concept of loyalty to an employer. This makes two-way communication increasingly important.

Alongside these changes, governments continue to disengage, off-loading many more community responsibilities on to employers and individuals. The government/industry partnership, especially in education, the environment and healthcare, looks distinctly lopsided.

Private Industry Councils in USA and Training and Enterprise Councils in the UK are partnerships between businesses, local government and national government, who do not all necessarily have the same agenda.

Reconciling these conflicting interests is a key role for public relations.

■ Changes in Business Needs

Effective community relations needs leadership from the top and must also involve the leaders of tomorrow. What that means in practice is that all staff levels in the enterprise have to become educated in the benefits and opportunities of community relations, and learn something of the responsibilities.

Quality of programmes is important, which does not necessarily mean extremely high quality. What matters is that the quality is right for the community and for the business. For instance, Time Warner's *Time to Read* is a national, volunteer-led programme to improve adult literacy in USA. A main aim for the community is to increase the number of competent readers: a main aim of Time Warner is to protect its own future market place, which depends on literacy – you don't sell many books and magazines to people who can't read. Other benefits included goodwill and staff development.

Another example: American Express ran a *Charge Against Hunger* programme, giving two cents to famine relief organisations for every Amex card transaction. In the UK, Tesco's *Computers for Schools* project gave tokens to customers based on the amount they spent. The tokens were handed on to the local schools for redemption. Benefits included the pooling of resources by several schools locally, to gross up the tokens for a better return and to share the hardware and software on a rota basis. Out of that collaboration came other joint endeavours and continuing community benefit.

■ Changes in Professionalism and Effectiveness

Community relations is not a 'bolt-on' activity, nor something a company takes part in just to feel good about. That is a part of it, of course; but unless the community relations function is managed, it can be a serious waste of resources. The first essential is commitment, and by that I mean formal commitment in a clear statement of the company's social vision. Next, there have to be clear, and clearly understood, objectives, with a programme for achieving them. All necessary resources have to be secured, whether from inside the firm or outside, and what cannot be provided by volunteers must nevertheless be provided. Well meaning amateurs are fine – some of the best results are achieved that way – but there has to be an underlying structure of professionalism, backed up by training. Retired ex-employees can be an excellent recruiting ground for community relations, reinforcing and extending programmes beyond the time available to paid employees. Partnerships, associations and affiliations can all add to effectiveness and professionalism.[8]

■ Consultation

Better information leads to better decisions. It is in your company's own interests to consult the people and organisations affected by its actions. Many of the guidelines for staff communication are just as relevant here.

Start your internal debates early so that you have enough time to take the results into account before you externalise. Make sure that everybody who needs to be consulted is consulted. If you think they don't need to be, and they think they do, it is you who needs to think again, just in case they are right.

Barbara Mills took over at the Crown Prosecution Service (CPS) in 1992. She found that too many casework decisions were being made away from the areas concerned, and there was over-centralisation in matters of personnel and finance.

In the eyes of the media the CPS lacked competence, and this led to a loss of confidence on the part of the public. Drastic restructuring of the CPS, from 31 areas to 13, and a vigorous policy of devolution and local delivery, were accompanied by a sustained programme of staff consultation, information, appraisal and development. CPS now concentrates on ensuring high standards in their core business of casework, decision making and court presentation.[9]

With public presentation treated equally seriously, CPS is, and is perceived to be, a better service.

■ What Made Banbury Cross?

In 1986, Cherwell District Council (CDC), in North Oxfordshire, decided to pedestrianise the main shopping streets in the centre of Banbury. There were two main reasons

- 'unacceptable environmental conditions' (mainly traffic congestion, noise and pollution)
- 'discouraging prospects for the future' (the threat to local shops posed by new out-of-town superstores and attractive neighbouring centres)

The Council concluded that pedestrianisation would:

- create a safer, traffic-free environment in the town centre, eliminate traffic congestion and resolve conflict between shoppers and motor vehicles
- attract more visitors to the town centre by creating a pleasant environment for shopping, tourism and commercial activities

Mindful that the new extension to the M40 motorway could bring visitors into the town but just as easily take residents out, CDC aimed to ensure and demonstrate that the pedestrianisation scheme would benefit shoppers, visitors and local traders alike. Draft proposals for the High Street/Market Place/ Parsons Street area were circulated, and surveys undertaken. Public response was apathetic at best, but 98 per cent of those who did reply supported the scheme. Response by the retail trade was more complex. It was clear that 88 per cent of High Street traders were in favour, but smaller shopkeepers, especially in the Market Place and Parsons Street, were not at all keen; these two areas were withdrawn from the scheme.

The proposals that went to public inquiry took account of survey results. Further changes were made afterwards, notably a traffic order giving pedestrians priority use of pedestrianised streets and allowing access by service vehicles before 10.30 a.m. and after 4 p.m. Disabled drivers, emergency services and bullion deliveries were allowed in at any time. Special arrangements were made for residents with on-site parking permits.

To avoid the Christmas shopping period, construction started in mid-January 1991. Work was completed in stages, so that shopkeepers could see the benefits. The idea was to minimise complaints, but there was a groundswell of resentment and criticism that took a long time to subside, even though very little of it seems to have reached the Council. Three years after, the main complaint was that Parsons Street had not been included in the final scheme;

that came from the Parsons Street traders. There was also a public perception – difficult to quantify – that vandalism and other crimes involving property had increased since and because of pedestrianisation. CDC found no evidence to support this. However, fear of crime is a national problem and the Council, in conjunction with town centre traders, introduced closed circuit television (CCTV) cameras into the pedestrianised area to reassure the public, deter potential criminals and help identify and catch any actual offenders.

In 1993, when CDC proposed a comparable pedestrianisation scheme for Bicester, there was a much stronger opposition from local traders. 'This time', said the Council, 'the PR effort included regular updates during construction work to keep local people informed of progress and timescales'.[10]

■ Conspiracy or Cock-Up?

Let what you are doing be clearly visible, so that nobody feels that it is just a formality. It is only when the results are genuinely in doubt that consultation is a credible process.

Getting the timing right is important. John Patten, when Minister of Education, allowed a three-month consultation period with universities for his document on the future of student unions. As the Committee of Vice-Principals pointed out, Patten chose the three months of the long vacation, which is precisely the time when the people most affected – the students – would not be at university to be consulted.[11] Maybe that was the idea: an example of the conspiracy theory of events. On the other hand, perhaps the Minister or his advisers just didn't think of it: this would be explained by the cock-up theory.

What do you think?

■ Cleveland Supertram

One of the most common causes of local objections to change is that people feel they haven't been consulted, or even informed, about what is going on. It is perfectly possible with modern techniques to provide everybody in the catchment area with an opportunity to have his or her say. Cleveland County Council managed it when, through Infopress, they consulted 236 000 households and 12 000 businesses on proposals to link up separate communities by a supertram system. The response rate, in what amounted to a referendum, was three times better than expected, although a significant number objected because their own area was *not* included in the supertram scheme.

Those who did not respond to the consultative programme were pre-empted of a favourite line of criticism or objection: 'Why didn't they ask *me*?'

■ The Environment

From the closing years of the twentieth century onwards, there are not likely to be any companies taking a stand against the environment; but that is a very different thing from having and promoting sound environmental policies.

What is required is realistic environmental actions, made visible. Staff, suppliers and customers need to be informed and enlisted into partnerships to extend and promote common environmental objectives. As the Advisory Committee on Business and the Environment (ACBE) points out, communication is vital. So is consultation.

The Institute of Management (IM) agrees with the DTI that the first stages of introducing effective environmental management are:

- enhancing environmental awareness within the organisation
- involving key members of staff in identifying the issues to be tackled
- making all employees aware of the firm's current environmental performance
- communicating to all concerned what the organisation's environmental aims, objectives, targets and programme actually are

Suppliers ought to be involved at all points of deliberation. There is not much credibility in your firm or client being environmentally sound if your suppliers are not.

Local community groups should be consulted and kept fully in the picture. As a professional manager, says the IM, you will want to ensure that your environmental policies and plans are communicated in a positive and proactive manner. You should not be intentionally misleading or suppress information.

Planning and regulatory bodies are an important audience. Stay in touch with them so that you can do more than the law requires before it is required, and so that penalties do not force the issues.

Of course your company is not one of those that takes advantage of less strict regulations in some other countries to dispose of products and materials that are subject to stringent requirements in the UK . . . is it?

Customers need to be kept aware of your environmental credentials through marketing activities. Your products, services and processes create minimal environmental damage, don't they? They can be used safely, can't they? Then say so.

Care for the environment can be a good selling point, so tell customers what can be re-used, repaired, rejuvenated, refilled or recycled: the '5Rs' of the ACBE.

As a good manager and a good public relations practitioner, you will want to ensure that all public communication is clear, unambiguous and true, with all relevant environmental, health and safety issues fully disclosed. In the words of the IM's guidelines, 'respect the interests of neighbours and the world community'.[12]

Now here are some guidelines for you and your company to adopt.

PORTFOLIO

Guideline 7.3 – Talking to family and neighbours

1. Illuminate the background. People need to know the context in which decisions are being taken.
2. Highlight the issues. There must be no doubt what the decisions to be taken are about.
3. Set out the criteria.
4. Define the constraints.
5. Make it easy for people to respond.
6. Allow enough time.
7. Be truthful. Peter Hunt, of Shell, spoke from experience when he said 'Never pretend a problem does not exist. Talk and listen. Understand and pre-empt environmentalists. Make friends with the media. Keep in touch with the appropriate Government committees. Monitor so that you are forewarned. Be aware of community discussions and take part in them honestly.'[13]
8. Be sure to collect and review *all* the evidence, paying equal attention to each voice. That doesn't necessarily mean attaching equal value to them all, but it does mean not starting with any forgone conclusions.
9. Come to the decision as quickly as you reasonably can, and report that decision to all concerned.
10. As you take any necessary action, keep people informed.
11. Monitor the feedback.
12. Good news or bad, the advice is still the same. Tell the neighbours before you tell the media, but only just before. Above all, tell the staff before you tell anybody else.

CHAPTER 8

The Third Sector

I deeply believe in the value of our kinds of organisations, where the profit motive is not paramount and which are not creatures of the City, but which are democratic, stand on their own two feet and are independent of Government.

Sir Dennis Landau[1]

■ Understanding the Economy

All economies are mixed economies. Even in pre-glasnost USSR, the state was not the sole authority on absolutely everything, nor were all economic activities and decisions the responsibility of an over-riding central planning authority. Likewise, even in the USA, private enterprise does not operate totally independently of government, nor are all economic activities and decisions determined entirely by the profit motive. Public relations takes place in the real world and PR practitioners need to understand the particular mix of the economy they work in.

■ Public and Private

Most of us are pretty clear about what the private sector in this country is and what it does. There may not be a watertight definition that covers all cases, and there may be legitimate doubts about the actual status of a few individual enterprises, but by and large we perceive the private sector as being made up of commercial organisations whose survival in the market place depends ultimately on their ability to make profits. Control lies with shareholders or proprietors, who are also beneficiaries alongside customers.

In the public sector, there is no bomb-proof definition. There is, however, a general understanding that though bodies financed by public money may, and often should, act in a more or less commercial manner, they are different in kind from those in the private sector. Control lies with government, national or local, and the benefits are reaped by the public, or selective sections of it.

There may be hybrids and cross-fertilisation arrangements, whereby private money may go into the public sector, and vice versa, in accordance with specific conditions and safeguards, but the essential character of the two sectors comes through.

Most of the examples and case histories of public relations looked at in this book belong in one or other of the two sectors, public and private, that constitute 90 per cent of the economy.

■ The Other 10 per cent

What of the other 10 per cent? It is made up of cooperatives, trusts, voluntary organisations, associations like the AA and the RAC, BUPA, PPP and WPA, credit unions, building societies, housing associations, mutual life societies, trade unions and professional institutions, NHS trusts, opted-out schools, charities and other fundraising bodies. They may appear to have little in common, but they are all engaged in economic activity to fulfil primary social objectives, community and national, and to serve their respective memberships.

■ Control and Benefits

This third sector is beginning to be recognised in the UK. It already exists in various forms elsewhere. France has its *économie sociale*, a neat triumvirate of mutual cooperatives, associations and a single government department. In Italy, the emphasis is very much on cooperatives. Portugal has a college – the Escolia Profissional de Economia Social – which teaches the management of non-profit organisations. The EU is interested in examining common needs and activities in members states, with particular reference to the legal, financial, management and educational implications.

Figure 8.1 positions all organisations – private sector, public sector and third sector – in relation to those stakeholders who have ultimate control and those who are beneficiaries of the services provided. Sometimes they are the same people.

■ Building a Higher Profile

The major public relations task for the third sector, every organisation in it and all bodies representing them, is to develop a higher profile. As Malcolm Hurlston pointed out at the Forum for the Social Economy, London, 1993, 'Much would be gained by fostering a climate in which policymakers and

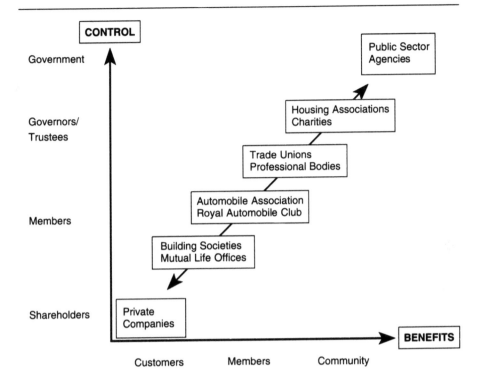

Source: © *MultiStrategies*, 1993, and reproduced with permission.

Figure 8.1   Control/benefit relationships

commentators give due notice to the many organisations which, while outside the public sector, are not private proprietary companies.'

This is being achieved through well-tried public relations techniques, such as:

● lobbying politicians
● influencing opinion formers
● educating commentators
● briefing the media

■ Correcting Misconceptions

Alongside this there is a need for a sustained effort to correct misconceptions, such as the well-entrenched belief that third sector organisations are inefficient. To counter this entails:

- constant vigilance
- media monitoring
- finding good and truthful examples of good management
- seizing every opportunity to 'tell it like it is'
- anticipating problems (there *will* be waste and inefficiency sometimes, there *will* be the odd case of fraud or misappropriation)
- having crisis management and damage limitation plans in place[2] (see Chapter 13)

Some third-sector organisations have got the message: the Co-op Bank, The Law Society and the RAC, for instance.

■ Co-operative Bank Financial Advisers

A series of financial briefings for women was put together by Co-operative Bank Financial Advisers (CBFA) from existing documentation, rewritten and offered to journalists as source material. The information was timely – women's changing role in society was affecting their financial position so that independent advice was in demand – and readable.

Each briefing cost £500 to research and write, and CBFA report that all got excellent media coverage. In addition many journalists asked if they could offer the briefings as a service to readers. This was done through a free helpline which gave women the independent financial guidance they wanted on such matters as taxation, pensions, credit, divorce and co-habiting.

As CBFA had hoped, and no doubt intended, the briefings also generated a considerable number of new business leads. What is more, they could be updated and re-issued at regular intervals, or whenever there was a significant development affecting women's finances.[3]

■ The Law Society

Some of the organisations in the third sector are among the oldest in the world, with deeply embedded traditional procedures. One of them, founded in 1739, decided it was time to get organised for the twenty-first century. The organisation is the Law Society, the solicitors' governing body. This is what happened.

The Society handles at least £60m a year. Almost half of that is income from the issue of annual practising certificates to 60 000 solicitors; the other half is largely accounted for by money paid into a compensation fund offering insurance to clients against fraudulent practice.

Investment business certificates are issued to 7000 firms; 30 000 accountants' reports are delivered from solicitors holding clients' monies; 4500 new solicitors are admitted each year, 5000 new students enrolled and 100 000 application forms processed.

This mountain of paper, with its workload peaks, was handled by the Law Society in traditional ways, temporary staff being taken on when needed. The first computer was introduced as late as 1973.

In 1993, Top-ix Business Systems were called in to assist in analysing the business processes so that information technology solutions to the problem of carrying on the regulatory function of the Society cost-effectively could be identified. A phased implementation strategy was agreed, and improvements became apparent almost immediately. Practitioners were kept informed of progress – for example, at the Annual Conference and Exhibition – and were made aware of the potential and actual benefits to them and to clients.

However, one result of rationalising and reducing the workload was that many of the regular temporary staff, taken on to deal with the peaks, would no longer be needed. The Society adopted a policy of complete openness towards those affected or likely to be affected. Discussions about the implications of the changes were very frank, and employment workshops were set up to talk people through their worries. The advantages of modernisation were achieved with minimum business disruption and personal distress.[4]

■ Strategy Shift

Just as organisations in the public and private sectors have to adapt to shifts in business strategy, so with those in the third sector. This is how one well-known association coped, by way of a professionally planned, labour-intensive joint operation with a leading public relations consultancy.

PORTFOLIO
Case 8.1 – Rescuing the rescuers

Analysis
The RAC's medium term business plan was to 'streamline and enhance its customer offering'. This involved closing most of the local offices, with several hundred redundancies; centralising customer service operations in five key locations; and relying very heavily on computer databases to support inquiry staff. There were very understandable and real risks of personal distress, industrial unrest and disrupted services, leading to the possibility that competitors would take advantage of these changes to improve their own positions.

Objectives

1. Eliminate any danger caused through unauthorised leaks of the plan.
2. By generous and fair policies, minimise the risk of staff disaffection and possible disruption to services
3. Allay any concerns on the part of external audiences such as motor manufacturers, and recovery garages
4. Reassure RAC members that the changes would benefit and not disadvantage them
5. Reduce the chance of the media and competitors focusing on the negative (job loss) aspects of the changes.

Strategy

1. Use RAC customer satisfaction research to highlight the extent to which the association is customer-driven
2. Emphasise service enhancement and innovative technology
3. Exhibit generous and fair treatment of departing staff
4. Communicate honestly, consistently and, whenever possible, face to face
5. Motivate remaining staff.

Consultancy
Paragon, working with RAC's own PR staff.

Budget
£69 196, of which £32 000 in fees.

Timetable
Phase 1   Initial briefing for the briefers (chiefly senior and middle managers)
Phase 2   Separate, carefully timed and sympathetic briefings for staff directly affected
Phase 3   Simultaneous mailings to important external audiences
Phase 4   Pre-emptive, low-key external announcement of main details and benefits of change.

Programme

1. Production of reserve statements, question and answer briefs, and a crisis management plan.
2. Production of 14 different tailor-made briefing packs and visual aids for use in Phase 1 and subsequently in Phase 2.
3. Phase 1 briefings all on one day.
4. Phase 2 briefings on one follow-up day, at staff's normal places of work.
5. Individual letters to all affected staff, tailored according to the impact of the changes on each one personally.
6. Briefing notes on redundancy terms to accompany (5) above.

7. Special edition of staff magazine with an upbeat assessment of the impact of changes. Production of this issue to be made under tight security conditions.

8. Handy pocket guide to remind managers of the key points to communicate.

9. Taped interview with Rescue Services Managing Director to be issued on a regular news tape to all patrolmen and women.

10. Tailored letters to be faxed on d-Day to all corporate fleet members and motor manufacturers.

11. National media announcement on d-Day, to be handled jointly by RAC in-house PR department and Paragon, with emphasis on benefits of change (including improved level of service).

12. National hot-line for members and others.

13. 24-hour, seven-day rota of Paragon and RAC spokespeople, for three months for instant response to leaks (internal and external) and immediate roll out of reserve communication plan if required.

Results

1. Successful carrying through of the changes with no disruption to members' services and no industrial action by staff.

2. Accurate positioning in the media of RAC's forward looking response to change.

3. Minimal adverse or negative comment by media.

4. Positive response of motor manufacturers, corporate fleet members, recovery garages and other interest groups. No significant concerns were expressed.

5. No commercial damage to RAC Rescue Service operations by competitors.

6. PRCA Award for Outstanding Consultancy Practice.

7. IPR Certificate of Excellence for Internal Communications.[5]

■ Non-Profit Organisations

Not only is the profit motive not paramount in the third sector, for many of its organisations it is non-existent. One of the most important characteristics of these non-profit organisations is that there can be two quite different systems of accountability. Paid staff are accountable to decision makers who are elected or appointed, either from an organisation's own membership or by recruitment from outside. Volunteer staff are often members who get things up and running themselves and are largely self-accountable. It is when those same volunteers get on the payroll that they can run into trouble.

Commercial organisations, and to an increasing extent those in the public sector, have relatively small numbers of staff, who ought to be adequately paid and in some cases are highly paid. Most third-sector organisations have even fewer paid staff but often have access to an extensive network of unpaid supporters. These may assist the organisation as volunteer staff, as collectors of donations, fees or subscriptions, as benefactors, donors or sponsors. Above all they serve on the councils and committees that run the organisations and make the final decisions on policy.

Like employees, volunteers must also be 'paid' – not in money, of course (it is often quite difficult to get them even to accept reimbursement of expenses) – but substantially in terms of satisfaction, recognition, expressions of appreciation and sometimes, it has to be admitted, of enhanced social status and contacts. Meeting the needs of these stakeholders is an important public relations objective.

Some third-sector organisations have enormous turnovers. They have to take particular care to steer clear of accusations of extravagance which, if proved valid, can be as damaging as accusations of fraud. The whole operation needs to be transparent, so that all concerned can feel that they know all is above board and that value for money is paramount. When something does go wrong, swift action is needed to admit the truth and put remedial solutions into effect.

Because many third sector organisations are promoting causes or carrying out public education work, the messages they deliver are crucial elements in their public relations programmes. If there are misconceptions, important sources of funding and support may never be tapped. Dr Barnardo's found that out when research revealed – or rather confirmed – widespread ignorance about the full range of that charity's work. Most people thought it was only for orphans. A change of name to plain Barnardos, simultaneous national and regional launches, a new graphic identity, a high profile Royal patron, front page news all over the country, a prime-time television feature: all this and more was needed to change perception and attract additional donations.[6] Even that was not enough and a strategy review was called for.

The key role played by members, supporters and volunteers in the third sector means that public relations programmes must be discussed extensively and agreed, before implementation as far down the chain of command – I use the term loosely – as possible. This is especially true of the smaller organisations where a good deal of time has to be allocated for democratic discussion and agreement of objectives. If this is not done, disaffected individuals who feel that not enough effort and time was given to their particular points of view can disrupt, not to say sabotage, a programme.

Once a public relations programme has been agreed, the public relations specialists must make it clear that they expect to do their job with the minimum of interference. They are inevitably over-stretched and underpaid, and need all their energy for the task in hand. This fact of life has to be conveyed to 'the great and the good' in ways which keep them interested and committed, but also at arm's length. Fortunately, they are often happy to take on a variety of tasks as honorary public relations officers. They can be extremely effective when those tasks may be undertaken while they are carrying out their normal activities and pursuing their usual interests.

■ Media Relations

Non-profit organisations get involved in what the media think of as 'human interest situations'. They can achieve remarkable results with slender resources. Their causes may be topical, or become topical. Membership associations, such as professional institutions and trade unions, can represent interests across a very wide spectrum. Some decisions and activities in the non-profit sector can affect people's everyday lives. For all these reasons, the media may show interest of their own accord. If so, the organisations should be equipped to respond rapidly and positively. If the media are slow to realise the news potential of non-profit organisations, they should be helped to recognise and act on the many opportunities available.

You don't need to spend a lot of money on keeping up-to-date with what's happening in the media. The Mothers' Union (MU), which has 165 300 members in the British Isles, aims to 'promote conditions in society favourable to stable family life and the protection of children'.

The MU Media Department covers the impact of all branches of the mass media on members and their families and monitors output, technical and commercial developments and legislation. Two-way contact is maintained between the MU and official authorities in broadcasting, press, video and advertising. Three times a year *Media News* goes out to about 4500 members and selected media organisations. The MU Media Department is also involved in the ecumenical Media Awareness Project, which publishes three bulletins a year.

This monitoring costs little more than expenses. The real costs are covered by countless unpaid hours by volunteers.[7]

■ Internal Communication

In membership organisations, each member is performing a public relations role. The messages that members receive and subsequently deliver must be well understood and consistent. The same is true for organisations promoting a cause. You will still get some individualistic, not to say idiosyncratic, interpretations. One way to make consistency a little more likely is to cascade the information, each well-informed layer being responsible for the effective briefing of the next layer.

■ House Journals

Many non-profit organisations find that a house journal is essential to survival. As well as playing a central part in internal communications, a regular publication can serve as a powerful link with external supporting and supportive groups. It can be a good way of building up media liaison. All publications, but especially house journals, can help define the organisation and establish its identity. The benefit to external relations is self-evident. It can be equally important as a motivator for the organisation itself and as a means of arriving at and maintaining a consensus on what really matters.

■ Events

Events are probably the best known and certainly the most visible of public relations activities in the third sector. Their fundraising and recruitment potential fulfil an essential need, bringing together everybody concerned. They confer prestige on the organisation, boost morale and provide feedback from members and other target audiences. They can provide excellent photo opportunities for the media, for house journals and for general public relations purposes inside and outside the organisation. Many charities could not exist without events. No matter that the funds raised may be so small that members and supporters sometimes feel they might just as well have had a whip round amongst themselves, or written out a cheque, rather than give so much energy and organisational time to putting on the event; what often matters more than the amount of money raised on the day is the effect that the evident grass-roots commitment has on substantial donors such as trusts, foundations and other grant-giving bodies.

■ Sponsorship

Valuable opportunities for partnerships with the private and public sectors can be provided through sponsorships, with all parties benefiting. Sponsorships can allow activities which would otherwise be ruled out altogether because of expense or financial risks. They can also extend a programme of public relations cost-effectively. There must, of course, be adequate public relations support. All these issues are covered extensively in Chapter 5 (Corporate and Financial Relations) and Chapter 10 (Media Relations). Voluntary and non-profit organisations, charities and pressure groups are among those in the third sector which provide educational material to schools. At present there are no guidelines on good practice but many of the points in the NCC's *Guidelines for*

Business Sponsors of Educational Material are appropriate to the third sector. They are summarised in Guideline 7.2, Chapter 7.

■ Third Party Endorsement

Opinion leaders and shapers, and famous people, can confer prestige, glamour or *gravitas* on organisations in the third sector. Their overt support and publicly-stated approval can stimulate attendance at events, boost recruitment, generate funds and attract media interest. It should go without saying (but still needs to be said) that non-profit organisations should take great care to select and approach people who will not turn out to be an embarrassment.

■ Advertising

Major charities make extensive use of advertising to increase awareness and stimulate donations. However, for most non-profit organisations, financial constraints mean that advertising may be difficult to justify. It must not be ruled out altogether because sometimes space is given free, as a form of donation.

■ Exhibitions

Exhibitions have much in common with events, as a way of reaching target audiences and involving supporters. It is particularly important that volunteers – and, indeed, paid staff where appropriate – should be helped to carry out stand-manning and other participation effectively. An amateurish performance can be worse than not being there are all. Clearly the exhibition stand itself should not be lavish, but it does need to be decently workmanlike. Sometimes it is possible for a charity to get a stand at a greatly reduced rate, or even for no payment.

■ General Expenses

Administration costs are a burden for many third-sector organisations, especially the charities. If these costs are met, wholly or in part, by other, richer, organisations, that can be to the advantage of all concerned. Enlightened self-interest can be a powerful motivator. Consider the case of Christian Aid Week, the UK's biggest charity week, whose administration costs over three years were funded by The Co-operative Bank. The Bank's donation of £500 000 paid for the printing of posters and magazines, as well as the 17 million gift envelopes distributed door-to-door during the Week.

The benefit to Christian Aid was clear; but what of The Co-operative Bank? Feelgood factor apart, the Bank 'heavily promoted its distinctive ethical stance as part of its marketing strategy'. That makes sense.[8]

■ Training

According to Jane Hammond, of Trident Training, public relations staff in the third sector should be as competent and well trained as those in the commercial or public sectors. Non-profit organisations are entitled to expect nothing less. Professional PR staff must ensure, in turn, that volunteers are properly equipped to carry out the honorary public relations function by training and briefing them, and by making sure that they have adequate support materials and services. All the people involved in the organisation are engaged in public relations whether they know it or not, whether they want to or not. Properly trained, briefed and supported, they can be an immensely effective PR resource.[9]

Customer and Consumer Relations

It costs 90 per cent of the gross margin on an existing customer to go out and get a new one.

David Perkins[1]

■ We are all Customers

We've all heard of the shop assistant who said 'No, we don't have any No. 3 widgets in stock. There just isn't the demand, and you're the fourth person I've told today.' The astonishing thing is that the story is true, not necessarily literally, but in the sense that it illustrates an attitude which is not uncommon, even in a recession.

It is generally accepted that only about 10 per cent of dissatisfied customers ever complain. These are the ones you and your firm have the best chance of satisfying and retaining, because they have identified themselves and defined a problem for you. Of the other, silent, 90 per cent, you can be pretty certain that only 10 per cent will ever buy from you again. The rest – that is, the overwhelming majority of unhappy customers – are lost, possibly for ever. Even if you could get them back, it would cost five times as much as keeping them happy in the first place, and therefore not losing them.

We are all customers. What do we do if we are satisfied with some product we have bought, or some service received? We tell a few people about it: maybe as many as half a dozen. If our expectations have been fully met, we feel good about spreading our satisfaction around a little.

Suppose we are not satisfied? Like most customers whose expectations have not been met, we feel disgruntled, and we spread that around, too: possibly to a dozen people, on average.

If our expectations are totally confounded, we feel mean enough to tell practically anybody who will listen. Our dissatisfaction with a specific product or service becomes in effect an attack on the company's reputation. Defending that reputation is what customer relations is all about.

■ The User-Friendly Bus

In many ways public transport systems the world over are alike, especially city bus services. In London, number 9s always hunt in packs; in the Midlands, late night buses stop running early. On almost any express route in the world, the vehicles pull away just before you reach the boarding point.

If you write to Customer Services to complain, what happens? You may get an acknowledgement and you may not: you may even be lucky enough to receive a reply within 48 hours from the Head of Public Relations, apologising for what happened, explaining why it happened and undertaking to do all possible to prevent it happening ever again. On the other hand, according to the late Gerard Hoffnung, you might find something like this in your in-tray.

Our drivers are trained in public relations and must be cheerful and friendly at all times. You have probably noticed that they smile and wave as they pass by.

Nor is this improvement only a matter of presentation. I am sure you will have come across our mission statement, WE GET THERE ON TIME, as indeed we do, and we are proud of that.

Of course, you will understand that this might not always be possible if we had to keep on stopping for passengers.

■ Quality and Value

Customer satisfaction is closely identified with perception of quality. Now, quality is a two-way relationship with two-way advantages: customers gain because the product or service more than meets their expectations; the provider gains because customer satisfaction often leads to repeat business. There is also the saving on not having to deal with complaints or put faults right.

Bad quality is always a cost: good quality pays for itself over time, especially if it is perceived in terms of value for money. As the *Dictionary of Modern Thought* points out, 'There are probably no more effective forms of promotion than increased value for money.'[2]

There are other values, but it is very difficult to measure them in any objective way because it is largely a matter of subjective judgement. What a customer *perceives* as good value *is* good value, for that customer. The better the relationship between supplier and customer, the more likely it is that good value will be perceived.

■ Enhancements

Building relationships with customers can be much easier if you offer them enhancements. It is pointless to offer customers anything they don't value, but there is considerable mutual advantage in offering them something which enhances the value of their purchase. No great cost need be involved.

Here are some examples: pay particular attention to no. 10.

1. *Add-on services* – most suppliers of kitchen units now put you in touch with fitters who will also design your lay-out for you. But if you want to carry out your own fitting, and lack the confidence or ability to do your own lay-out, some manufacturers will provide you with a computer-generated design at nominal cost, or even free.
2. *Complementary deals* – another kitchen unit manufacture also runs a catalogue sales operation on kitchen accessories.
3. *Contracting* – yet another manufacturer contracts to sell compatible kitchen appliances made by a different manufacturer altogether.
4. *Exclusives* – if you are a heavy spender, they will supply you with 'exclusive' gold-plated sink-taps 'at no extra cost'.
5. *Information* – many of the companies selling personal financial products offer additional and general information. The fastest movers mail you a computerised interpretation of the Budget no later than 24 hours after the Chancellor's speech.
6. *Integration* – Prudential and National Breakdown each offered motorists a particular specialism (insurance in the case of Prudential; assistance from National Breakdown). Together they offered an extra option: an integrated insurance and assistance package.
7. *Rewards* – regular spenders are rewarded with bonus points, trading stamps or some other tangible recognition of their loyalty.
8. *Shoppers Clubs* – join one and receive a steady stream of information, samples, special offers, and all manner of enhancements.
9. *Societies* – if you belong to a gardening society, or other special interest or affinity group, you can often get special offers and special treatment in return for access to your own data bank.
10. *Your additions* – the enhancements you think up yourself are likely to be the most valuable to your own customers, because you know most about their needs . . . don't you?

■ A Customised Magazine

Securicor Cellular Services keeps in touch with its 125 000 business and consumer customers through a quarterly 16-page colour magazine, *Dialogue*.

Readers can specify their own customised edition by picking any two subjects from four options: Personal Finance, Home & Garden, Travel & Leisure, and Motoring. That's six different versions of the same issue, each according to reader preference. Advertisers get options, too: in this national magazine they can include inserts by geographical or postcode area.

■ Educational Leaflets Add Value

As some of the previous examples suggest, information can be a very attractive enhancement. Here is a case where providing educational leaflets in a carefully controlled way added significant value to products that were otherwise largely undifferentiated.

PORTFOLIO
CASE 9.1 – *Insurance checks*

Analysis
Abbey National, formerly a building society and more recently a bank, was generally recognised as a leading provider of mortgage and banking services. For the company's insurance products – travel, buildings and contents, personal pensions – there was no such general awareness.

Objectives

1.   To position Abbey National to the media and public as a major provider of insurance services
2.   To raise awareness of the company's insurance products and differentiate them from the competition
3.   To position Abbey National to the media and public as an authority on insurance, and as an automatic source of insurance information and comment to all journalists.

Strategy

1.   To add value to Abbey National's insurance products against the largely undifferentiated products of competitors, by producing a series of three educational leaflets: *Travel Check*; *Home Check*; *Pension Check*
2.   To create news for the company's products and so secure editorial coverage by offering these Abbey National Insurance Checks through the media, backed up by research.

Consultancy
Cohn & Wolfe.

Budget
£45 000 fees plus £36 000 expenses (total £81 000).

Programme

Summer 1992	To coincide with media interest in holidays and travel, *Summer Travel Check* was launched at the end of July 1992, and was still in demand in September.
Winter 1992/93	1. To coincide with media interest in winter travel and skiing holidays, *Winter Travel Check* was launched early in December 1992. It was still in demand in March 1993.
	2. To coincide with the media's interest in the weather and seasonal problems, one Check was launched in mid-January 1993. Copies were still being distributed as late as June 1993, in response to requests.
Spring 1993	To coincide with the media's pre-Budget financial focus, *Pension Check* was launched in March 1993, a week before Budget Day. Interest was short lived but intense (over 130 media mentions by the end of March 1993).

For each of the above phases there was a special media package, including:

- press notice
- photograph or cartoon
- syndicated radio tape
- offer of pre-agreed numbers of appropriate *Insurance Check* for readers/listeners/viewers
- round-up table comparing competitive products with Abbey National's own
- availability of media-trained people to take part in interviews and phone-ins
- background material, such as pension examples

Evaluation
1. Positioning as major provider of insurance services:
   308 articles in national and regional media; combined circulation 58.5 million; in over 80 per cent of the articles, Abbey National led the feature
2. Product differentiation:
   17 per cent of the articles featured the Abbey National competitor product comparison table
3. Positioning as an authority on insurance:
   89 per cent of the articles covered the research results
4. Added value:
   15 000 readers/listeners wrote in for one or more of the Insurance Checks
5. Journalists' reference point:
   a 'significant increase' in number of unsolicited media calls to Abbey National's Press Office and to Cohn & Wolfe

6.   Consumer Products Award in the IPR 1994 Sword of Excellence awards
7.   PRCA 1994 Award for Outstanding Consultancy Practice
8.   Galaxy 1993 Gold Award for Product and Service Marketing
9.   *PR Week* 1993, Award for Best Use of Design (runner-up).[3]

■ Will the Cow (& Gate) Jump Over the Heinz?

Between 1990 and 1991, baby-food brand leader Heinz saw its share of the market fall from 34 per cent to 30 per cent. Over the same period, the Cow & Gate share went up from 21 per cent to 26 per cent.

Then, in 1993, Cow & Gate made a bid for an increased share of the £100m market in foods specifically for toddlers, and also went for a slice of the £1bn spent on adult foods consumed by toddlers. The whole range, including meals in jars and low-sugar juices, was backed by a £3m marketing support campaign, with television and press advertising, sampling and direct mail to 300 000 mothers. In addition, Cow & Gate linked up with the British Dental Health Foundation (BDHF) with a BDHF message on packages, and a 400 000 leaflet campaign to mothers and pregnant women, advising on dental health.[4]

What Cow & Gate were doing was communicating with customers, direct and through intermediaries, but not with consumers. Toddlers certainly watch television but I doubt if they read leaflets much, or study information on packages. To customers, the message being communicated was about caring and responsibility, and being a better parent, helped of course by Cow & Gate and evidently endorsed by the BDHF.

■ Skipjack

Messages are funny things, however, and what is being sent may not always be exactly the same as what is being received. Quite small inconsistencies can matter.

Sainsbury's *Skipjack* tuna is caught on pole and line, because net fishing is fairly indiscriminate and can catch or do damage to other fish, including endangered and non-food species such as dolphins. That's a good example of a caring and responsible company doing right by its caring and knowledgeable customers, isn't it? You would think so.

Then why did the *Skipjack* can label have a design with a fishing net background? Not important, you may say, but I wonder if Sainsbury would agree. At any rate, they had the label redesigned and it is now netless. Not only that, there is a 20-word flash that says to customers 'Sainsbury's tuna is caught with a pole and line rather than being netted, thus avoiding danger to other marine life.' This is a direct and overt appeal to the ecologically and environmentally concerned customer.

■ Family Decision Making

Research in the 1970s showed that buying decisions concerning some widely consumed goods were made with the participation of the whole family: father, mother, children. More recently, the so-called *triangle of influence* allocated a percentage score to each family member, proportional to that member's degree of influence. Six main zones of influence were identified:

- husband's influence
- wife's
- children's
- husband and wife joint decision
- husband and children joint decision
- wife and children joint decision

Research in 1991 indicated that when electronic products were bought for the household, children were the main influence on the purchase of video games (61 per cent influence), whereas the wife's influence was predominant when it came to dishwashers and food processors (69 per cent and 67 per cent respectively). Only one item of the 12 surveyed was husband-dominated. Go on, guess. That's right: satellite-television aerials (72 per cent).

Children also had 10 per cent or more influence on the purchase of video cameras (13 per cent), video cassette recorders (19 per cent), CD players (24 per cent), and personal computers (35 per cent). But if you differentiate between children younger than 12 and those over 12, the picture changes significantly.

Under-12s had less than 10 per cent influence on the purchase of vertical freezers, microwave ovens, dishwashers, answering machines, satellite aerials, colour televisions, video cassette recorders, food processors, CD players and video cameras and 11 per cent influence on the purchase of personal computers; but they exercised a whacking 41 per cent on the purchase of video games.

Over-12s, by comparison, had a huge influence on the purchase of video games (74 per cent), and personal computers (70.5 per cent); a considerable influence on CD players (45.6 per cent), video cassette recorders (33 per cent), and video cameras (28 per cent), and even on colour televisions (16 per cent), food processors (15 per cent), answering machines (15 per cent) and satellite dishes (12 per cent). In fact, in only three purchases was their influence less than 10 per cent (microwave ovens, dishwashers and vertical freezers).[5]

Interesting information, yes; but how to use it? Well, there are implications for budgets and media choices. It might make sense to spend the biggest proportion on advertising to those who exert the main influence in buying. So you might target a third of the advertising budget for video cassette recorders to teenagers, and a quarter to their mothers. Another way of using the data might be to split the total budget for promotion and sales so that 44 per cent went on advertising to men, 23 per cent on advertising to women, and 33 per cent on teenage media relations.

As with all numerical data, the numbers do not make the decisions, you do: but your judgement can be strengthened by intelligent use of the figures.

■ Industry Decision Making

In organisational buying, it may not be the Buyer or Purchasing Officer alone who makes the decision to purchase, or even has the authority to do so. Buying is actually done by a decision making unit (DMU) which does not necessarily have a fixed membership. For instance, the people who decide that a new machine is needed may not be exactly the same as those who decide where and when to get it.

According to marketing lecturer and consultant Dr David Jobber, five roles have been identified in the structure of the DMU.

Users	Those who actually use the product
Deciders	Those who have the authority to select the supplier/model
Influencers	Those who provide information and add decision criteria throughout the process
Buyers	Those who have the authority to execute the contractual arrangements
Gatekeepers	Those who control the flow of information (for example, secretaries, who may allow or prevent access to a DMU member, or a buyer whose agreement must be sought before a supplier can consult other members of the DMU).

For very important decisions the structure of the DMU will be complex.[6]

It can be difficult and costly for the sales force to reach all the people in a DMU, or even to identify them with any precision. They are, of course, important stakeholders, and the public relations approach of recognising and reconciling the wants and needs of different stakeholders can get good results. You need to reach them through the channels they respect, with messages they find acceptable.

■ Influencing Workforce and Customers

When a Finnish company decided to invest in a costly new machine, they had to train their staff to accept and use it, while persuading customers to place advance orders for the new output. It was a complex operation, carried out over three years. The company was Kymmene Corporation, whose Kymi Division manufactured paper in Finland, Germany, France and the UK.

PORTFOLIO
Case 9.2 – *Beating them on paper*

Background
Kymi decided to invest $200 000 000 in a new machine which would make them the biggest and most technologically advanced paper maker in Europe.

Technical problems were formidable: the aim was to install and run the machine in smoothly, getting up to target production levels fast.

The personnel problem was to train and motivate the 2700 men and women in the workforce to accept the new machine, learn to use it in minimum time and maintain the firm's high quality standards.

As for customers, the need here was to keep them informed of progress and persuade them to place substantial orders early.

Programme

October 1987	–	start staff training
January 1988	–	advance notice to customers
February 1988	–	staff training completed
November 1988	–	machine goes on line
November 1988	–	major event for customers
February 1989	–	official start-up
Spring/autumn 1989	–	direct mail/advertising campaign

Personnel project

1. 24 one-day training sessions, 9 a.m.–4.30 p.m., each attended by an average of 130 staff, spread over five months (October 1987–February 1988).
2. Each training day consisted of 13 sessions, covering the whole production process from receipt of raw material to delivery of finished product.
3. Customer opinion captured live on video in Finland, France and the UK, and presented at the training sessions.
4. At the end of each day, there was a draw for a trip to England to meet sales staff and customers.

   Kymi report that the rate of participation in these events was as high as 95 per cent.
5. Features in the company's house journal and advertisements in the local press supported the staff training programme.

Customer project

1. January 1988: letter to customers telling them of the start-up programme.

2.   300 key customers and their wives/husbands invited to an event to be held in November 1988, one week after the machine was due to go on-line.
3.   November 1988: the White Gala was held in a Paris hotel. According to Kymi, 'The aim was to provide an unforgettable experience. The star of the show was paper.' Two dance performances, a video fantasy, a solo singer and a laser show added up to five hours altogether.
4.   November 1988: machine went on line.
5.   February 1989: the President of the Republic of Finland's official start-up of the machine was attended by about 300 major customers and opinion formers. The same dance group performed. Extensive press and television coverage was obtained.
6.   Spring–autumn 1989: direct mail and trade journal advertising was carried out in the leading market countries.

Results

1.   The machine was run in at world record speed, beating the previous best (seven months) by a clear four months
2.   The workforce adapted well, maintaining the usual high quality output
3.   Sales forecasts were exceeded by 24 per cent in the first two months
4.   The project won Kymi an award from the Confédération Européenne des Relations Publiques (CERP).[7]

■ Key Buyers

Sometimes the buying decision is made by a few, readily identified people – the key buyers – even though the product may be consumed by millions. Terry's Suchard, leading manufacturers of confectionery, identified three main categories of customer: wholesalers, newsagents and the major grocery multiples. Within those there was a total of about 60 key buyers, each of whom was sent an audio cassette of a comic radio interview. The tapes had entertainment value, but the real purpose was to convey a targeted invitation to attend one of a programmed series of shows that ran four times a day for three weeks.

Each show was interactive, the buyers being encouraged to intervene and chat with the entertainers. New products were launched and samples distributed. Every show was different, each being tailored to a specific client's interests, purchases and market position in relation to the sector as a whole. To dispense hospitality and talk business, 25 account managers from Terry's Suchard were on hand. Professional show callers helped to make sure that the apparently impromptu dialogues between clients and performers developed along the most fruitful lines for the company.

A good time was had by all, existing relationships were strengthened and new ones formed.[8]

■ Voters are Customers

Even when the number of customers is potentially very large and diverse, relationships can be personalised. Political parties use specific, targeted mail to get through direct to their customers and potential customers: that is, to you, the voter. The better their database, the more cost-effective their mailings, particularly when reinforced by constituency workers who are well informed about those issues that concern you as an individual.

So the next time you are thinking of filling in one of those fun questionnaires you find in magazines or on the back of product guarantees, think again. In describing your lifestyle, you are probably identifying yourself as a target for very specific political propaganda. As a voter you may not care much for that.[9]

Of course, as a public relations practitioner you may see things in a different and more favourable light. This is particularly likely to be so if you work for a political party in a marginal constituency.

■ Internal Customers

In some organisations, the public relations department is seen as making vital a contribution to overall performance. If your department is perceived as an administrative overhead, what you need is an internal public relations campaign, to raise your profile and shift yourselves into the vital category.

Here's how you do it.

PORTFOLIO
Guideline 9.1 – Gaining credibility inside your firm

1.	Research	— to establish who are the customers (segmenting)
		— to establish what they need to fulfil their business objectives
		— to establish current perceptions of performance
2.	Consultation	— to agree service standards
3.	Analysis	— to identify a clear mission
		— to develop clear values
		— to create the 'brand'

4.	Communications	–	to develop a communications plan
		–	to share best practice
5.	Continuous improvement	–	of people in the function (professional development)
		–	of products
		–	of processes
6.	Feedback	–	at all stages

Note that establishing a clear identity, a clear understanding amongst internal customers of what the PR function stands for (and its aspirations on their behalf), is critical to gaining credibility.[10]

When is a Customer not a Customer?

The public sector is going through a phase of pretending that it is the same as the private sector. Largely this takes the form of using the same language, like talking about 'customers'. Is this realistic?

This is what Valerie Strachan, Chairman of HM Customs and Excise, had to say. 'We collect indirect taxes and we try to stop the smuggling of drugs and other prohibited and restricted goods . . . one can reasonably suppose that an individual business, or an individual traveller, would just as soon not be our customer at all.' The Department deals with this in a way which is becoming increasingly popular in the public and newly-privatised sectors.

> We . . . need to plan for the quality of our service to individuals, and to measure it. This is all Citizen's Charter territory. We are now signed up to a Taxpayer's Charter, a VAT Charter Standard, a Traveller's Charter, an Excise and Inland Customs Charter Standard, and are about to release . . . the Customers Charter Standards for Importers and Exporters. All contain measures of service against which we can be judged. But we have to find a better word than customer.[11]

It may be difficult to take seriously the suggestion that the Inland Revenue or the Audit Commission or the VATman have customers. But what about local authorities? Many of these now believe that they are marketing-led and try to behave accordingly: Brent Council, for instance, which employs 10 000 people and has a turnover of £400m a year.

Brent sees its main customers as

- residents of the borough (existing: new: potential)
- local businesses (existing: new: potential)

- council employees (existing: new: potential)
- other employees in the borough (existing: new: potential)
- council members
- visitors to the borough
- other social agencies in Brent
- voluntary sector organisations
- opinion formers (central government: local government: others)
- the media

■ Southern Electric

The population of Brent is around a quarter of a million. Southern Electric's customers – domestic, industrial and agricultural – add up to 2½ million.

The Company guarantees specific minimum standards of services on: responding to meter, voltage or account queries; keeping appointments; connecting a supply; restoring a failed supply; quoting for a new or altered supply; dealing with main fuse failures; and prompt payment of £20 compensation every time they fall down on any of these guarantees, plus a further £20 if they fall down on that last one. The Company's retail shops have their own customers' charter, and neither they nor the contracting subsidiary are subject to the guarantees.

There is a *Careline* service of information and advice for customers with special needs, such as reliance on electricity to operate home medical equipment. For customers with impaired hearing who have access to a text telephone, *Careline* receives and transmits typed messages.

A range of leaflets for customers covers subjects such as services for older or disabled people, and handling complaints. Taken together, the leaflets add up to the code of conduct on which the guarantees are based. The standard language is English, and summaries in Hindi, Punjabi and Urdu are also issued. In addition, there are summaries in large print and on audio tape. Surveys showed that 'some 90 per cent of customers who were asked said they were satisfied with the overall quality of service they received. More than half were 'totally' or 'very' satisfied, with only 4 per cent 'not satisfied'.[12]

In percentage terms that looks gratifyingly small, but it still means 100 000 unhappy costumers. Southern Electric are the first to admit that they need to go on improving.

■ Competitors as Customers

There is nothing that says a competitor cannot also be a customer. The Energis telecommunications network between cities and towns, piggybacking on the powerline network of its parent National Grid Company, was quick and cheap to install. That made it a formidable competitor to BT and Mercury, not for local calls but in the long-distance and international markets. However, for Energis to be available to users anywhere in the country, there had to be local loop networks, and these were provided by others, notably BT. The more successfully Energis competed with BT, the bigger customer it became of BT.

Realistically, Energis could not expect to succeed simply by offering the same service as its competitors at a lower price. That would have led to a price war, which the bigger and longer-established rivals would probably win. Differentiation was the answer. Energis went for customer-driven services, whereby companies have the flexibility not only to specify exactly what service they want, when and for how long they want it, but actually to put it in place themselves through computer software.[13]

■ Professional Users

If you aim to sell technical products to professional users, you need to target your customers precisely, find out all you can about how they could use the products and give them accurate, comprehensive and usable information. That was the approach adopted by Polaroid.

PORTFOLIO
Case 9.3 – Doing the business, instantly

Analysis
Polaroid's Image System camera, which had been designed with the business user in mind, had been purchased by a range of users in the business and professional sector. Polaroid needed to increase sales of instant film in this same sector.

Objective
To position the Polaroid Image System as an efficient and effective business tool for professional users in the most promising areas of the business sector.

Strategy

1.   To establish how professional users actually used instant photography in their day-to-day working lives.
2.   To promote case histories of successful applications.

Consultancy
Infopress, working with Polaroid's marketing department.

Budget
£20 000 approx.

Programme

1. Identify specific customer groups which already used Polaroid products and had a potentially high film usage.
2. Extract contact names, professional and business addresses from Polaroid's information bank of purchasers' registration cards.
3. Identify from existing business users a Key Business Group area, drawn from

antique dealers	estate agents
architects	interior designers
art dealers	landscape gardeners
bankers	management consultants
building contractors	surveyors
caterers	town planners
engineers	

4. Issue 'screening' questionnaire to potential invitees to check how they used the Image System camera.
5. Invite individuals using the camera in interesting or beneficial ways to join the Business Users Group. Give all new members a Polaroid wall clock and free film.
6. Send detailed questionnaire to Users Group members to identify wide range of specific business application ideas.
7. Compile and structure informative case studies to convey a series of targeted messages to each professional audience.
8. Interview selected Group members at work, highlighting unusual application ideas.
9. Liaise with trade, business and chamber of commerce publications, including some exclusives.

Results

1. Business Users' Group attracted over 50 members in one year from the target professional areas. Total membership in 1990 was 60. By 1991 it had risen to 100.
2. More than 30 case studies were placed in over 20 target trade and business titles.
3. Sales leads arose from editorial coverage through business-reply service.
4. Group members tested prototype products and advised on communication messages to professional users.
5. Leads into other professional associations beyond the original targets were identified and followed up.[14]

■ Customer Centres

As we showed in Chapter 4, one very effective use of research is to present the results as justification for setting up a Centre, Bureau or other authoritative source of knowledge, advice and help. Sometimes such centres have, or seem to have, a measure of independence. Others are unequivocally branded, as in the case of Sensodyne.

PORTFOLIO
Case 9.4 – A sensitive subject

Analysis
Research showed that people with sensitive teeth needed access to advice on how to deal with the problem on a day-to-day basis. The experience of manufacturers Stafford-Miller confirmed this.

A specially commissioned survey to identify the main issues highlighted general lack of understanding about the nature and causes of tooth sensitivity, indicated how many people suffered from it, and the action – including no action – they took to relieve it.

Objectives

1. To provide a branded advice service to consumers
2. To promote the service to sufferers and the wider public
3. To generate requests for further branded information and samples.

Budget
£30 000, including all fees, printing, production and other costs.

Consultancy
Counsellor, of High Wycombe.

Strategy
The main strategic decision was to set up a branded advice centre as the base for a wide-ranging, branded, educational programme and a mechanism for distribution of samples.

Programme

1. Carry out research outlined in the Analysis section, above
2. Set up the Sensodyne Advice Centre
3. Launch the Centre at a London press event, held at the British Dental Association, with a leading dentist and dental hygienist explaining sensitivity and ways of relieving it

4. Demonstrate the effects of sweet, sour, sharp and hot foods on sensitivity
5. In conjunction with the launch, contact all regional radio stations and offer information
6. Where possible, set up interviews with local speakers
7. Arrange individual briefings at the offices of media unable to attend the launch
8. Supply branded lifestyle photographs to the press
9. In response to requests, send branded leaflets and Sensodyne samples direct to consumers.

Results

1. Radio coverage: 12 stations, 8.8 million listenerships
2. Press coverage: national tabloid, four trade journals, six consumer magazines; total circulation 5.1 million
3. Flow of inquiries at the Sensodyne Advice Centre averaging 17–20 per day
4. Distribution of 10 000 leaflets and/or samples forecast by end of first year
5. BDHF Award for Best Consumer PR Campaign for a Dental Product or Service.[15]

■ Influencing Perception and Increasing Consumption

Trade organisations that go in for generic promotions have the dual task of changing the image, or at least influencing general perception, and of persuading customers to buy more and consumers to consume more. Nothing is served by one brand increasing its share of the market at the expense of other brands. All have to benefit, against other generics. Here is one such case.

PORTFOLIO
Case 9.5 – Add a banana

Analysis
Generic promotional body The Banana Group was concerned that for 10 years banana consumption had been virtually static. A two-pronged campaign was started in 1983, focused on a schools education programme to the main consumers, children aged 5–9, and sponsorship of a cycling team to emphasise the energy-giving character of the fruit. Limited television advertising in 1991 continued the theme of an energy-giving, convenient snack food.

By 1992, overall sales of fresh fruit were declining by 4 per cent on average. To go against this trend, and maintain the dramatic and sustained growth in banana consumption experienced since 1983, a new approach was needed.

Objectives

1.   Influence the consumer's perception of bananas
2.   Encourage increased consumption from 20lb per head per year to 25lb within five years.

Strategy

1.   Identify breakfast as a 'vital meal occasion' which gives consumers, especially children, the energy to perform well
2.   Give the public positive reasons for adding a banana to their diet
3.   Target opinion formers and education sector with dietary and nutritional information
4.   Maximise impact of sponsored cycling team
5.   Support supermarket trade and independent greengrocers
6.   Generate banana industry support for activities of The Banana Group.

Consultancy
Beechey Morgan Associates (appointed in 1991, although Jane Beechey herself had also masterminded the 1983–9 campaign).

Budget
£160 000; plus £100 000 on sponsorship and schools education pack.

Programme

Consumer breakfasts	– Audience Selection research into children's breakfast eating habits
	– *Banana Breakfasts* booklet as editorial giveaway and as material for features on bananas
	– Third-party endorsement by celebrity television doctor, Hilary Jones
	– Press breakfast to launch campaign
	– Radio and television interviews and features, national and regional
	– Syndicated radio tape.
Opinion formers/slimmers	– Fact-file *The Nutritional Banana* for presentation to key trade, nutrition, education and slimming audiences
	– Coverage in main slimming publications, highlighting bananas as a good food for slimmers

– Continuance of presentation of existing
education packs for primary school-children –
the main consumers

– New education pack for senior children,
underlining energy-giving nature of bananas.

Cycling/sporting
– Regular news releases on the team's successes
– Biking stickers for trade promotions and
editorial giveaways, linked to road safety for
cyclists through better concentration arising
from high-energy food
– News releases and feature material using third
party endorsement by sports stars.

Trade/industry
– Trade press briefings, regular news releases
and interviews
– Regular newsletters
– In-store giveaway booklets
– Point-of-sale material to 6000 retailers.

Results

1. National and regional television and radio coverage with equivalent
advertising value (EAV) of £2.7m
2. National women's magazine coverage, EAV £1.2m
3. Regional newspaper coverage, EAV £100 000 +
4. Recommendation by Weightwatchers and other slimming organisations
that bananas are a suitable food for slimmers
5. Bananas rated Britain's most widely consumed fruit by several competent
bodies
6. Continuous increase in banana consumption by more than 50 per cent
since start of 1982 campaign, or 8 per cent year-on-year, in a slack market
for fresh fruit generally
7. Banana consumption up by 2.5 lb per head (halfway to the five-year target)
in one year
8. Certificate of Excellence in 1993 IPR Sword of Excellence awards.[16]

CHAPTER 10

Media Relations

What's going on, and have we got the best stories?

Rupert Murdoch[1]

■ What Story?

Whatever medium they are working in, from national television to house magazine, scientific journal to local freesheet, journalists have four main interests:

- a good story.
- a story that is better than their competitors'
- a story that is better than their competitors' and also true
- a story, better than their competitors', that is true and also in the public interest

And the greatest of these – by far – is a good story. The question is, how can you make sure it is *your story*?

■ Know your Media

In the UK alone there are at least 16 000 media listings. You can add another 12 000 or so for Europe, and perhaps a further 16 000 worldwide. Nobody can be sure just how many there are, but the scale is staggering. Figure 10.1 gives a reasonably reliable impression of how things were in 1994, and some idea, not necessarily accurate, of how they can change.

The first and obvious point to make is that there is likely to be at least one specialist publication on almost any subject you can think of, including your own. The second is that in the general media you will find a whole range of specialist correspondents or editors, from city to farming, transport to economics. General news, specialist news, consumer features and background pieces all eat material, and all have to be fed. The more precisely you target your message, the more likely it is to be published.

Table 10.1   Media Statistics

Some media listings	1992	1994	Direction of apparent change
UK			
National newspapers	28	28	no change
Regional newspapers	2464	2938	up
Business/professional/consumer magazines	9896	9311	down
Media organisations	316	306	down
Publishing houses	685	1451	not comparable
Media services	664	788	up
Directories/reference works	2248	2115	down
Broadcasting	n/a	361	
Other media	n/a	210	
Europe			
Newspapers	2578		
Periodicals	8736		
TV/radio/cinema magazines	258		
	11572	12343	up
World			
Newspapers	5468		
Periodicals	10369		
TV/radio/cinema magazines	545		
	16382	16635	up

Note: These figures may not give an accurate picture of trends and changes in the media industry, especially in the Europe and World categories. It is impossible to be fully comprehensive, and apparent upturns could simply be due to an increase in data sources.

Source: Acknowledgements to Benn's Media.

Sometimes, of course, the media will target you, especially when you may not want them to, because of a crisis or scandal or some other problem. Chapter 13 discusses what you do in such circumstances. In other, more normal, times, you have to do most of the work, which is odd, because the media actually *need* your news.

What *you* need is a thorough grasp of the pros and cons of the complete range of media relations techniques. This chapter deals with some of them. Although press and broadcasting have many points in common, there are enough differences to justify considering them separately.

■ The Press

As many of the case histories and examples in this book show, press editorial can help a company in all kinds of ways. Here are some of them:

- create direct sales leads
- provide effective support for the sales force
- increase the potential customer base
- reach specific target audiences
- launch new products or services
- create product or service awareness
- improve the competitive standing of a company
- encourage the right business environment
- reinforce company reputation

The strength of editorial coverage is its credibility and independence. The weakness is that because you are not paying for the exposure, you do not control it; you have to depend on good working relationships. It is not always easy.

PORTFOLIO
Guideline 10.1 – What the journalists say

1. In-house PR people often do better than consultants because of their greater understanding of the organisation and being close to the horse's mouth
2. Consultants should get closer to their clients and speak with authority, rather than constantly having to refer back
3. PR people should be effective facilitators rather than a source
4. Too often PR people are obstructive and miss opportunities, failing in their promise to respond on time
5. Develop personal relationships with journalists but remember it is two-way: 'bring something to the party'
6. Journalists like information aimed specifically at them, rather than blanket releases
7. Be short, sharp and factual
8. If more background is wanted it will be asked for
9. Cut the waffle on the phone
10. Don't ring in the late afternoon or Fridays – unless it's important.[2]

■ What the Editors Say

26 per cent of press notices are badly written

63 per cent of press notices are not appropriate
37 per cent of press notices are sent too late
60 per cent of press notices have no news value
26 per cent of press notices are misdirected[3]

■ Press Notices on Target

You can see why people say that press notices are an inefficient method of media liaison, but don't you believe it. Glasgow-based consultancy Flora Martin Public Relations ran a comprehensive, precisely-targeted press release programme as part of a marketing and education campaign for Academy Computers, specialists in CAD.

A general press notice went to 16 media magazines and correspondents, and 10 computer/CAD journals. A series of tailor- made announcements on specific aspects of CAD targeted consulting engineers, through a selected media list of 22; design engineers (media list of 20); and architects (11). Academy's specially built seminar suite was promoted through press notices to a dozen business magazines and correspondents, while individual seminars – for example, on CAD and timber-framed buildings, and on CAD in the stone industry – were targeted to the appropriate trade and technicals. Financial matters were given special attention when information on the leasing of CAD systems, maintenance agreements and training costs was released to 28 national newspapers, business/ financial magazines and computer journals. Staff appointments to Academy Computers were announced to the trade press and local newspapers.

Flora Martin's press relations effort was by no means confined to press notices, successful though they were. One-to-one briefings of selected journalists led to interviews and features; and, when the company opened an office in Manchester, there was a photocall on the set of Granada television's long-running soap opera, *Coronation Street*.

The full story of the campaign is told in Case 3.3, Chapter 3.

PORTFOLIO
Guideline 10.2 – What kind of press notice?

Not all press notices are of the same kind. Here are some of the more common.

1.   Hard news   e.g., new treatment for AIDS
                        e.g., election of the US President
                        e.g., beginning of new television soap
                        e.g., latest Royal indiscretion

It doesn't have to be important. It does have to be perceived as news by news editors. That is their decision, not yours. Whenever possible, a picture and caption should also be available.

2.   Background briefing   e.g., international comparisons of AIDS treatments
                             e.g., key stages in the successful Presidential
                             campaign
                             e.g., profiles of producers, writers, actors
                             e.g., matrimonial histories of Royal and friend

These 'stories behind the news' help the journalist to understand what is going on. They are not necessarily for immediate use, but be prepared to see them in print or on television sooner or later.

3.   Invitation   e.g., to a Press Conference
                             e.g., to a Press Reception
                             e.g., to a facility visit

Give enough information to persuade journalists to turn up but not so much that they don't need to. Those who do attend get the full story, including any discussion or question-and-answer exchanges. They have the chance to secure interviews, quotes and pictures for themselves. Those who do not attend get all the documentation, press packs and so on after the event and make the best they can of it.

4.   Picture story   e.g., specially shot picture of controversial civic
                             sculpture
                             e.g., archive picture of client's premises or process
                             100 years ago

Double captioned. One is not for publication and tells the picture editor what the subject is and how to get copies. The other is much longer and, when put together with the picture, tells the story. That is the one that is meant to be published. Watch the copyright position (see Commissioning Photography, later in this chapter).

5.   Double hander   e.g., extracts from a speech, plus the full text
                             e.g., conclusions of a survey, plus the full research
                             report

Can be hard news or background briefing. News editors will be more interested in the extracts and conclusions. Features editors, especially on relevant trade journals, may want the lot.

6.   Diary item   e.g., appointments, job changes, new contract

Very short, often with a picture, these items can pick up useful coverage in a range of media, from local radio and newspapers to trade and professional magazines. If the person is perceived as important enough, the item can make the nationals.

7. Advance notice   e.g., forthcoming exhibition, conference, film première

Intended for publication. A first bite at the cherry, to be followed up at the time of the event with hard news.

8. Operational Note   e.g., advance notice of how to have access to a confidential Parliamentary Paper in advance of presentation to the House

Make it clear that this is not intended for publication.

PORTFOLIO
Guideline 10.3 – Writing a press notice

1. A press notice, sometimes called a news release, is intended to be read not by newspaper readers, but by people in the newspaper business.
2. Tell them what the story is about in your *title*. It is a waste of time to write a *headline*: they'll do that.
3. Put the date on it (the date they'll get it, not the date you wrote it).
4. Tell them who you are in the masthead.
5. Tell them who to get hold of for further information, and how.
6. White paper, A4 size, double spaced, wide left hand margin, one side only.
7. Number the pages. Type '/more . . .' at the bottom of each page except the last, where you type 'end'. Repeat the title at the top of each continuation page.
8. No underlining, because that is a printer's mark, meaning *set in italics*.
9. Be brief. Be factual. Be accurate. Check everything at source.
10. Encapsulate the whole of your story in the first paragraph – the intro – of your press notice. It may be all an editor can use, or even has time to read.
11. Add further qualifying and explanatory information in the next paragraph.
12. If you have a genuine quote, which actually adds something to the story, use it. Get permission first. Identify clearly the name and relevance of the person being quoted.
13. Bear in mind the needs of radio and television. They do like brief 'sound bites' and 'screen bites'. If you can offer them someone to interview, a site to visit or a picture to take, say so.
14. Finish off with the practical data: where to send for the report/buy the widget/attend the event/sign up for membership, or whatever it may be.
15. Details not intended for publication, such as phone numbers (day and night) of two contacts, help editorial staff. Notes to Editors can include

background facts, availability of interviewees, photographs: all the operational nuts and bolts.

16. When to embargo? Don't, unless it will help the press, or you have to for legal or other compelling reasons. Read Guideline 10.5 on media provisos.[4]

Figure 10.1 shows the construction of a press notice, such that an editor can slice sections from the bottom up and still have the apex, the point, the sharp end of the story.

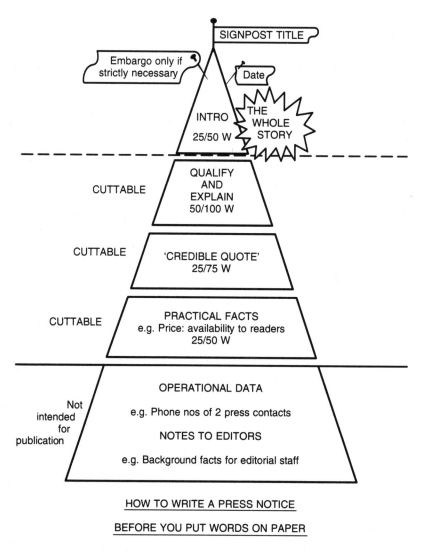

Figure 10.1   Slicing the triangle

■ Feature Articles

You can put a lot of time and effort into writing features that may or may not get used. What are the chances of success?

About 55 per cent of regional newspapers accept readymade feature information.[5] That means that 45 per cent do not, which is fractionally better than a 50:50 chance. You can greatly improve those odds if you telephone the editor first, talk it through and agree an approach and outline content.

With magazines of all kinds, from academic to consumer, the position is complex. Some are happy to take unsolicited material, especially if it is in the name of someone well known in the subject area of that particular journal. The narrower the subject area, the more likely the acceptance. However, most magazine editors prefer to discuss possibilities, often at length and usually over the telephone, before deciding what it is that you have and they want.

Once the preliminaries have been settled, and all concerned know what is to be written, editors will give you a deadline for receipt of copy by fax, electronic mail, through the post or hand delivery.

There are differences between writing a press notice and writing an article. The main ones are touched on in the following guidelines.

PORTFOLIO
Guideline 10.4 – Writing a feature article

1. An article is usually written at the invitation of an editor or by arrangement.
2. It is intended to be published in its entirety, and is written so that it is not readily cuttable.
3. Who is an article written for? The reader. Who is a press notice written for? The editor or copy taster.
4. The intro to an article has the sole purpose of hooking the reader. A press notice intro encapsulates the complete story. Article intros are probably written last, whereas press notice intros are usually written first.
5. The title is part of the article and is meant to be published. Unlike a press notice heading, it is not simply a signpost, but a hook. Key points can be made in a stand-first.
6. The structure of an article is sequential, unlike the press notice triangle.
7. Articles are written to a specified length, press notices to the shortest possible length consistent with doing the job.
8. Whereas a good article fleshes out a synopsis, a good press notice pares it down.
9. It is often advantageous for an article to be attributed to a named author, who may or may not be the actual writer. Press notices are not attributed to anybody, though all quotations within them must be attributed.

10. As much thought should be given to illustrations as to words.
11. Do not try to make an article do the work of an advertisement. Ration the number of times you mention your client or company. Three times is too many.
12. Get 'off the page' cleanly. Leave the reader with a clear memory of your message and a favourable image of your client or company. Finish on an up-beat.
13. Check all facts at source. Take nobody's word for anything. Verify it for yourself.
14. If permissions/authorisations/acknowledgements are needed – say, for the use of copyright material or a quotation, or attributing a thought or attitude to a person or organisation – get them yourself.

■ Commissioning Photography

Take notice of this warning by Adrian Berkeley, Editor of *The Photographer* magazine. 'When you buy a print or a transparency from a photographer, that is all you buy – even if you, personally, have commissioned the photograph. You do not buy the copyright with it.'

Berkeley points out that the owner of the copyright has the exclusive right to copy, or authorise the copying of, the photograph and to exhibit or publish it. All copying, exhibiting or publishing of any copyright work without the authority of the copyright owner is a civil offence. Any breach of copyright in the course of trade or business is a criminal offence.

Of course, you don't have to buy the copyright in order to use the picture. Normally, in with the fee, you are granted a 'licence', which may be written, oral or implied by circumstances. For a further fee, you can usually get a licence for wider or additional uses. However, if the licence is intended to be exclusive – with sole rights to reproduce, publish and exhibit – that has to be in writing and you would expect the fee to be higher.

Outright assignment of copyright must be in writing, and is bound to be expensive, because you are in effect depriving the photographer of any further income from that particular work for half a century. Fortunately, there are not many occasions when you will actually need to buy the copyright of a photograph.[6]

■ Seven Days a Week

An important development in national newspapers is the emergence of beefed-up Saturday editions. In the early 1980s, Saturday was the lowest selling day for the dailies. Then *The Independent* launched its 'weekend newspaper', published on Saturday, and things were never the same again. (Later, there was also a *Sunday Independent*.) Sales of the Saturday edition rose to 14 per cent above their Monday–Friday average. Other dailies were quick to get in on this new market, and the *Daily Telegraph on Saturday* soon sold 20 per cent more than its Monday–Friday average.

They were all at it. The *Guardian's* Saturday edition was outselling its Monday–Friday average, also by 20 per cent, while the *Daily Mail's* biggest seller (by 17 per cent) came out on Saturdays. Even *The Times* did better on Saturdays, topping its Monday–Friday average by 2 per cent.

Bulky as these weekend and lifestyle papers are, they do seem to be read. Property, holidays, motoring, personal finance, the arts, books, business: the lifestyle possibilities are being steadily developed. What is more, sales of hefty Saturday papers do not seem to be having too damaging an effect on sales of the just-as-hefty Sundays.[7]

The clear message to the public relations practitioner is that media relations with the national press are now worth serious attention seven days a week.

■ Giving the Press What they Want

You may think you know what editors want. That is, after all, part of the expertise of public relations. Don't be too proud to make sure.

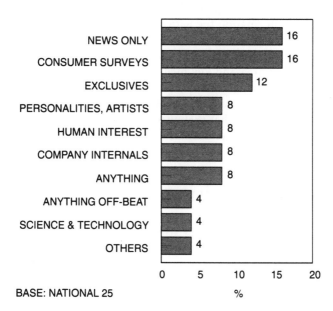

BASE: NATIONAL 25   %

Source: Reproduced by permission of Two-Ten Communications.

Figure 10.2 Public relations input the nationals prefer

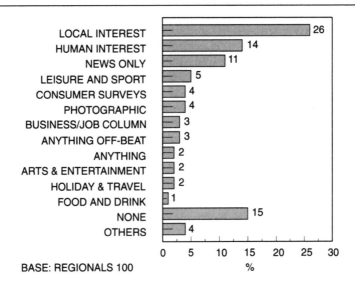

BASE: REGIONALS 100

Source: Reproduced by permission of Two-Ten Communications.

Figure 10.3   Public relations input the regionals prefer

A survey by Two-Ten Communications in 1993 showed marked differences between the type of information the national (Figure 10.2, p. 169) and regional (Figure 10.3, above) press would like to receive from PR sources.

That is useful general guidance. You will want to make it more precise and specific to your subject area and key media, like LeFevre Williamson did. The Oxford based consultancy conceived the idea of a pictorial media hook for client Lombard Natwest. They defined their target media, asked the relevant business and picture editors what they wanted and then gave it to them. Read all about it in Case 5.1, Chapter 5.

■ Radio and Television

In any medium it is important to know who to talk to. In broadcasting it can be vital. National radio and television networks are organised very much like newspapers, with highly responsive newsdesks, reporters, copy tasters, specialist correspondents, researchers, editors and so on. Of course you must get to know the individuals who really matter to you, but they do have back-up; if the person you want isn't available, there is usually somebody else to talk to.

Then there is the additional dimension of the technology, which brings in presenters, interviewers, producers, directors and personalities. On top of that are the unique advantages and hazards of going on-screen or on-air, live or recorded, and the interaction of the phone-in.

Sound and visuals are an essential ingredient, especially for stories that are not self-evidently of national interest.

Regional television and radio operate in much the same way and can often be a way into the national networks.

All this works more or less within the original Reithian structure of information, education and entertainment.

To a very large extent, everything I have said about national and regional broadcasting is also true at local level. The difference is that far fewer people are involved and they tend to suffer from the traditional cricket umpire syndrome: they wear several hats. There is absolutely no substitute for getting to know them personally. Of course, you cannot, and should not, expect any favours even if you are a friend or neighbour: that would be unprofessional, to say the least.

National or regional, television or radio, get to know their deadlines.

■ Syndicated Tapes

By 1994, radio broadcasting was reaching huge audiences. In fact, 150 independent stations attracted at least 21 million listeners a week, while 39 local BBC stations pulled in more than 10 million. In addition there were three national and five network services.

From the point of view of PR practitioners, there were obvious attractions in putting out syndicated tapes. The question is, were there equal attractions from the point of view of the broadcasters? The best way to find out was to ask them.

That is exactly what broadcasting consultants Radio Lynx did, sending written questionnaires to 38 BBC and 91 independent local radio (ILR) stations. There was an 86 per cent response from the BBC and 84 per cent from ILR. The main finding was that, as a matter of policy, 57 per cent of BBC local radio stations, and 40 per cent of ILR services, never used syndicated tapes. That does not mean 'very infrequently'; it means 'not on any occasion'.

Another finding was that 36 per cent of BBC stations and 59 per cent of ILR stations in the survey indicated a very limited use, which in many cases meant hardly ever.

For stations that did use syndicated tapes, the criteria were

- news value
- production values
- local angle
- celebrity contribution
- duration (an average of 2½–3 minutes, though music-based programmes preferred much shorter items).

Problems included too much branding; too long; of no interest whatsoever; of no relevance to local audiences; badly produced.

An important use of syndicated tapes by the broadcasters is as story leads. Properly handled, these can benefit the PR professional. As long as your story gets broadcast, does it always matter that much if the tape itself does not?

As you might expect, your syndicated tapes might also be used by the broadcasters as sales leads. Their reasoning is that if getting on the air is important to your PR strategy, maybe you can be sold some advertising, to make sure.

So it is clear that the odds are loaded against syndication. Nevertheless, according to Lynx, 'when the . . . format is right and the content relevant, syndicated tapes can work'.[8]

For confirmation of that, read about Abbey National's Insurance Checks campaign (Case 9.1, Chapter 9, and Table 14.2, Chapter 14).

VNRs are obviously more recent than radio tapes. They became established in the USA in the 1980s but have been viable only since about 1992 in Europe, where the UK leads the field. Budgets and usage vary widely and it is important to guard against over-expectation. According to Steve Garvey, of Reuters, VNRs of specialist or regional interest, costing £5–£7000, frequently score two or three hits, and in a number of cases have been even more successful. In Chapter 12 you will find a couple of examples of effective use of VNRs which cost £10 000 or less.

If your story is potentially of national or international significance, you need audiences in the millions and must be prepared to spend considerably more than £10 000. Should your target audience be worldwide, and your project long term and sustained, it is possible that you might need a VNR budget in six figures. Even then, there can be no guarantees. But when the story, treatment, format and delivery mechanism are dead right, VNRs can be very cost-effective indeed.

■ Interviews

Anybody who is likely to be interviewed by any of the media – press, radio, television – needs training. Let nobody persuade you otherwise. Media training should be carried out by specialist professionals. You will find the addresses of some of them in Appendix B.

■ Media Events

An event is a happening that seems important to those who are present at it. A media event is one that is made to seem important to those not present. The essence is to involve people, direct or vicariously, in a stimulating and satisfying experience, and at the same time generate approving attitudes towards your company or client.

If you want people to take a particular action at an event – join something, buy something, whatever – you have to make it easy for them to do so.

An event which is highly and visibly successful always has a by-product: improvement in staff morale.

Here are five steps to a successful event:

- plan thoroughly, and well in advance
- communicate with all concerned
- coordinate so that things happen when they're supposed to
- implement in precise detail
- evaluate honestly and without undue delay

Small or big, it is essential that the scale of the event is consistent with the scale of the enterprise. Small organisations look ridiculous trying to run massive events, and big organisations look mean running modest events.

Be professional and meticulous. Success lies in the accumulation of spot-on detail, at the expected time, in the expected place.

■ Relevance

A media event for a pen manufacturer might be an autograph party, where famous guests happily sign their names on promotional or souvenir literature. If they were all the winners of the Booker Prize still living, that might make 20 seconds on national television. A local football hero could sign programmes at 50p a time for charity. Afterwards, the charity could auction the very pen with which the famous name was written. That kind of item ought to be worth 1½ minutes on a regional news magazine programme.

On the other hand, you're not likely to win much support for a religious organisation through an event that centres on a night out at a gambling casino. But all things are relative, and even the vicar's mother might have a flutter on a raffle to raise funds for church roof repairs. (It's one of the mysteries of life that all church roofs always need repairs.) Put the vicar on the roof, in hard hat and dog collar, and you have the makings of a photocall and possibly a local television item.

Sometimes an exceptionally clever, or brave, or lucky, campaign succeeds against all reason. Tommy's Campaign may be one of those. Decide for yourselves: read the story in Case 14.2, Chapter 14.

■ Product Demonstrations

Unless your product happens to be an atomic bomb, demonstrating it may not in itself be a media event, but you can help to make it so. For example, if your product is a new play-and-learn activity game for schools, you could hold an inter-schools event in a significant catchment area, laying on a real live demonstration with real live children: then run an inter-schools competition, with the winner getting the product free, and others getting supplies at a big discount.

Coordinate this with advertising in the teachers' press and editorial on local radio and in the local press, with photocalls. Pay special attention to timing, and think of ways of making your activity game easy to buy. You could tie up a coupon redemption scheme with the local branch of a household name store chain. Enlist the support of home–school associations. Think about getting into parish magazines and community newsletters: that is real grass roots territory.

■ Taking the Product to the Media

During the busy periods of seasonal confectionery, all the manufacturers are competing for coverage in the trade press. Rather than call the media together to preview their new range, Mars took the products to the journalists. Paragon customised an exhibition trailer, loaded it with samples and promotional material, and sent it on the road for a two-day tour of the key trade journals. Individual press briefings were given by Mars specialist staff. The activity resulted in 18 significant items in the target press, including features and exclusives.[9]

Mirage International Systems, manufacturers of specialist personal computer monitors, launched their new range of multi-platform monitors in London. Journalists didn't need to be there. Mirage arranged for lunch to be delivered to selected PC journalists at their own desks, followed by a conference telephone call, with a speech by Mirage managing director Kevin Butterworth, and then an opportunity for questions and discussion.[10]

A nice idea, and none the worse for having been done before, as in the 1960s, when Mary Noble, of Peter Roderick Public Relations, sent a quarter bottle of champagne to beauty journalists asking them not to open it until further notice. Three days later each journalist received news of a new lipstick colour, a sample, and an invitation to drink to the success of the product with the champagne already provided.[11]

To promote their 1993 winter collection, Chanel sent a hand-made box full of flowers to fashion magazine editors, plus a handsome promotional brochure wrapped in hand-made paper.

Direct-line insurance brand Guardian Direct used its owl logo in a talking press notice. A tape-recorded message to journalists transformed the company's 0800 phone number 282820 into tu-whit, tu-whit, tu-whoo. The live original of the logo, a European eagle owl, figured prominently in photocalls.

■ The Essex Brewer

When T.D. Ridley & Sons, a family-owned Essex company with a string of 65 local pubs, wanted to raise their profile and establish themselves as a significant participant in community life, they became *Ridleys the Essex Brewer*. With new livery and new signage, the company advertised on bus sides and poster sites. They ran a horse-drawn delivery vehicle as a touring road-show, complete with trad jazz and Victorian wenches. Advertisements were placed on local radio. Sales promotions in pubs were backed by a major information programme to staff and tenants. Central to the whole operation were two sports competitions, both naturals for a brewing company. The Ridleys Cricket Campaign had Player of the Month and Player of the Season Awards, sponsored commentaries on local radio, perimeter advertising at the County Ground, plus competitions and awards in association with the local press. In the winter months the Ridleys/*Essex Chronicle* Darts Awards took over, with the same involvement with local media.

The campaign, by consultancy Welbeck Golin/Harris, made a major contribution to increased sales: up 6 per cent overall, and by as much as 300 per cent for some brands in some pubs. It also won an award for outstanding consultancy practice.

■ Advertorials

Although the interventionist tendencies of some newspaper proprietors and multi-media tycoons might suggest otherwise, it is still the case that editorial matter, its objectivity and integrity are entirely the responsibility of the editor. What goes into editorial matter is determined by editorial judgement based on editorial values.

Advertisements are paid for by advertisers and should be clearly recognisable as such. What goes into them is determined by the advertiser, based on promotional values.

Advertisement features and special supplements use editorial matter to support advertising. The two strands should be handled separately, with no implication that advertising in the feature or supplement will secure favourable editorial.

Advertorial is a particular combination of advertising and editorial, usually on a single theme or group of related themes, paid for by the advertiser but looking like editorial. Three questions need to be asked.

1. Are advertorials effective?
2. How are they perceived by readers?
3. Are they legitimate practice for PR professionals?

In 1993/4 National Magazines and the Research Business Group carried out a qualitative survey of readers of eight Natmag titles. The aims were to understand what the consumers thought of advertorials and to explore their role in an advertiser's communications strategy. The research showed that advertorials can:

- change perception of a product
- encourage a second look at a product
- involve the reader more fully with the product
- achieve product sampling

Readers were shown to:

- enjoy advertorials as a form of communication
- appreciate that advertorials often provide more information than a 'normal' advertisement
- see them as added value advertising with a significant potential reward

The success of advertorials depended on:

- the personal relevance of the product
- the fit with the reader's motivations for magazine purchase
- the product category relevance

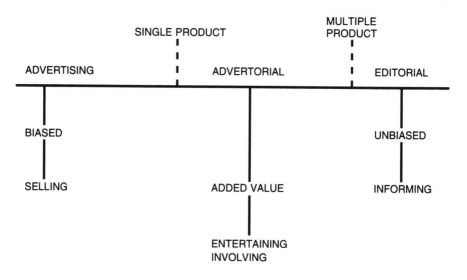

Source: Reproduced by permission of National Magazines.

Figure 10.4   Readers' perception of advertorials

- the fit with the editorial style, content and image of the magazine
- the balance between information and selling
- their visual appeal

The style and content of the advertorial determined how it was perceived. On the whole, a single-product promotion was seen as closer to advertising, and a multi-product promotion as closer to editorial (see Figure 10.4).

That answers the questions on effectiveness and readership perception quite satisfactorily.[12] On the question of legitimacy for the PR practitioner, the IPR, the Chartered Institute of Journalists and the National Union of Journalists all emphasise the distinction between advertising and editorial. They warn of the possible risk of confusion to the reader and undue pressures on the PR practitioner, but conclude that with careful thought and discreet inquiry we can judge for ourselves the validity of any proposition. Files are kept on borderline cases, and transgressing publications are identified.

As long as editorial integrity is maintained, and readers are not misled, advertorials can be a valuable and ethical option in a public relations programme. In the case of womens' magazines it is becoming the preferred option.

■ Infomercials

Since the mid-1980s there has been a new development. Infomercials are television advertisements that resemble programmes.

In the USA, infomercials are typically 30 minutes long, often in the format of a television chat show. They generate total sales of $1–5m a year. Initially, the advertisers were small and individualistic, not to say cranky, and the ads appeared on cable and local television in the cheap midnight-to-dawn time slot. Then the big brands got interested in infomercials, and leading advertising agencies set up units to produce them.

In the UK, cable and satellite were the first to introduce infomercials. Then *Focus on Ford* appeared on national terrestrial television, with familiar faces as presenters and guest celebrities, and with a factpack mail-out in response to freephoned requests.[13]

There are some difficult questions here. If viewers consciously recognise that they are ads that look like programmes, fine; but can infomercials work in that way? If viewers do not see them as ads, but as straight information or editorial, are infomercials honest and truthful? There is as yet no research corresponding to the survey on advertorials, and every public relations practitioner, consultant and adviser will have to form a view and take a position on this issue. Infomercials are legal and, unless they are banned – which seems unlikely – they will not go away.

■ No Guarantees

Events are often central to a sponsorship deal, especially in sports. The Football League signed an estimated £3m sponsorship deal with Endsleigh Insurance. The event had to:

- be prestigious
- have the right geographic spread
- offer promotional opportunities during the year
- be a tried and trusted event

'The Football League meets all these criteria,' said Mike Naylor, of Endsleigh. The deal involved:

- title branding
- match day programme promotions
- advertisement hoardings
- corporate hospitality opportunities at all games
- sponsorship of end of season Wembley play-offs.[14]

Media exposure was at the heart, but even spending £3m did not give Endsleigh guaranteed television coverage as of right. The only way to be absolutely certain of getting that would have been to advertise.

■ Sponsorship Credits

ABSA has an excellent Media Crediting Checklist, which is reproduced here with their permission.

PORTFOLIO
Checklist 10.1 – Media crediting

1. Establish clear objectives for the media credits.
2. Never guarantee media coverage.
3. Establish the business target group (nationals, Sundays, regionals, trade press).
4. Coordinate with arts groups target press.
5. Draw up a comprehensive list of press targets identifying cross-overs between arts and business.

6. Allocate responsibility for particular press sectors and contacts. Arts groups can assume this responsibility and fail to utilise the sponsor's resources effectively.

7. Maximise resources between sponsor's press office and arts group.

8. Generic press release paper for the sponsorship is an advantage. Otherwise use the arts group press release paper and add sponsor logo.

9. Announce partnership in short press release and send to all press contacts. Include the sponsor's name in title (if possible) and opening and closing paragraphs. Highlight sponsor's name in bold throughout the press release.

10. Ensure profile of sponsor's name is on all printed material peripheral to the event (for example, posters, programmes, signage, invitations).

11. On press nights include specific information about the sponsorship inside the programme on a separate sheet. The presence of a press desk for the collection of journalists' tickets is an opportunity to stress the importance of the media credit.

12. Use visually exciting photographs to get picture coverage. Early morning photocalls are labour intensive but can pay off in good coverage. Picture coverage is of particular interest to most sponsors.

13. Arts sponsorship is not in itself news. If an angle to the sponsorship exists (ground-breaking activity, large sum of money) pursue this through feature writers.

14. Target feature material to Sunday papers, supplements and magazines. One exclusive could be a better option than three possibles.

15. Marketing and trade press will almost certainly cover a new sponsorship, but work well in advance of publication date. Prepare any press work and contact well in advance.

16. Regional press will give a better return on time invested. The value of this to a sponsor with regional offices may be greater than national coverage. Touring productions have a particular attraction for regional press, as does the story of a local business supporting the arts.

17. For large-scale events the hire of an independent television/video crew may be worth considering, in order to circulate the footage. The extra expense is considerable but it usually pays off in coverage.

18. Radio coverage of the event is easier to obtain on the arts front, but accreditation of the sponsor will need careful negotiation.

19. Do not promise media credits. They are subject to a variety of imponderables.

20. Take part in the ABSA media crediting campaign, whereby details of our members' sponsorships are sent to arts editors and correspondents in advance of the opening. For further details contact ABSA's Press Manager.[15]

It will be obvious to you that the ABSA checklist can readily be modified to suit a variety of circumstances other than arts sponsorship.

■ Sponsorship in Regional Newspapers

At national level, it is usually clearly understood when sponsorship is taking place, as many of the examples in Chapter 5 confirm. At regional level, with the local penetration and loyal readership of the regional press, it may not be so clear cut. Letters pages, weather forecasts, crosswords and horoscopes are regularly and frequently sponsored in a wide range of regional media. More ambitious projects include television listings, sports reports and features on holidays, gardening and leisure. Readers' clubs of various kinds, education sections, science inserts, business pull-outs and financial specials are all doing a job for their sponsors. From weekly property supplements to one-off budget blockbusters, the range is expanding and there is still plenty of potential for growth. Sponsorship combines well with advertising in mutually reinforcing packages. Costs vary widely, and some very good deals are being negotiated. It is essential that editorial integrity is not compromised.

■ Deadlines and Provisos

One of the most difficult facts of life for a public relations manager to accept is that it is the journalist, and ultimately the editor, who decides what is a good story. They may well conclude that the real story is the one you don't want told. Expect them to make every effort to get it.

Never tell journalists something you don't want them to use. Just make sure, before you start, that they know what is attributable and what is non-attributable. That applies to press, radio and television. The following guidelines should keep you on the right side of the media.

PORTFOLIO
Guideline 10.5 – Media provisos

1. Always be scrupulously fair in your dealings with the press, radio and television.
2. Do not impose an embargo to make your information seem more important than it is, or just to suit your own or your client's convenience.
3. An embargo is justified only if it helps the media to overcome disadvantages such as those due to different lead times, deadlines or time zones.
4. Never break your own embargo.
5. Observe the Stock Exchange rules and other established practices on the release of price-sensitive information.
6. Never tell lies.

7. There is no such thing as 'off the record'. All information given to journalists is publishable.
8. Recognise that 'no comment' is nowadays taken to be a comment.
9. Anything you say, including background information, may be attributed to you or your organisation. If you don't want it to be attributed, specify clearly at the start that the information is 'non-attributable'.
10. If you don't want it published, keep it to yourself.[16]

■ An Insidious Practice

During the 1990s, there was a growing tendency for publishers to levy a charge on freely offered editorial material. Sometimes they wanted to be paid for publishing press notices; more usually, the money purportedly covered the costs of producing colour separations.

Taking a lead from the IPR Professional Practices Committee, an unprecedented alliance of five separate organisations, representing the disparate interests of public relations practitioners, journalists and advertisers, joined forces to oppose and condemn these radical departures from established publishing practice. A joint statement issued in February 1995 (Appendix C) likened publishers' demands for cash for coverage to 'the corrupt media deals which have become institutionalised in some countries' and pointed out that 'the value to advertisers and readers of journals known to offer paid space under the guise of conventional selected editorial is already diminishing and will continue to do so'. Whether you believed that to be realistic or optimistic depended on where you were positioned.

If you were a journalist, you could have found yourself under pressure from your employer to go against your conscience and abandon your personal commitment to accepted editorial principles. If you were a PR practitioner, your client or employer may have expected you to compromise your own professional standards: for if you did not, you could be striving to get media coverage through creativity and skill while your competitors were unethically buying an advantage over you.

The Professional Practices Committee of the IPR put in several years' work defending and advocating professional integrity. In the words of the joint statement 'charging for colour separations, for news items and similar material *where this is not an advertisement, advertorial, or other overtly sponsored feature* . . . appears to have no justification. It blurs the distinction between advertising and editorial, and undermines a central argument for public relations'. It was also in breach of the Codes of Practice adopted by all organisations contributing to the February statement. These were:

- the Institute of Public Relations, with 5000 members
- the Public Relations Consultants Association, whose members employ 4500 people
- the National Union of Journalists, almost 30 000 strong
- the Chartered Institute of Journalists, membership around 1500
- the Incorporated Society of Business Advertisers, with 850 member organisations.

With this powerful consortium refusing to have anything to do with it, how long could the insidious practice of charging for editorial and colour separations survive? The real question is, will it be replaced by other questionable ploys to boost publishers' revenue?[17]

■ A Sense of Proportion

We must agree to treat the media seriously, but we do not always have to be solemn about it.

Fred Plester, a leading regional editor with a light touch, understands exactly what is news. This is what he says.

Dog kills cat is not news.
Boy kills cat merits just one paragraph because boys can be beastly.
Girl kills cat is worth two paragraphs because girls are less beastly.
Mouse kills cat is front-page funny, in bold.
Nun eats cat is a page 3 lead.
FERGIE FRIES CAT is a splash, but only in a bad week.[18]

CHAPTER 11

Organising and Training for Excellence

Knowledge is not the main thing, but deeds.

Jewish saying[1]

■ What Kind of Organisation?

If there was a best way to organise public relations, everybody would be doing it, but they aren't, because there isn't. What determines the difference is often just the sheer size of the organisation. An international pharmaceutical giant might find that what works best is to have one type of structure for its brand PR and another for corporate affairs. For the brands, public relations would simply be a sub-function of brand marketing, with the specific tasks of marketing support and customer relations.

You would expect the corporate arrangements to be more complex. Under a Vice-President for Corporate Affairs there could be half a dozen or so Directors, responsible for Media Relations, Government Affairs, Investor Relations, Internal Communication and so on. Each Directorate would run a group of activities; for example, Media Relations would certainly cover Press Office, Broadcasting and Monitoring, and possibly other functions such as Speech Writing. Several PR consultancies would be engaged, for Corporate Identity, Government Affairs and Investor Relations at the very least.

A somewhat leaner machine could run public relations for a trade association. A Director and his or her Personal Assistant; a Deputy Director who was also Head of Strategy and Chief Press Officer; a Press team of two, and a Public Affairs specialist, plus a departmental secretary (who might well be the hardest worked of all).

A small, specialist public relations consultancy could typically employ two or three consultants and the same number of support staff.

Right down at the nittiest and grittiest end, proprietors and managing directors of very small firms do just about everything themselves. That includes public relations, whether they realise it or not.

Which kind of organisation do you work in?

■ An Excellent Partnership

Toyota is by far the biggest Japanese automotive manufacturing company and number 3 in the world rankings. Europe is the world's largest market for automobiles, and the company has manufacturing plants in Burnaston, Derbyshire, and Deeside, Wales. Scope: Communications was ranked number 28 in the *PR Week* list of the top 150 UK public relations consultancies in 1995. Differences of scale and culture notwithstanding, Toyota and Scope organised for excellence in public relations. This is how.

PORTFOLIO
Case 11.1 – Anglo–Japanese cooperation

1. Broadly speaking, Toyota's PR in the UK is divided as shown in Table 11.1.

Table 11.1   Toyota's UK public relations

Audience	Toyota entity	PR support
Opinion formers	Toyota Motor Corp. London Office	1. In-house communications managers 2. Scope
Employees and local community	Toyota Motor Manufacturing UK Ltd (manufacturing plants)	1. In-house communications team 2. Scope (specific issues only)
Customers	Toyota (GB) Ltd (UK Distributor, 75 per cent owned by Inchcape)	1. In-house communications team

2. Toyota Motor Corporation International Public Affairs in Tokyo is supported on UK and European issues by TMC London Office.
3. NV Toyota Motor Europe Marketing and Engineering SA in Brussels (TMME) is supported on pan-European corporate issues by TMC London Office; on manufacturing issues by Toyota (UK); and on distribution issues by Toyota (GB).
4. Toyota (GB) is responsible for product advertising in the UK.

5. Specific projects carry their own budget and the corporate community involvement activity is separately funded jointly by Toyota Motor Corporation, Toyota (UK) and Toyota (GB).
6. All budgets are developed based on consultation and consensus between Toyota entities and Scope.
7. On a day-to-day basis, the Scope team – Deputy Managing Director, Associate Director, Account Manager and support functions – interfaces with TMC London Office General Manager and TMC London Office Corporate Communications Manager. In addition, the Scope team, where necessary, interfaces directly with senior executives and in-house communications teams at TMUK, TGB and TMME.
8. Table 11.2 shows who does what.

Table 11.2   Toyota public relations interfaces

Scope	TMC Japan International Public Affairs	Toyota UK	Toyota GB
Deputy MD	General Manager TMC London	Managing Director Toyota UK	Managing Director
Associate Director	Corporate Communications Manager	Director Human Resources & Communications	Marketing Director
Account Manager	TMC London Support Team	Corporate Affairs Manager	PR Manager
Account Executive		Toyota Corporate Affairs Department	TGB PR Department
Scope Support Team			

9. The different Toyota entities and Scope meet:

*   *Quarterly* strategic meeting with senior executives
*   *Monthly*   working meeting to co-ordinate activity
*   *Daily*   contact by phone and meetings to implement programme

10. Twice each year, progress of Toyota's UK Project is reviewed. Papers charting progress and future planning are prepared by TMC London Office and consensus is gained with TMUK and TGB. These papers are taken back to Japan and thoroughly reviewed with senior management at TMC International Public Affairs in Tokyo.[2]

■ Professional Organisations

Public relations is moving towards being a profession, with the four main characteristics shared by all professions:

- a body of knowledge and recognised skills
- regulated entry
- enforceable code of practice
- sense of mission or calling

Competent public relations practitioners should always behave in a professional manner. The structures within which they work satisfy Professor Charles Handy's criteria, being 'flat organisations; most have only four steps to the top layer of status, and that results in a long list of names at the top . . . but the work is organised in groups, teams, sections or faculties'.[3]

You often find in consultancies, and to a growing extent in-house, that public relations is carried out by project groups, where the leader is by no means always of a higher rank than the rest of the team.

Handy has some useful observations on another aspect of organising for excellence. 'Few organisations', he points out, 'use their professionals for things that other people can do equally well . . . the professional organisation, to be viable economically, has to be accompanied by the contractual organisation.'[4]

A vital skill in the management of PR is to combine one's own personal excellence with the purchased excellence of an outside collaborator or supplier.

■ Identifying Skills and Attitudes

You can find examples of very successful PR operators who have never had a day's formal training in their lives. Some of them are brilliant, and would have succeeded anywhere, anytime. Others have been lucky. Most people are not able to rely on either brilliance or luck. What they need is a solid professional grounding and a planned career development; how to get it is the question. What did the IMS have to say?

As you might expect, the most important aspect of performance in post is *achievements*: actually getting the tasks done. This is closely followed by the *management of people*, which is achieving through the achievement of others. *Judgement* and *flexibility* are also rated pretty highly.

It is only when we get to the fifth-ranked requirement of performance in post that there is any mention of *professional and technical skills*. More about this later.

The last two items on the list of requirements are *organising ability* and *initiative*.[5]

PORTFOLIO
Checklist 11.1 – Knowledge and skills

At the level of professional starter – that is, people who are developing their public relations career as assistants and junior executives – the IPR and PRCA identify specific skills and knowledge they class as essential. To those already itemised in Chapter 2 as pre-entry requirements, add the following.

Knowledge

1. The roles, responsibilities, value systems and reporting structures of the public relations function, both inside the organisation and with outside bodies such as the press, local and national government and the trade unions
2. The roles, responsibilities, vocabulary, techniques, ethics, law and regulations of public relations, marketing, advertising, research, behavioural studies and production of printed media
3. The roles, responsibilities, vocabulary, techniques, ethics, law and regulations of sponsorship, sales promotion, direct marketing and broadcasting
4. The structure, priorities, distribution, basic economics, organisation and operation of manufacturing and service industries, financial institutions, the public sector, local and national government, voluntary organisations and member organisations.

Skills

1. Editorial writing in connection with photocalls, interview calls, news releases, photo captions, briefings, feature material
2. Script planning and writing
3. Understanding public relations objectives and strategies
4. Identifying publics (the 'stakeholders' concept)
5. Selecting media to reach identified publics
6. Media liaison techniques and operation
7. Understanding the differing emphasis of different market sectors such as consumer, technical and financial
8. Editorial planning and monitoring
9. Handling editorial inquiries
10. The basis of photography and how to brief a photographer
11. Planning and organising events
12. Selecting, planning and organising sponsorship
13. Editorial promotions such as competitions and special offer advertising
14. Negotiating editorial features and interviews
15. Briefing designers
16. Print selection, briefing and production management
17. Audio/visual briefing and production management

18. Exhibition planning and management
19. Capabilities of desktop publishing
20. Reviewing and implementing emergency plans
21. Presentation techniques
22. Networking with clients, colleagues, contacts
23. Time management
24. Delegation and supervision.[6]

If all that seems rather formidable, do not be put off. It is learnable if the will is there, and the opportunities are found. If you can't find them, create them.

As the junior executive moves on and develops into a fully operational professional, the quality of knowledge and skill increases over time. In addition, other areas of knowledge and skill are required (for example, risk, issue and crisis management; strategy and policy making; budget setting and financial control). The question is, as well as learning on the job, what other ways are available for acquiring the knowledge and skills you need at the appropriate level?

■ Training for Performance

Much of learning on the job is simply keeping your eyes and ears open and picking things up as you go along. But there is much more to it than that, and the best employers, in-house and consultancy, run structured training programmes. Sometimes these programmes are done entirely from the organisation's own resources. More often and more usefully, specialist trainers are called in. Their expertise may be used in one of two ways: either the trainees go to the trainers, or the trainers come to the trainees.

Professional and trade bodies in the communications business put on courses, and so do a number of commercial undertakings. You will find some useful addresses in Appendix B.

Here is a practical example of training for excellence in a local authority.

PORTFOLIO
Case 11.2 – Cascading to excellence

Analysis
In the 1980s, local government services were under attack. Through government legislation, notably compulsory competitive tendering, everything from housing to maintenance, education to street cleaning, transport to refuse collection, was to be exposed to market forces. Few local authorities had the requisite staff,

expertise or budget to meet 'a need that nobody felt they had'. Brent Council was no exception.

Objective

To get marketing on the agenda so that it became part of the daily life of everyone working for Brent Council.

Strategy

By means of cascading, to provide audiences with enough targeted information and training for them to see the whole of the Council's operations from the point of view of the customer.

Programme

In each of the four years 1990–94, a specific target audience was identified. Each was either significantly wider than in the preceding year or was trained in greater depth.

Customised packages addressed each recipient direct. A detailed, high-quality and customised manual was created to meet the information and training needs of the top three tiers of management, who had no background in public relations or marketing.

Follow-up training and audio-visual presentations reinforced the messages and broadened the audience.

In the final stage of the campaign, video and training packages were delivered through facilitators to the entire workforce of 8000 people.

The cascade nature of the programme is illustrated in Table 11.3.

Table 11.3 Brent's training programme

Year	Target audience	Production	Cost (£)
1990	A dozen senior managers (one per department)	Bought-in, high quality, customised marketing training	20 000
1991	Sixty senior managers (about five to each department)	Production and dissemination of Brent's first corporate marketing plan, written by the 12 managers trained the previous year	1000
1992	Two hundred senior managers (the top three tiers in the organisation)	High quality, ring-bound Marketing and Communication Manual, aimed as a do-it-yourself guide to marketing/ advertising/communications	5000
1993	As a result of restructuring, the number of senior managers in the organisation halved. This year's plan was aimed at 100 senior managers, the equivalent of those 200 from the previous year, and to build on what they would have gained from the manual	(a) High quality training programme of roughly equivalent quality to that delivered to 12 people in 1990 (b) The production of an attractive audio-visual presentation on marketing by a dozen senior managers. Shown to over 300 people internally	15 000

Year	Target audience	Production	Cost (£)
1994	The entire workforce (8000 staff)	An internally produced training pack, with video – to be delivered by in-house facilitators (trainers) to entire workforce between February and June 1994	14 000 (except for training time)

Source: Reproduced by permission of *IPR Journal*.

Budget
£60 000 over four years.

Results

1. Brent Council became customer-focused
2. Internal business units were committed to spending 1 per cent of income on marketing
3. A self-financing Ad-Shop provided marketing services to the internal business units, leading to a high success rate when they were subjected to market testing or voluntary competitive tendering
4. Two Charter Marks were awarded to the Council
5. The campaign won a major award in the IPR Sword of Excellence 1994 awards
6. Brent Council's reputation began to turn round from 'inefficient, corrupt, poor service delivery, bad industrial relations' towards 'centre of excellence'.[7]

■ National Vocational Qualifications

Throughout the world there is increasing interest and involvement in vocational qualifications that are based on nationally agreed standards of competence independent of the learning process and assessed through direct observation at the candidate's place of work.

National vocational qualifications (NVQs) are awarded, for example, in the member states of the EU, in Oman and in Bahrain. Comparable systems operate or will operate in New Zealand, Australia, the Irish Republic and Spain, among others. In North America, there is considerable Canadian interest, and USA involvement is at Presidential level, while in South America, Mexico and Argentina are pursuing their own vocational education and training schemes.

English and Welsh NVQs and their Scottish equivalent (SVQs) are obtainable at five levels, covering a whole range of competencies from basic craft through to professional/middle management. For public relations NVQs, these levels broadly correspond to the five levels of the IPR/PRCA Education and Training Matrix. For example, at NVQ level 3, competence must be demonstrated in implementing a communication campaign; contributing to the development of PR strategies; managing media relations; producing copy; maintaining business relationships; providing information and advice towards meeting organisational objectives; and contributing to the health and safety of the working environment. In addition, contributing to the obtaining of specified supplies *or* contributing to the organisation of events and promotions *or* contributing to the management of reputation is assessed.

Level 4 covers much the same subject areas, with the emphasis on managing and evaluating them, rather than contributing to them.[8]

The joint awarding body for NVQs in public relations is CAM (Communication, Advertising and Marketing Foundation) and RSA (Royal Society of Arts). Outcomes should perhaps be treated as elements in a modular set of building blocks.

■ Writing: A Fundamental PR Skill

Most journalists care about words. That may seem hard to believe, especially when you read some examples of butchered copy, but mostly they do. So if you want to have any kind of rapport with journalists – and you do, otherwise why would you be in public relations – treat words as if they matter to you. That advice applies equally to every readership, each with particular needs, assumptions and expectations. Nothing fancy is called for: just plain competence, and I do mean plain.

PORTFOLIO
Guideline 11.1 – Writing style

There is no one style of writing that is always right for every purpose. The right style is the one that is most appropriate for the reader, most consistent with the content, most credible when the source is considered.

However, if you use the following guidelines sensibly and flexibly your own writing style should benefit, whatever the occasion.

1. Cut out all words that aren't necessary. Why write about your company's 'future plans'? A plan is something the company intends to happen, so how can it be other than 'future'?
2. Cut out all the adjectives, and put back only those that are strictly necessary.

3. Use simple, short words, such as 'begin' or 'start', not 'commence': 'about', not 'approximately'.
4. Use short sentences, mostly between eight and twenty words. If you need more than twenty words in a sentence, consider whether you might need two sentences.
5. Use short paragraphs. If a paragraph has more than five sentences, consider whether you should move one to the next paragraph.
6. Write in the active voice, not the passive: 'when we had done that', not 'it having been done'.
7. Be positive and specific: 'We have 49 per cent of the market', not 'More than half the market belongs to our competitors.'
8. Guard against jargon, hackneyed phrases and foreign words that have not been fully absorbed.
9. Vary your pace, colour, rhythm, vocabulary. Make your readers keep on wanting to know what happens next. That is as important in an annual report as in a paperback thriller.
10. Remember that the person who decides whether writing is successful or not is the person reading it. Don't be backward in applying these guidelines to this book. I guarantee that you will find less than 100 per cent compliance.

■ Getting it Right

If you are not sure of the difference between *infer* and *imply*, you may well use one when you mean the other. Getting it wrong can set up a barrier between your reader and you, and there are surely enough impediments already.

You may think that the opposite of *antagonist* is *protagonist* but it isn't, and many (I wish I could say all, or even most) journalists know that.

When a professional accountant gets the figures wrong, credibility gets dented; likewise when a public relations professional gets the words wrong. In some circumstances, a simple spelling mistake can be very damaging, not so much because wrong spelling can affect understanding – that's comparatively rare – but because it can alter the way you are perceived. You see, many people who can spell, including clients, believe that this makes them superior to those who cannot. Certainly a report or proposal containing spelling mistakes implies that the compiler – you? – is either careless or doesn't know any better. Either way, confidence is eroded, and that is no basis for a businesslike relationship.

Fortunately it is very easy for almost anybody to improve their spelling. It does not require much intelligence to do so. The first stage is to recognise that spelling mistakes are indeed mistakes. Computer spellchecking programs will do that. Another way is to read more of everything and anything, on the principle that if you can see the correct spelling in print often enough, you will eventually twig when your way is wrong.

Whatever you do to identify the faulty spellings, learn and practise the right ones until they become second nature. Then practise them some more.

■ Creativity Training

According to the IM, 'creativity and innovation are often regarded as high risk activities which are difficult to manage'.[9] Well, yes, they might be regarded as high risk and difficult: but that's only because they are.

The IM's solution is to advise companies to focus on existing strengths rather than engaging in high-risk diversification. A better way might be to reduce the risks associated with creativity by shifting the odds in its favour. Encouraging creativity, especially in the communication business, can be a way of getting more for your money.

Arthur Koestler once said that the creative act does not create something out of nothing; but uncovers, selects, reshuffles, combines and synthesises ideas, faculties and skills that are already there. The more familiar the parts, he argued, the more striking the new whole. Edward de Bono called it lateral thinking. You don't need a special name for it, and you can learn to do it.

Give creativity every chance to flourish by exposing your brain to the widest variety of stimuli and absorbing as many as possible. As it happens, your brain is not very efficient at keeping track. Nothing personal: it's true of all of us, and it is precisely that inefficiency which mixes and mingles impressions, blurs and blends images, so that we make connections and juxtapositions that can be illogical and not all sensible. But since when was creativity sensible?

I am not using the word in the sense of the so-called creatives in advertising agencies: the people whose job it is to produce memorable advertisements, and who are usually kept well away from the client. Maybe that's because 'memorable' advertising often seems better at serving the interests of the agency than at meeting the needs of the client.

■ Reference Banks

If you want to be more creative, you need to invest in constantly updated reference banks. These will reside partly in your files, but mostly in your own head, where words and images can get together in unexpected ways.

Checklist 11.2 lists a number of sources of raw material for a visual reference bank. The most important entry is that final one.

PORTFOLIO
Checklist 11.2 – Visual reference bank

Look out for, and really look at, any or all of the following. Note the location of particularly interesting examples.

AMUSEMENT ARCADES	– they still show the influence of folk art
ANTIQUES FAIRS	– quite different (in range, style, atmosphere) from antique shops
ANTIQUES SHOPS	– a crash course in visual styles of the past
ARCHITECTURE	– styles, materials, juxtapositions
ART BOOKS	– for top-notch printing in every colour-range imaginable
ART EXHIBITIONS	– today's avant-garde is tomorrow's advertising style
BARROWS	– folk art again
BOOK JACKETS	– for ideas on how to convey a complete story in one picture
BOUTIQUES	– the clothing equivalent of contemporary art
CARBOOT SALES	– everything from the utilitarian object to the 'What is it?'
CASUAL CLOTHES	– cheerful, not always cheap
CATALOGUES	– every page a lesson in selling
CITY GRAPHICS	– see street graphics
COMICS	– story telling with the minimum of words
COMPETITORS	– a very important category. If you don't know what your competitors are up to visually, how can you possibly aim to be better than they are?
COMPUTER MAGAZINES	– inventive and exuberant icons
DERELICT SITES	– for intriguing fragments and surreal compositions
DESIGN PERIODICALS	– full of creative imagery
EPHEMERA	– everything from bus tickets to price tags
FETES AND FUNFAIRS	– more folk art
FLYPOSTING	– instant impact
GRAFFITI	– a contemporary form of folk art
GREETINGS CARDS	– something for everybody
HOARDINGS	– large scale and sometimes impressive
HOLIDAY BROCHURES	– glimpses of what others find exotic
LIFESTYLE MAGAZINES	– funnier than many comics
MUSEUMS	– some brilliant visualisations
NAMEPLATES	– domestic, professional, industrial lifestyle symbols
NEON SIGNS	– nothing by day, beautiful or vulgar by night

NOVELTY SHOPS	–	vulgar at all times
OTHER PEOPLE'S IDEAS	–	better to poach a good visual than to originate a bad one
PERFORMANCE ARTS	–	the live action equivalent of comics
PERIODICALS	–	and not only those in your own subject area
PRICE TAGS	–	especially the hand-lettered type
ROCK CONCERTS	–	where often the visuals are more interesting than the music
SATELLITE PICTURES	–	birds' eye views of birds' eye views
SIGNS AND SYMBOLS	–	attention grabbers, especially when used out of context
STREET GRAPHICS	–	a city street is a mass of visuals, some legitimate, others not
THEATRE AND CINEMA POSTERS	–	like king-size book jackets
VANDALISM	–	it's a fact of life and some of the results are visually interesting
VIDEOS	–	promotion techniques are over-used but still have mileage
XMAS DECORATIONS	–	acceptable bad taste
YOUR ADDITIONS	–	and deletions, too

Better still, make reference banks entirely of your own. What, for instance, would you put in a verbal reference bank? No, I don't mean one full of spoken words and phrases: that would be an oral reference bank. What I mean is an extension of the traditional reading list (which usually has a clear theme) into a gloriously unsystematic, ramshackle list of sources of words, and combinations of words, to feed and stimulate the mind. It would not be at all surprising if many of the sources in your visual bank occurred again in your verbal bank.

A Press Relations reference bank would include notes and cuttings on good ideas in action, and remember that if it was a good idea once it can be a good idea again (see Chapter 10). If it worked for somebody else, why can't it work for you? But beware of stunts and gimmicks that draw attention to themselves.

■ Skills for the Future

In our enthusiasm for creativity, we must not forget that we are also concerned with managing, now and in the future. Looking to the beginning of the twenty-first century: what are the management skills you will need then? Try this checklist.

PORTFOLIO
Checklist 11.3 – Managers in the twenty-first century

Leading opinion formers have identified various skills for the manager of 2001.
Which of these skills have you got? How will you acquire those you haven't
got?

> Strategic thinking
>   (e.g., longer term, broader perspective, anticipating)
> Verbal communications
>   (e.g., coherent, persuasive)
> Understanding the role of information and information technology (IT)
> Financial management
>   (e.g., role and impact of key financial indicators)
> Organisational sensitivity
>   (e.g., cross functional understanding)
> Listening skills
> Sensitivity to others
> Facilitating others to contribute
> Responding to and managing change
> Coaching and counselling skills
> Risk assessment in decision-making
> An orientation towards total quality/customer satisfaction.[10]

If you look at specific training needs in public relations, you find that corporate
strategy heads the list. Here are the results of a survey undertaken for the IPR in
1993.

PORTFOLIO
Checklist 11.4 – Training in the twenty-first century

Members of the IPR interested in training were asked what courses they
wanted. The following 14 were most in demand and are listed in order of
preference.

Course	*Percentage demanding*
Corporate Strategy and Public Relations	83
Introduction to Corporate Relations	49
Employee Communications	48
Working with Radio & Television	48
Effective Presentations	46
Public Relations and the Law	43
Project and Time Management	41

Government Relations	39
Managing People	39
Business Communication	38
Event/Exhibition Planning and Management	34
Finance for the Non-Financial Manager	32
Community Relations	32
Consumer Public Relations	25[11]

■ Unix to Apple

We have seen in Chapter 8 how the Law Society introduced changes in new technology. At about the same time Beaumont & Sons, Solicitors, became convinced that their specialism in aviation law would be improved if they switched from their Unix system of information technology to user-friendly Apple Macintosh. Beaumont's IT manager, Emma Farrant, planned a 16-week change-over, involving installation and training for three audiences: administrators, fee-earning lawyers and secretaries.

First to be trained were the administrators. The idea was to get them up and running before anybody else, so that the firm would keep on ticking over as others were pulled out for training. The administrators also acted as back-up when needed.

Fee-earning lawyers were next, in groups of about five, for one day's training. They were encouraged to stay in-house for lunch 'so that they wouldn't drift off to discuss their insecurities with others'.

Secretaries were trained for three days, not because they were three times less intelligent than the lawyers, but because they had at least three times as much to learn. They also had to unlearn the old system, which the lawyers had never even got round to trying to learn.

While the groups were in training, the IT manager went round their offices, taking out the old machines and installing and setting up their replacements. So when lawyers and secretaries went back to their desks, there were the brand new Apple Macintoshes which they were able to use immediately.[12]

Good training practice? Yes, and very good public relations practice.

■ Train Everybody

Every member of every organisation deserves to be trained in PR, starting with those who interface with the public. I'm not sure that even a superlatively trained receptionist can actually win significant business for your firm; but I'm absolutely certain that a badly trained or untrained one can lose it.

CHAPTER 12

Paying for Public Relations

There are only two sorts of management decision that matter – the ones about money, and all the others.

Anon[1]

■ 'Just Put in What you Think'

In January 1994, the Department of National Heritage confirmed that it would spend £1m on two campaigns to do with the 50th anniversary of the D-Day landings of June 1944. One campaign, in the USA, was to be handled through the British Tourist Authority. The other, UK based, was to be 'a major high profile campaign through a coordinated series of events involving people of all ages, including schoolchildren, across the country'. At best the briefing for potential consultancies could be described as vague, with no clear guidelines on costs. The winning agency was expected to 'advise on and implement this campaign . . . act as a clearing house for ideas; establish contacts with the commercial world, seeking sponsorship where appropriate, and come up with good ideas'. The Department was quoted as telling a consultant, 'We're talking about half a million [pounds] but just put in what you think.' As *PR Week* pointed out at the time, 'all this had to be achieved with just 19 weeks to go before the D-Day Anniversary. By calling on extra reserves of Dunkirk spirit it will get done, of course . . . but the Heritage Department's approach smacks of amateurism.' Lowe Bell Communications won the account. It was reported that their fee was £62 500. If so, they certainly earned it.[2]

Had you been looking for a textbook example of how not to do it, you couldn't have chosen better. The objective was unclear: was it to *celebrate* or *commemorate* the D-Day landings of 50 years ago? Public reaction and pressure almost aborted the whole programme before it even started. As for research and consultation – well, either there wasn't any, or it was perfunctory. Was any serious thought given to resources? There seemed to be a general assumption that whatever was needed would be available. About the only thing the Department got right first time was the original D-Day date, and there weren't any options on that.

Ultimately the D-Day programme was reckoned to be a success, though this judgement was subjective. As far as the public was concerned, and especially

198

those who pay taxes, there were no objective criteria against which effectiveness could be evaluated. The only popular test appeared to be whether or not Dame Vera Lynn would sing. She did, though much later than scheduled, and all was well. Hard bitten journalists were heard to say that the commemoration got more coverage than the D-Day landings themselves back in 1944.

■ Principles of Budgeting

If a D-Day budget principle could be detected it could perhaps be summarised as: 'We really ought to be doing something. Here's quite a lot of money. Now what?'

There has to be a better way; in fact there are several. Here are four of the most common:

- relate PR expenditure to turnover, revenue or profit
- relate PR expenditure to marketing or advertising expenditure
- compare your PR budget with others
- base your PR budget on the actual job to be done

■ PR Expenditure Related to Turnover, Revenue or Profit

An organisation that sees public relations as an essential and integral part of all it does might decide to apportion a percentage of turnover or sales revenue or profit, or income from donations, or new capital raised, or some other financial expression of the totality of the enterprise.

When you compare industry's PR expenditure with turnover, you get a very wide range of ratios. In recent years one firm in four spent up to 0.1 per cent and one in 25 spent 3 per cent or more. The great majority – about two out of three – committed themselves to something between these two extremes. The larger firms tended to allocate less proportionately than the smaller ones, but more in absolute terms, of course.

It was estimated that IBM had budgeted £2m on a combined advertising and PR campaign to boost the company's image as a leading software provider. IBM sells about £300m of software in the UK, so the advertising/PR expenditure would be 0.66 per cent of that. The PR element amounted to 0.033 per cent of sales revenue, at £100 000.

Direct health sales food company Cinergi was estimated to have earmarked £50 000 for PR support of its network of 6000 independent distributors. That was 2.5 per cent of the company's turnover.

If Cinergi had budgeted the same percentage as IBM, there would not have been enough money to buy each of their dealers a first-class postage stamp. If IBM had budgeted the same percentage as Cinergi, they might have achieved their objective more decisively.

Northern Telecom, Canadian-owned contender for the *Bowman* battlefield voice-and-data communications system contract, was believed to have set aside £100 000 for a public affairs and government relations programme. Northern Telecom were aiming to win a slice of the £2bn Ministry of Defence order. The size of that slice was unspecified, but if it was 50 per cent – £1bn – that would be in line with the estimated PR fee of over £400 000 allocated to Dewe Rogerson for advising the government on its £4bn sell-off of its remaining 40 per cent stake in National Power and Powergen.

Cable operator Telewest was thought to be planning a $1.6bn flotation. If so, it could have been worth £200 000 in fees to Dewe Rogerson, Telewest's corporate PR advisers.

Dewe Rogerson won the £100 000 account for the partial privatisation of Spain's largest electrical company, Endeso, which was expected to raise £1bn.

Financial Dynamics' financial relations programme for property developers The Argent Group was estimated at £30 000 fees and expenses. Argent had £100m net assets, and there was general speculation that a flotation might have been in the offing.

The Royal National Institute for the Blind (annual turnover £50m), reckoned it could afford to spend £50 000 on a campaign to shift attention away from handicap and disability, focusing instead on opportunity and equality.

■ PR Expenditure Related to Marketing or Advertising Expenditure

Where public relations is classed as one of the marketing functions, that will usually determine how the money is allocated: perhaps as marketing support, perhaps as a sub-section of the advertising spend. Once again, there is tremendous variation.

30% of firms spent up to 5% of the advertising budget
32% spent more than 5% but less than 20%
20% spent between 20% and 50%
Only 4% spent more than 50%[3]

American construction toy manufacturer K'Nex had an estimated £70m share of the market. The firm's European launch programme was budgeted at some £500 000, of which 80 per cent was spent on advertising and 20 per cent – £100 000 – on a familiarisation campaign through The Communications Group.

Romania's pilot privatisation programme was worth £500 000 in fees to a consortium of banking, accountancy, law and PR firms. Of this, the PR fee was reckoned at £100 000.

■ Comparing your PR Budget with Others

In a fiercely competitive world, what others do will largely determine what you do; so what your rivals spend on public relations will have a big influence on what you spend.

Shortly after the Cosmetic Surgery Unit of Guys Hospital launched a £30 000 promotional campaign, the main non-surgical alternative was launched by the European Association of Aesthetic Medicine through – wait for it – a £30 000 promotional campaign. Coincidence? You tell me.

Compare your PR budget with other PR budgets: self-referentially, by looking at previous budgets within the firm; competitively, by looking at the PR budgets of comparable organisations outside the firm. You may find the section on budget brackets useful.

The most popular budget seems to be £100 000, which is enough to show serious commitment but shouldn't scare the pants off the accountants.

■ Basing your PR Budget on the Actual Job to be Done

Calculate the PR spend in terms of the objectives to be attained and by costing the actual tasks to be performed. This works best when not referred to previous budget levels. Start from a zero base each time.

PORTFOLIO
Guideline 12.1 – Task-directed, zero-based budgeting

1. Identify the change you want to bring about
2. Estimate the benefit of changing against the cost of not changing
3. Plan a programme of activities and events to achieve the required change
4. Justify the programme, and each element in it, in terms of its contribution towards securing the benefit of the change
5. Cost the programme item by item
6. Operate the programme and control the costs
7. Measure results achieved against intentions
8. Feed corrections back.

■ Budget Brackets

There is no typical budget for public relations. Good work is done for less than £50 000, and sometimes much less. In fact, Magellan Medical Communications charged the Neurological charities nothing for handling their PR, while The Voluntary Organisations Communications Advisory Service offered free PR advice to small charities.

Equally, good work can be done for more than £500 000, and sometimes much more. An increasing number of budgets now go beyond £1m (the 'magic million').

It can be useful to look at the budgets in terms of brackets. Let's keep it simple, choosing only five:

- under £50 000
- £50 000–£100 000
- over £100 000 but under £350 000
- £350 000–£750 000
- over £750 000

If you have a general idea of what others pay to achieve their objectives, you are more likely to recognise value for money when seeking to achieve your own.

■ Budget under £50 000

Although many PR consultancies have concluded that it is not worth their while to pitch for accounts worth less than £50 000, a great deal of activity goes on with budgets under that. For instance, East Sussex County Council ran a one-day conference on the archaeological potential of the coastline. Archaeologists, academics and council employees attended this Heritage Coast Forum. When they walked out at low tide to inspect a sunken wreck off Hastings, selected journalists had been tipped off. There was also a photocall. The in-house mini campaign secured features in two national newspapers, and coverage on local television, for a budget of £1000.

Up in County Durham, Easington District Council's in-house team ran a campaign to clamp down on dog fouling. Press attendance at a presentation to the environmental health committee was followed by the release of striking posters, designed by a specialist firm. All the local media picked up the story, plus Sky television, the Press Association and Channel 4. The budget was £7000.

Campaigns centred on VNRs can cost no more than £10 000. BT Northern Home Counties wanted low-key PR for their sponsorship of a veterinary nurse at a wildlife hospital. A £3500 VNR by Creative Touch Films was used on BBC, Anglia television and Central television. The RAC's VNR, produced by SMS and promoted by the in-house team, generated 16 television spots for a car crime campaign, for a budget of £5000.

WDC spent 13 per cent of its total public relations budget on the awareness campaign described in Case 6.3, Chapter 6. That amounted to £10 000, and the Council made it go a long way by teaming up with nearby Buckinghamshire College, part of Brunel University. This approach fitted in with Wycombe's partnership policy. Students of advertising at the College responded to the opportunity of project work on a real-life campaign, coming up with the slogan 'We make every penny count', and designing some highly effective posters.

Academy Computers, specialist dealers in CAD applications, spent £13 000 through Flora Martin Public Relations on an awareness campaign. This budget was 13 per cent of the total marketing, advertising and education budget of £100 000. Academy Computers' sales went up by 33 per cent and turnover rose from £3.6m to £4.5m. It would be very difficult to compute a direct percentage relationship between the £13 000 PR budget and the £900 000 gain in turnover, but it's a fair bet that the client was very pleased with the consultancy's award-winning performance (see Case 3.3, Chapter 3).

PORTFOLIO
Case 12.1 – Something to show for the money

Background
Eureka!, the first museum for children in this country, had been at various stages of planning for many years and all the traditional PR launches had already been used. When the official opening date was announced a year ahead, journalists were understandably sceptical. There were practical difficulties: the museum was still seeking funding; museum staff were already fully extended; most exhibits could not be installed until the last minute; even mock-up photography was not possible until a couple of months before opening.

Objectives
1. To maximise limited resources through partnerships and joint ventures
2. To attract 200 000 visitors in the first year.

Budget
£16 000 fees: £15 000 photography and production costs.

Consultancy
Northern Lights, of Harrogate.

Programme
1. Partnership with Leicester School of Engineering and Manufacture, to generate publicity targeted at business people (potential sponsors) and teachers (to plan school visits). Schools were asked to take part in Eureka! research of exhibits. Leicester School analysed the results.
2. Tailored stories were fed to specific press segments – design, education, research, nursery provision, the rejuvenation of Halifax, where the museum was sited, and so on.
3. Newsletters and updates were drip-fed to the national press, to culminate in major articles at the official opening.
4. Press preview day, and individual visits for all key national press.
5. Publicity partnerships with sponsors of major exhibits (for example, M&S, BT, Nestlé).
6. Official opening by HRH The Prince of Wales.

Results
1. 200 000 visitors within three months of opening, 460 000 in the first year.
2. By the opening date, 10 000 schoolchildren had pre-booked visits.
3. 80 schools took part in the Leicester School of Engineering and Manufacture joint research project.

4. Media coverage included national and regional television and radio; 16 features in national newspapers and over 70 in the regional press; about 40 trade, business and educational journals; a dozen consumer magazines; and the newsletters of all the major sponsors.
5. Yorkshire Publicity Association Award for Best Publicity for a Charity.[4]

■ Budget £50 000–£100 000

The National Children's Home became the NCH in 1987, but the change of name did not do enough to correct misunderstandings about the charity's work, and that didn't help fundraising. There was a pressing need to develop a new identity more expressive of the full range of work undertaken by NCH, including areas of social concern such as child abuse and homelessness. The strategy developed with Fishburn Hedges was to involve all stakeholders in the planning and execution of the new identity.

Of all the options considered, the internal favourite was NCH Children and Families, but this was over-ruled. The final choice – NCH Action for Children – was introduced in stages, at first within the charity. A PR hook claimed that modern research showed that the 1½ million families living on state benefit today could not afford even a Victorian workhouse diet of gruel. Subsequent headline coverage provided a public lift-off platform for the new identity. Fishburn Hedges worked on the campaign at a special discount rate (estimated to be around £50 000).

Other campaigns at £50 000 were the Black Country Development Corporation's account with David Clark Associates; Solent and Severn Inns' programme of media relations, crisis management and quarterly in-house newspaper, through Leedex PR; Southern Electric's financial relations contract with Citigate; and the TUC's widening of political links, masterminded by Burson Marsteller, in the run-up to their autumn conference.

Shandwick had the job of raising the profile of the IT software developed by Neilsen, the number 2 market research company in the UK with a turnover of £44m. Campaign fees were £60 000.

For £70 000, Premier Relations ran a generic campaign for the Association of Contact Lens Manufacturers, aiming to extend their £42m market.

The merchandising arm of Warner Brothers, film distributor, aimed to have six Studio Stores up and running in the UK by Christmas 1994, to add to the 56 in the USA. Dennis Davidson Associates won the account, with around £75 000 in fees.

Handel Communications' healthy eating campaign for the Health Education Authority targeted lower-income groups. The £80 000 campaign included a roadshow, competitions, a joint promotion with a national newspaper and editorial spots on television and radio.

Here is a cluster of fifteen campaigns, each budgeted at £100 000.

- BT's business-to-business promotion of visual services. Consultancy, Scope: Communications
- Capital Region USA – three American tourist authorities combined to attract visitors as an alternative to Florida. Consultancy, Representation Plus.
- Gateway 2000, American manufacturer and direct marketer of IBM-compatible personal computers. Promotion to PC users in the UK. Consultancy, Text 100.
- Hay Personnel Services, recruitment consultancy. Integrated communications programme. Consultancy, The Communication Group.
- Henkel, the German chemical giant. Raising the profile of its DIY adhesive brands in the UK. Consultancy, Iain Smyth Associates.
- IBM's pan-European exploitation of information technology systems as used at the Olympic Games. Consultancy, The Rowland Company.
- Investment in People – to make the Investment in People mark the accepted training standard for employers. Consultancy, Burson Marsteller.
- Jersey, Channel Islands – to promote the Island's status as a financial centre and as an international tax haven. Consultancy, Shandwick.
- Lincolnshire's new university, due to open in 1996. Advice on fundraising initiatives and public consultation. Consultancy, Burson Marsteller.
- London Clubs, the international casino group. Investor relations, in run-up to possible flotation. Consultancy, Lowe Bell Financial.
- Mazda Cars' media relations campaign extended beyond the motoring press to consumers. Consultancy, The Quentin Bell Organisation.
- Mondex UK electronic payment system promoted through trade and consumer media. Consultancy, Band & Brown.
- Motorola's promotion of mobile phones and paging services, plus sponsorship of a cycle team for the UK stages of the Tour de France. Consultancy, Amanda Barry.
- Station Bravo – a series of stunts to attract 24–45-year-old viewers to this cable television station. Consultancy, Lynne Franks.
- Tring International, budget price CDs and audio cassettes. Expansion into consumer PR. Consultancy, Key Communications.

PORTFOLIO
Case 12.2 – The scent of success

What would you think it costs to launch a new scent, perfume or fragrance? According to Elf Sanofi, the controlling group of Yves Saint Laurent, it took Fr100 000 000 to launch *Champagne* perfume worldwide. They got back twice that in sales over three months, even though the wine-makers made sure through the courts that *Champagne* had to be called something else in France.[5] That is serious money; but what about launching a new 'popular' Beauty International scent to teenage girls, and getting shops to stock it?

Objectives

1.   To launch *Tribe* and to sustain awareness among 13–18 year old girls
2.   To encourage initial orders by the retail trade, and major stocking up for Christmas.

Strategy
To talk to teenage girls in their own language, both through their 'own' media and direct at events.

Budget
Trade launch £51 000 (including £10 000 consultancy fee); plus *Take That* tour, £12 000.

Consultancy
Paragon.

Programme

1.   Roadshows at four nightclub venues. This was a joint venture with *Just Seventeen* magazine
2.   Sponsored 12-concert tour by 'teenscream' band *Take That*
3.   Research report linking scent with sexual attraction
4.   Stand at Clothes Show
5.   Competitions
6.   Product sampling
7.   Editorially supported promotions
8.   Local radio
9.   Advertorial
10. One-to-one briefings, press packs and photography for trade press, women's press and youth press.

Results

1.   39 million cumulative opportunities to see (COTS) in consumer media, 70 per cent of them in key teenage media
2.   54 000 teenagers reached direct via sponsorships and Clothes Show
3.   555 800 COTS in trade press
4.   Total cost per 1000 OTS was £1.29
5.   During the six months of the launch period, sales of *Tribe* into retail outlets were 60 per cent more than the company had budgeted for.[6]

■ Budget over £100 000 but under £350 000

To move the market away from totally refined sugar to the more versatile non-refined type, Billington Sugar commissioned Richmond Towers for £150 000. The PR programme included trade and consumer relations, exhibitions and editorial promotions. Mobil's *sans frontières* pan-European staff communications project through Paragon cost about the same (see Chapter 7).

Swedish pulp and paper giant Assi Doman's pan-European campaign of industrial media relations and corporate identity was budgeted at £200 000. The consultancy was Manning Selvage & Lee. The Bahamas Tourism Office's UK and European PR account was provisionally budgeted at the same figure. Also at £200 000, GCI carried out an international media relations programme for Budget Rent A Car. The trade and consumer account for Robinsons soft drinks was secured by Spreckley Pittham for a budget of £250 000. Cameron Choate and Partners won the £285 000 launch account for Armand Hammer's Dental Care brand baking soda toothpaste. The campaign began with mailings to the dental health profession, plus editorial in the specialist press. The next stage was communication with retailers, followed by consumers.

■ Budget £350 000–£750 000

Food poisoning and food safety are big issues and the Food and Drink Federation took the lead in the national Foodlink campaign. The starting point was a MORI survey. The findings were presented to opinion formers and the national media at a London seminar. A House of Commons exhibition was staged in the same week. Local authorities took part in regional events during Food Safety Week. Major retailers were also involved. In-house PR teams did the whole programme for £350 000, including the MORI survey.

The Malaysian Timber Industry Council decided it was good at conserving its forestry, a major national asset, and wanted this to be clearly and fully understood throughout Europe. Hill & Knowlton's brief was to cover Germany, Scandinavia and the EU, including the European Parliament at Strasbourg. The business was estimated to be worth an annualised fee of around £400 000.

At £500 000, healthcare communications agency Medical Imprint had the job of promoting Pfizer's anti-rheumatic Tenidap, through an education programme, media relations and presentations to opinion formers.

The motor-cycle industry's two representative bodies are The Institute of Motor Cycling and the Motor Cycle Industry Association. Together they budgeted £600 000 for trade promotions, industry-wide marketing and the International Motorcycle Show.

■ Budget over £750 000

The Police Federation's £1m campaign to stave off unwelcome reform is outlined in Chapter 1, and Worldcom's £2m consumer information programme for the EC is described in Case 6.4, Chapter 6.

US whitegoods manufacturer Whirlpool's pan-European consumer campaign earned Ketchum PR up to £2m a year in fees.

McDonald's 1993 PR budget of £2.1m included media relations, roadshows, support of the Keep Britain Tidy Group, and pre-opening lobbying on proposed new restaurant sites. Actual restaurant openings were handled by McDonald's marketing department

The DTI campaign to promote open systems of information technology (Case 14.3, Chapter 14) had the aim of changing awareness, understanding, attitude and behaviour. These classic public relations objectives involved publications, audio visuals, advertising, exhibitions, speeches and demonstration projects. The total budget was £14m, in two phases. In the first (four-year phase) £6.1m was spent on the umbrella programme, and £5.9m on technology modules. The 'marketing' spend, which was actually mainly public relations, accounted for about 17.5 per cent in each case, totalling £2.1m over the four years. In the second phase, probably £750 000 of the total £2m was spent on public relations strategy: a hefty 37.5 per cent.

According to reports in *PR Week* on 17 February 1994, external work accounted for less than 1 per cent of the W.H. Smith Group's annual PR budget of £4.45m.

The huge privatisation programme of the French government – 20 firms in four years – aimed to bring in £27bn. The PR allocation was in the region of £15m.

■ Informed Guesswork

Sometimes a consultancy (or a client, or a company, or a government department or a local authority) is unwilling to disclose the cost of a particular campaign. One has to respect legitimate confidentiality but it is often possible to estimate the budget. The figure for LeFevre Williamson's award-winning pictorial 'media hook' campaign for Lombard Natwest was withheld. However, by studying Case 5.1, Chapter 5, one could reasonably guess that the cost was certainly not less than £25 000 but probably not more than £50 000.

On a larger scale, the undisclosed cost of The Rowland Company's campaign to secure a £5bn contract for Devonport Dockyard (Case 6.2, Chapter 6) could not have left much change from £500 000. If it did, the client got a bargain.

■ Cost Justification

Whatever budget principle you adopt, you need to justify what you spend in terms of what you get. That means careful and realistic analysis, as with the Royal Tournament (spelt out in Case 3.5, Chapter 3). PR consultancy Kestrel Communications was called in to reinforce the existing marketing effort, increase the total number of seats sold and so generate increased net revenue. Specific targets were set and both objectives were achieved with handsome margins.

There is an analysis of what elements worked best (and worst) in Table 14.3, Chapter 14.

Do not assume that this says anything about the relative merits and cost-effectiveness of different PR techniques generally: the data refer solely to the specific case of the 1993 Royal Tournament.

You have to cost and justify not only the whole programme but every significant element in it. What contribution is being made towards carrying forward the required change? How does the cost of doing it compare with the benefit?

■ Costing Procedures

Before you can control costs, you need to record them. You could use an off-the-peg system, or create one to fit your specific needs. Either way, consider how best to make use of information technology. But before actually buying or creating any cost-recording system, be clear about the purpose of what you are doing: is it costing a product or service? Pricing? Overall cost control? Maximisation of resources?

Define your cost centre and classify your costs into such categories as:

- direct
- indirect
- fixed
- variable
- controllable
- uncontrollable
- separate
- shared

Look at your procedures (for example, estimating) and improve them. This is not a once-and-for-all process. Allow for variable behaviour costs with different levels of activity: for instance, a big increase in core activities ought to be reflected in higher fixed and direct costs, and a corresponding decrease in those discretionary overheads which tend to add cost but not value. Try to avoid having to deal with very small figures. Group them in some useful way. To get a quick idea of how things are shaping, round your figures. Greater accuracy can come later.

Describe everything clearly. Monitor everything continuously. Compare variances. Anything exceptional or unusual should be quickly investigated. Take whatever action is called for.

■ Salary Costs

Public relations is, as they say, a people business. As a rule of thumb, the gross income of a PR consultancy should be least twice its wages bill, although in 1994 the figure was a little less (between 1.8 and 1.9 times). This is based on all employees and therefore the people who work with clients have to generate enough in fees and mark-up on rechargeables to cover their own salaries three or four times.[7]

In-house corporate overheads can be 100 per cent in a small firm, 200 per cent in a middle-sized company, and 300 per cent in a big one.

The significance of these 'multipliers' is set out in Tables 12.1 and 12.2, which give 1994 average and top salaries at five levels in consultancies and three in-house, and applies multipliers of two, three and four. You will see that

Table 12.1   In-House Salary Costs

	PR Director	PR Manager	PR Officer
Average age	43	38	33
Average salary (£)	42 044	27 137	18 309
× 2	84 088	54 274	36 618
× 3	126 132	81 411	54 927
× 4	168 176	108 548	73 236
Top 10% salary (£)	83 249	46 070	27 977
× 2	166 498	92 140	55 954
× 3	249 747	138 210	83 931
× 4	332 996	184 280	111 908

Source: PR Week, 31 March 1995, in association with Media Appointments.

Table 12.2   Consultancy Salary Costs

	Chairman/ Man. Director	Board Director	Account Director	Account Manager	Account Executive
Average age	43	38	33	29	25
Average salary (£)	38 212	40 435	28 032	20 328	15 252
× 2	76 424	80 870	56 064	40 656	30 504
× 3	114 636	121 305	84 096	60 984	45 756
× 4	152 848	161 740	112 128	81 312	61 008
Top 10% salary (£)	75 332	79 999	45 726	30 291	29 166
× 2	150 664	159 998	91 452	60 582	58 332
× 3	225 996	239 997	137 178	90 873	87 498
× 4	301 328	319 996	182 904	121 164	116 664

Source: PR Week, 31 March 1995, in association with Media Appointments.

chairmen, managing directors and board directors of consultancies, and in-house PR directors, could cost nearly a third of a million a year each in salaries combined with corporate overheads: that's over £215 an hour. Assuming a seven-hour day and a 220-day year, why not work out the 'per hour' and 'per minute' salary costs that would apply to you? You may be in for a surprise.

Clearly the more that corporate overheads can be controlled, the more cost-effective the operation. Some overheads are pretty well fixed (those that are generated by essential core activities which must be carried out and directly supported). The scope for improvement lies in discretionary overheads.

■ Paying for Consultancies

Consultancies base their fees on time spent in the service of clients. That includes management, executive and administrative time. Provided it is legal and agreed by all parties, any fee basis is acceptable. The most common are:

- an agreed annual fee for an agreed PR programme, payable quarterly or monthly in advance
- a retainer plus fees for individual projects up to a pre-set limit
- a minimum fee plus hourly costs up to an agreed maximum

We have already discussed the significance of salary costs.

Fees do not normally cover disbursements and expenses, which can be billed separately, covering such materials and services as:

- accommodation, travel and subsistence
- advertising artwork and mechanicals (pulls, proofs, reductions and so on)
- audio visuals
- design, artwork, print
- events, conferences, exhibitions, displays, roadshows
- film and video production
- media monitoring
- messenger services
- photocopying, stationery
- photographs, prints
- postage, telephone, fax
- press materials, production, distribution
- research

When materials and services like these are bought in from outside contractors, they are recharged to the client at cost plus a mark-up (currently 17.65 per cent), payable in arrears.

Consultancies have to finance their own operations but not costs incurred on behalf of clients. However, consultancies are held by their suppliers to be solely liable in law: hence the importance of prompt payment.[8]

Advice on client/consultancy agreements and methods of remuneration is available from the PRCA and the Incorporated Society of British Advertisers (ISBA). You will find their addresses, and extracts from a specimen PRCA contract, in the Appendices.

■ Cost of Materials and Services

Whether you are buying direct from a supplier or through a consultancy, you need to know the typical costs of the different public relations materials and services, and the relative cost of the different techniques.

That is a Portfolio page you should put together yourself and constantly update. Take a unit of cost – say, £1000 or £5000 – and check what you can typically get for it. How many hours of consultancy time? How many A4 pages of print? You could approach it the opposite way and base your Portfolio page on what activities typically cost: one minute of video, say, or 1000 A4 leaflets, or an hour of consultancy time, or a photographer for half a day. Perhaps it would be best to do both.

Other information about costs can go into your portfolio. For instance:

- the Local Government Group of the IPR estimates that as a rough guide it costs 10p per household or business to reach everyone
- transferring slides or video to film is possible, but expensive, compared with transferring slides or film to video, which is easy and at reasonable cost
- the US-based International Exhibitors Association reckons that while the cost of a rep's sales call can reach £250, exhibition leads usually cost around £38. The cost of a sale from 'conventional' marketing activity can be more than £600; sales generated from exhibitions cost less than £130[9]

Remember, you must keep your portfolio up to date once you've started it. That way you'll have a permanently useful costing tool.

■ Budget Checks

Let's be quite clear about what a budget is. It is the sum of money which, if managed properly, will enable us to carry out a programme of action and so achieve specified objectives. I'm not suggesting that is in any way an official definition. What it does is to focus our minds on the essential relationship between the money and the objectives, with the programme as the means.

If we find that we are having to spend significantly over our budget, then something has probably gone wrong with the programme. The same is true if we find we are spending significantly under budget. (The other possibility is that our estimating was incompetent.)

The two extremes in budgeting are:

- do what you must and pay what it costs
- do what you can for the money you've got

Most budgeting practice lies somewhere between the extremes, being mainly task-based but subject to cost limits. Janet Salvoni, of Paragon, summed it up as 'a price for every job and job at every price'.

Some of the ideas and examples in this chapter and throughout the book should help you on the road to becoming good at budgeting. Experience and training will accelerate your progress.

Here are three simple guidelines.

1. Controlling the budget arises from controlling the programme, not the other way round
2. Use the budget to fund outcomes, not inputs
3. Budget checks are actually programme output checks.

CHAPTER 13

▌Public Relations in a Crisis

Never assume that things will get better.

Sam Wauchope[1]

■ What Qualifies as a Crisis?

The kind of problems that all managers have to face, including public relations managers, can be technical or tactical, strategic or analytical. The way to arrive at usable answers is to ask sensible questions, but beware of the 'illusion that when problems are easy to state and set up . . . they are then easy to solve'. [2]

Simple questions do not necessarily have simple answers, and even when they do, getting at them can be anything but simple. Nowhere is this more true than in the area of uncertainty known as crisis management.

Not every unexpected happening is a crisis, and not every crisis is entirely unexpected. It is the potential result that matters. You could define a crisis as a moment of danger, or suspense, which has the capacity, if not resolved, to do serious harm. The moment of danger could have taken some time to develop, perhaps as the result of a series of problems none of which was big in itself but which, in the aggregate, reached crisis point almost unnoticed; or it could be a sudden catastrophe that took everybody unawares with devastating consequences.

To qualify as a crisis, the potential harm should be enough to do damage to the financial standing of an organisation, or its business performance, or its reputation, or its major stakeholders. In extreme cases, all of these can be at risk. The most extreme case of all is when human life is lost or hangs in the balance.

Here are some examples, from devastation by bomb to product tampering, where it could not be assumed that 'things will get better'. But that does not mean that things stayed bad or got worse. In fact, they did get better, because they were made to.

You could say that helping things to get better is half the job of a PR practitioner. The other half is making sure that all those affected know about it.

214

■ Disaster: Piper Alpha

All disasters are calamities: and nearly all are sudden. Response has to be fast. Here is crisis PR expert Kate Graham's diary for the evening of Wednesday, 6 July 1988, the first 15 minutes of the Piper Alpha oil platform disaster, 120 miles off the coast of Scotland, north-east of Aberdeen.

2205 approx.	Call received at home from local journalist, asking about a rumoured explosion on board Piper Alpha.
2210	Left for Occidental Petroleum (Caledonia) Ltd (OXY) head-quarters at Bridge of Don, Aberdeen.
2215	Arrive at HQ, retrieved Emergency Response file and went to Media Response Room being set up by communications staff.
2220	Holding statement prepared and ready for issue, including dedicated Press Room telephone numbers.

Within that 15 minute period a television newsflash had appeared nationally on ITN: as a result, the news of a potential disaster flashed round the world. By the time I got to the Media Response Room, every emergency phone line was ringing and the main switchboard was swamped. Response was on a 24-hour basis and the first Press Conference was held in Aberdeen at 9 o'clock the following morning, 7 July.[3]

The story of Piper Alpha is well known: the intermeshing of operational and communications policy, the arrival of world famous troubleshooter Red Adair on 8 July, the heroic efforts to rescue survivors, the daily availability and accessibility of the President of OXY, the misinformation and disinformation that had to be countered, and all under the unremitting attention of the world's media.

Most important of all was the tragic loss of 167 lives. That was the real disaster and, in spite of all the company did to mitigate the effects, they are still being felt today throughout the oil industry.

■ Recovery

Disaster recovery specialists offer a package deal aiming to provide all that is needed should disaster strike. Because they originated as computer back-up services, companies in the disaster recovery business are particularly strong on information technology. Computer disasters, and consequent loss of security of information, can make a severe dent in a company's public image.

Good communications with key stakeholders are essential – that means within the company, with customers and suppliers, and with the media. Some disaster recovery specialists, such as Comdisco, carry out an immediate client audit of all communications. That is after the crisis, but communication is equally important before there is even the hint of a crisis. John Brien, of Sears Womenswear, summed it up well when he said: 'The whole of the business should understand what it needs to do in the event of a disaster.'[4]

Let us look at a practical example of disaster and recovery and learning from experience.

■ Disaster: Commercial Union

Commercial Union Risk Management (CURM) is a wholly owned but independent subsidiary of insurance giant Commercial Union. CURM's specialist knowledge and practical experience has helped clients of CU in more than 60 countries. As you would expect, CURM developed detailed contingency plans for every branch of CU throughout the UK, designed to mitigate the worst effects of a disaster, to maintain trading and to reassure staff, clients and shareholders that all that should be done is being done. Staff at all levels need to know what is expected of them; suppliers of equipment and services need to know how they can best be of assistance; while customers and intermediaries need to know where to turn for their continuing service requirements.

All this was severely tested on the night of the St Mary Axe bomb in the City of London, 10 April 1992. Here is CU's own diary of what happened and what they did about it.

PORTFOLIO
Case 13.1 – Crisis timetable

FRIDAY 10 APRIL 1992
2118　Bomb exploded.
2140　Television pictures broadcast – St Helen's, the Commercial Union Head Office, evidently badly damaged.
2220　First crisis meeting held, at home of CU's UK Managing Director.
2330　CU representatives on site, inquiring about injuries and extent of damage.
　　　Injured staff released from hospital.
2240　Disaster recovery plan activated. Senior management team contacted to fix meeting next morning.

SATURDAY 11 APRIL
0730　Crisis meeting in Croydon of 12 directors and senior managers.

All communication links, including the telephone switchboard for the entire London area, had been lost.

The four prime considerations were:

- how to reinstate telephone links for the 3600 extensions in the London area offices by Monday morning
- how to accommodate the 650 CU staff previously located in the building
- how to provide them with the necessary telephones, computers and furniture
- how to inform customers and intermediaries about arrangements for Monday morning.

1000   By reference to the disaster plan, those present established:

- that the switchboard could be reconstituted at CU's computer centre near Croydon
- that data requirements could be met by linking the mainframe to new screens in new locations
- contact with BT and IBM to reinstate communications and order extra equipment
- contact with supplier of office furniture and equipment
- the need to cascade information down through the organisation, so that all 650 staff would know what was expected of them on Monday
- staff numbers in each business area and the amount of CU office space available in and around London
- that market requirements meant that certain staff had to be relocated within the City straight away
- that, as an investment house as well as an insurance company, a replacement trading floor would be needed by Monday morning

1200   A member of staff had been allowed into St Helen's and advised that the damage was even worse than the police had reported. The building would be out of commission for a least a year.

1300   Managers started relaying details to their staff of where they should report to on Monday morning: some to provide essential client service, others to make necessary preparations for the rest of the staff for the following day.

1400   New computer terminals (over 500 lost), telephones (over 650 lost) and other office equipment and furniture ordered for delivery on Sunday.

1500   Press release issued including mobile telephone numbers of CU PR staff. Advertising space booked in the national press for Monday.

1900   Alternative venue established and advertised for the AGM due to be held on 14 April at the Baltic Exchange, which had suffered even worse damage than St Helen's.

SUNDAY 12 APRIL

0900   The crisis team continued to direct operations from Croydon.
         Loss adjusters allowed access to St Helen's.

1200   All staff now notified of their location and duties for Monday morning.
         Equipment and furniture delivered throughout the day to designated
         locations.

1400   Switchboard reconstituted, ready for use by CU staff on Monday
         morning.

MONDAY 13 APRIL

0700   Adverts appeared in the national press, confirming that it was business
         as usual.

0800   CU Asset Management, the Group's investment arm, trading from new
         offices.

0900   Staff affected now providing customer service from new locations, with
         access to CU information systems including the sophisticated electronic
         mail facility.
         Wider management meeting held for senior staff in London area.
         Additionally, all CU staff country-wide were provided with broad
         briefing via e-mail, so that they could answer local inquiries from
         customers and media.

TUESDAY 14 APRIL

0900   Of the 650 staff previously based in St Helen's, 631 were working as
         usual, the others being either away sick or on holiday.

1200   At the appointed time for the AGM, a quorum of shareholders met as
         close to the original venue as deemed safe by the police and passed a
         resolution to reconvene at the new venue.

1400   AGM held as though nothing had happened.[5]

■ Learning from Experience

Almost exactly a year later, a terrorist bomb exploded at Bishopsgate. It was
10.24a.m. on Saturday, 24 April, and the damage was enormous. Firms which
found themselves in serious trouble asked themselves the simple question 'How
soon can we recover?': that is, how quickly could they get back to where they
were before the disaster? The answer for many was business as usual on the
Monday morning after the Saturday bomb. Learning from the experience of the
St Mary Axe disaster, three out of four City organisations had contingency
plans in place.

■ Not Always Sudden

Much crisis management work will be pedestrian, plodding and excessively obvious, but, unless it has all been planned in advance, in meticulous detail, and thoroughly rehearsed, the chances are that public relations will be largely overlooked, or relegated to a wholly responsive role. At the other extreme, the public relations approach may be over-protective and defensive.

In May 1994, *PR Week* reported that Nynex Cablecomm was facing a torrent of complaints. Local councils, MPs and homeowners were protesting at wrecked roads, flooding, water shortages, gas leaks, an explosion and general chaos attributed to the workgangs that were carrying out Nynex's £2bn cabling operation. The cable-licensing authority, the DTI, had also been inundated with complaints.

Nynex thereupon identified public affairs as a key area of business, recruited a new in-house manager of government relations, hired lobbying consultancy GJW, and strengthened the company's regional PR and community relations capability.

This impressive line-up engaged in a strategic programme of public affairs, paying particular attention to relations with the DTI, the select committee on fibre optics, and the 75 MPs, 12 MEPs and 41 local authorities in the areas covered by Nynex's 17 cable television franchise.

■ Not Just Firefighting

Crisis management extends well beyond dealing with immediate problems. Business as usual within three days is, of course, an excellent achievement, but what of the longer term? Stakeholders must have confidence not only in a company's ability to recover fully, but in the fact of recovery itself. Credibility, as we have noted elsewhere, is an essential of good public relations. Likewise, loss of credibility is a different sort of crisis and a prime cause of bad public relations.

The security firm, Group 4, hired Shandwick to recapture public credibility after many weeks of scathing press criticism. The first priority was to repair the damage done to Group 4's corporate reputation since its subsidiary, Group 4 Prison and Court Services, took over the prison escort contract in Humberside and East Midlands. In less than eight weeks, eight prisoners escaped or were 'accidentally released'. A prisoner died in custody. There were lurid press stories of typists doubling as drivers of vehicles taking prisoners to and from jail.

Shandwick's director, Tom McNally, said: 'obviously the priority is to correct the adverse publicity and misinformation . . . but we are not just firefighting, we are helping to turn the long-term positioning of the company'.[6]

This was to be a long slow job; but within a year the worst of the sniggers had subsided, jokes at Group 4's expense were becoming rarer, and repositioning was under way. The improvement was not necessarily permanent.

■ Product Tampering

Mercury injected into oranges, glass found in baby food, cyanide in headache remedies: product tampering is an ever present risk. It does not even need to be true to cause a crisis. If your company suspects, for whatever reason, that a product has been tampered with, act fast, but do not over-react.

PORTFOLIO
Guideline 13.1 – Crisis on the shelf

Product tampering – true or false? Whether you think you know the answer or not, this is what you do.

1. Assess who needs to know, and what they need to know. In particular what do the public need to know to protect them? Make sure they get that information. Alert all the proper authorities. Keep a tight control over anything that might help copycats or false claimants.
2. Weigh very carefully whether a product needs to be recalled. Taking it off the shelves may be a useful temporary measure. Learn from others. When the scare story broke about syringes in cans of Pepsi Cola, the company did not recall the product. Instead, they convincingly argued that no syringe could get into a can of Pepsi at the processing plant. They clinched it by showing a video of a customer caught in a retail outlet in the act of putting a syringe into an open can.
3. Because research shows that many customers do not notice even very obvious tampering, draw attention to tamper-evident packaging if you have it, especially if you can also show that you are improving it. If you haven't got tamper-evident packaging, get it.
4. Stay alert. Keep monitoring the situation as it develops and review all precautionary measures. When it is all over, tell the world what the company did and why.
5. It is always best to treat every threat or report of product tampering as if it were the real thing. Only when it is proved to be otherwise should you disbelieve the story. And even then, be sure that you can demonstrate to those concerned, in a way which will convince them, that there is indeed no crisis and never has been.

6.   With benefit of hindsight, most stories about product tampering turn out
     to be false, or exaggerated, or downright confidence tricks. Very few
     represent a true crisis. But play it safe.

■ Product Purity

In 1990 what the *Sunday Times* called the 'double whammy of recession and a
contamination crisis in America' hit Perrier, world market leader in bottled
water. Strongly marketed and heavily advertised, in the 1980s more than
200 000 000 bottles of Perrier a year were being sold in the UK alone, a 60 per
cent market share. Then came the discovery of traces of benzene in bottles of
Perrier exported to America. The firm promptly withdrew its product all over
the world, and for four months rival brands had their chance to grab a bigger
share of the market.

Recovery for Perrier was steady, and by 1994 the brand was back to 70 per
cent of its pre-crisis sales. Where it would have been without the crisis is
anybody's guess. All the other leading brands increased their sales, so you could
reason that market patterns were changing anyway. Still bottled water became
more popular than fizzy, at least in the UK, partly because of another crisis: this
time over the purity, or rather impurity, of tap water.

Perrier and Evian remained market leaders, but in the UK a British brand
moved from obscurity into third place. How it was done is explained in Case
3.4, Chapter 3.

■ Hostile Take-Over Bids

Any company can be vulnerable to take-over and needs to have a good idea at
all times of where a predatory bid is likely to come from, and why. Would your
company fill a gap in the predator's business mix? Is your market share
attractive to a competitor? Does someone want to move into your market/
territory? Has your management/technical team got skills that the other side
needs?

Identifying the likely attackers will help you prepare your defensive plan well
in advance: but, of course, sometimes a predator comes out of the blue.

As always, you need to be clear what your objectives are. They may not
always be what they appear to be. When Citigate handled the public relations
for Granada's £735m hostile take-over bid of LWT, the predator already owned
17 per cent of the equity. Not much doubt about Granada's objective. But what
about the defence? Financial Dynamics and their client LWT had three clear
objectives:

- stress LWT's independence
- question the value to shareholders of being part of a leisure group (Granada) instead of a real television company (LWT)
- discredit the Granada bid as grossly undervaluing LWT

However, it was possible to conclude from media speculation and subsequent events that LWT had already accepted that they would be taken over, and their hidden objective was to push up as high as possible the price that Granada finally paid.[7]

■ Inner Strength

In most crises – terrorist attack, plant shutdown, hostile take-over, staff cuts, relocation, natural disaster – what happens inside the company can make all the difference. If inner communication is strong and people understand what is happening, they will be better equipped to deal with whatever the crisis brings.

Strong inner communication is a defence against hostile take-over bids. 'Staff and management reactions to the approach will be so hostile that even the most resolute of pursuers is likely to rethink their strategy. Observing this reaction, shareholders are likely to be more loyal. They will not want to back a loser.'[8]

Relocation can be a crisis for families who feel their livelihoods will be threatened if they don't move, but stand to lose their sense of belonging if they do. Kate Lye, of Smythe, Dorward, Lambert, stresses the need for corporate openness. 'You have to show the strategy behind the move. Otherwise, if decisions aren't justified, it undermines management integrity and people's security.'[9] The same is true for redundancies and staff cuts, with the added dimension that you also need to generate the right environment for any staff who remain.

■ Staying in Control

Keeping control of the process and the information is essential if your company does not want to find itself at the mercy of mushrooming rumours. Put the same team in charge of internal and external communications because messages need to be fast and consistent. That means making the best use you can of all the communications technology available – desk top publishing, electronic mail, CCTV, bicycled video, satellite television – whatever it takes. Let all the staff see the support the company is giving. That will reassure everybody, and not only those within the company.

Set up information hot lines, counselling services and job-lines into other employers. Make sure there is plenty of good, clear, information on redundancy packages. It is not only a case of helping your own, or even of ensuring that employees on the way out are not a public relations liability when they are gone.

If internal communication is handled badly, or ignored, the effect on morale can be as disastrous as the most uncharitable media criticism. The time to start that internal communication programme is during the good times, because when things start getting bad it is already too late.

■ The Ultimate Rollercoaster

What constitutes a crisis for one organisation may seem pretty low-key and small scale to another, but none of them is exempt and all need to be prepared for the worst (which need not stop them hoping for the best).

The Lynx Public Relations award-winning programme for the world's biggest rollercoaster – known as The Ultimate (and why not?) – at Lightwater Valley, Ripon, spanned two years. First the pre-launch build-up, then the launch itself, getting the visitors in, minimising any local hostility by a charity link that gave money back to the community, coordinating with advertising and marketing, positive media relations, competitions, educational liaison: all the well tried elements were there. But even the best regulated theme parks are vulnerable to accidents and other untoward incidents, so a crisis management capability was built in from the start, through a system of staff evaluation (how well would each one cope with a crisis?); a manual of guidelines, contacts and procedures (helping everybody to cope better); and special training in media relations for selected people (information management is an essential part of crisis management). Consequently, when minor operational hitches occurred on the giant rollercoaster, potential negative reporting was de-fused.[10]

■ Kwik-Fit

Long running public relations programmes are increasingly open to the likelihood of hitting a crisis. That is what happened to Kwik-Fit, leaders in the automobile fast-fit industry. For five years, working with Edinburgh-based consultancy Dunseath Stephen, their promotion of family safety on the road won awards, raised large sums of money for charity and built a solid reputation for the firm as a responsible organisation. It was all good for business, too. Then came crisis.

A *Which?* magazine survey of the fast-fit industry was about to come up with the shattering conclusion that Kwik-Fit was the worst performer. Consternation and panic? No.

Kwik-Fit immediately issued a chairman's statement spelling out the steps being taken to put things right, so that when the *Which?* findings were published, Kwik-Fit's remedial action was reported at the same time. The company's share price held, and sales actually went up, but that was not the end of the crisis. Strident complaints from a relatively small number of dissatisfied customers began to appear. The company and its consultancy had their work cut out to persuade an initially sceptical press to show restraint, but they did. 'When the storm abated', said the consultancy, 'we got back to our positive work.'[11]

■ Other Crises of Business Life

Kidnapping of key personnel, or members of their families, and the ensuing ransom demands, are more common in some other countries than in the UK. The life of a hostage is always at risk and, although the official line is that ransom should never be paid, there can be many reasons for not taking that advice. In such cases, the main public relations contribution could very well be to keep it out of the media. There should certainly be a contingency plan.

Sometimes a crisis is self-inflicted. Would you have believed a story that appeared in the press on 1 April 1993 to the effect that an international company was running a sales promotion with giveaways worth more than receipts from sales of the product? It was no April Fool's joke, but a genuine offer that meant anyone buying a £100 Hoover vacuum cleaner could claim two free return air tickets, London/New York, worth £500. The response was huge, and the company had problems delivering, so that profits and reputation were both damaged.

Customer crime – from shoplifting to grand larceny – is not at all uncommon, and sometimes it may reach crisis proportions. Maximum publicity may deter others, but it could also encourage copycatting. As in all crisis management, the very highest levels in the company must be involved in defining the policy, authorising the resources and being accountable for what is done.

There are situations in which a threat, a rumour or an allegation may be enough to cause a crisis. Bomb threats can stop trains; allegations of fraud can close banks; rumours on the Stock Exchange can generate panic. The machinery for dealing with these may differ in detail from each other and from each of the examples in this chapter.

Can there be any common ground?

■ Some Principles

The most important principle of crisis management is to think ahead. Anticipate and pre-empt so that the worst never happens.

That isn't always possible, so the next requirement is to have a crisis management plan that briefs and trains a crisis management team.

Alongside the action, but in no sense a substitute for it, is the management of information.

Underlying all should be the realisation that a crisis rarely destroys a company.

Sooner or later things get back to normal, or near normal, and life goes on.

With the help of Kate Graham let's develop these principles into a set of guidelines.

PORTFOLIO
Guideline 13.2 – Crisis management

Each organisation needs its own crisis management plan which is specific to itself and therefore unique. Nevertheless, there are some well tried principles that every organisation needs to be aware of. Use them as a starting point for your own plan.

1. Crisis management is the responsibility of top management.
2. Recognise and assess the potential crises in your organisation.
3. Secure the active involvement of senior management in crisis prevention, planning, operations and communications.
4. Set up a crisis management team. Prepare a written plan and procedures to be followed before, during and in the aftermath of, a crisis.
5. Identify what outside resources may be available – former employees, consultants, crisis experts – and know exactly how to get them, if needed.
6. Allocate responsibilities : who does what, who has authority for what, and so on. Make sure that there will be enough trained people.
7. Constantly revise, update, rehearse and test the crisis management plan, procedures and team.
8. Set up an early warning system so that the signs of an impending crisis are recognised immediately.
9. The over-riding priority is to deal with the crisis itself, and especially the safety of people.
10. The company, through its senior management, must accept responsibility, take action and control the flow of information. No excuses, no fudge, no jargon, no 'no comment'.
11. Be prepared for 24-hour manning of your Press Room. Media interest can be instant and abundant. Inaccurate and speculative information can be spread via media sources within minutes of a story breaking. If the media do not have accurate information from you, they will get whatever they can from whoever and wherever they can.
12. Get an initial statement out fast. It may not be able to say much but it ought to ensure a uniform response by confirming times and locations, for

example, of an accident, and such other factual data as is available. The initial statement should also confirm telephone numbers for media inquiries and, if appropriate, separate numbers for inquiries from relatives. Close liaison is essential between the supervisors of the Media Response team and the Crisis Control Unit.

13. Press statements should be dated, timed and numbered, and contain only accurate and verified information. There should be no undue delays in the release of information.

14. Ensure that the Media Response team has background information, photographs and videos available for issue to the media as required.

15. Senior company representatives, notably the Chief Executive, should be trained in interview techniques and be ready and willing to meet the media either at news conferences or on an individual basis, according to need.

16. Misleading, biased and inaccurate opinions, comment and reporting should be tackled and corrected with minimum delay and no fuss.

17. Stay calm. There are very few cases of a crisis or even a disaster putting a company out of business, though some have come pretty close to it.

18. The public don't get too upset about companies losing lots of money. It is a different story altogether when human lives are involved. Be extra-sensitive to this dimension. Demonstrate what is being done to reduce risk, safeguard lives and help relatives.

19. Be alert to the needs of all interested parties: individuals in danger; customers; consumers; employees; the local community; finance providers; contractors. Identify them and their concerns. Look after their interests.

20. As things return to normal, turn your attention to the longer perspective. What relationships have suffered and need rebuilding? Has the damage to reputation been fully assessed? What needs to be done to restore market confidence?

21. Will there be an independent inquiry? Should there be an internal inquiry? What crisis plans and procedures ought to be amended? What operational changes are necessary? What lessons have been learned and what use will be made of the new knowledge?[12]

■ After a Crisis

Julia Thorn, Chairman and Chief Executive of Paragon Communications, points out that the best measure of successful crisis management is that events never assume the scale of a crisis. People's memory of bad news lasts much longer than their recollection of good news.

The messages you want to see emerging are positive, such as:

- the company has an excellent safety record
- this was a rare lapse and out of character
- senior executives were on site very quickly
- the top men or women were accessible and open
- action was immediately taken to rectify damage, assess compensation and so on
- there was no attempt to cover up or minimise

What you don't want to see are criticisms such as:

- the company was caught with its pants down
- response was slow
- top people did not get involved
- the company went on the defensive and would not admit that anything was wrong

Media coverage needs to be monitored continuously for balanced reporting, and any gaps dealt with, but the vital measurement is the effect on the company's principal stakeholders: consumers, shareholders, employees, neighbours, and others.

It may take time, but if the crisis is well managed, recovery should follow. Regular measurements will confirm this.

CHAPTER 14

Evaluation

The evaluation process starts long before the first activity in the programme begins.

Julia Thorn[1]

■ What is Evaluation?

If you have followed the advice in this book you will agree the importance of:

- setting realistic PR objectives and quantifying them when possible
- relating PR objectives to business objectives
- planning a detailed programme of activities
- allocating an adequate budget and controlling it

The process of evaluation is essentially that of measuring achievement against intention in each of these areas. All attempts at evaluating public relations have to face up to the same problems and find solutions.

First, what results can actually be measured? The answer has to be those that are, or are capable of being, quantified. *Second*, what do we do about results that can't be measured? Answer: apply value judgements to assess their quality. *Third*, what methods will we use to measure and assess? Answer: those that are known to work. *Fourth*, what use will be made of the evaluation? Answer: feedback and action.

The quality and quantity of the information available to you has far reaching effects. You might get by with hardly any information to go on, as long as you guess right. If you have good information, your chances of getting good results are much improved, though not guaranteed. The one certainty is that if you base your actions on bad information, you are going to experience bad consequences.

228

■ Results that Can be Measured

If you have quantified your objectives you should be able to quantify your results, using the same criteria. For example, you could measure:

- percentage shift in awareness
- growth in number of inquiries received
- reduction in number of complaints
- frequency of reports in target media
- opportunities to see or hear a particular message
- improvement in market standing relative to competitors
- time taken to achieve specified share of market

In each of the following examples, one such quantitative measure was used.

Introduction of the new 10p coin on 30 September 1992 was handled by Shandwick Communications for HM Treasury. This represented the final passing of pre-decimal coinage. Two months before d-Day, awareness of the new coin by the general public was measured by Gallup as 19 per cent. Research just before 30 September measured awareness at 91 per cent. This huge increase was achieved without undue public criticism or negative perceptions (see Chapter 1).

Independent Financial Advisers (IFA) normally expect to receive about 100 inquiries a week on their telephone hotline. A local radio campaign, organised by Radio Lynx Productions and featuring 21 down-the-line interviews backed by station-specific material, boosted the weekly average number of calls on the hotline to more than 700.[2]

United Parcel Service promoted its *Europe Business Monitor* as an annual source of essential information to the media and the academic, business and government communities in Europe, North America and the Asia-Pacific region. The associated direct mail campaign – part of a comprehensive programme by Edelman PR Worldwide – produced high response rates, topping 12 per cent in the UK and Germany, whereas the average for all direct mail is perhaps 2 per cent.[3]

In 1985, ICL was perceived by the retail trade as number 5 in the league table of suppliers of retail technology such as electronic point of sale systems (EPoS). By 1988, an award-winning PR campaign by Paragon had moved ICL into the undisputed number 1 position, ahead of former leaders IBM and NCR. This was confirmed by independent research.[4]

Measurements of this kind are often carried out by independent research specialists. However, evaluation by professional researchers can be out of the question for the many organisations short of money, especially those in the third sector. Other barometers, such as rise or fall in membership numbers, changes in recruitment patterns, increased attendances at functions, letters of support, level of subscriptions, donations and other funding are all quantifiable measures of actual behaviour. What could be more direct than that?

■ A Weighty Decision

Beware: direct measurement is only effective if the right quantities are being measured. The Emperor Qin Shihuang, 259–210 BC, decided all affairs of state, great and small, himself. He standardised Chinese laws, measurements and colours, established a national network of roads, abolished the feudal system, reformed land ownership and rebuilt and extended the Great Wall of China. Paperwork must have been a problem because he ratified a proposal that all historical documents pre-dating his own regime should be destroyed. He also simplified and standardised the system of writing.

His own personal method of measuring results was interesting. He had documents of state weighed every morning, and worked until he had handled a pre-determined weight. He verified this by having them weighed again at the end of the day.[5]

■ Results that Cannot be Measured

Quantitative measurements are about dimensions with numbers on them. But what about quality? That is more a matter of value judgement, and is related to expectations. What quality of service do you expect from a PR consultancy or your own in-house PR department? How can you tell if you are getting the right quality? Research carried out in Scotland early in 1994 considered 20 criteria for expectations of quality of service and ranked them in order of importance as perceived by purchasers and by PR consultancies.

Both sides agreed on the primacy of 'reliability' and 'meeting deadlines'. Both put 'creativity' in sixteenth position. No other qualities were perceived as being of equal importance to clients and consultancies, though in most cases there were only a few places in it. The biggest discrepancy by far was in the way that the two sides regarded 'chemistry'. Consultants placed it fifth, whereas it was at the bottom of the list as far as clients were concerned. The criteria and their rankings are set out in Table 14.1. These results suggest that although there is broad agreement between clients and consultancies on the criteria by which the latter's quality of service might be evaluated, there are enough differences to keep life interesting.[6]

Some of the qualities are quantifiable to an extent (you can count the number of deadlines missed), but how do you measure 'creativity' or 'chemistry'? Even though they do not contain value *words* such as good, bad, right or wrong, they are in fact value *judgements* and therefore they can be evaluated. For example,

Table 14.1   Expectations of service quality

By purchasers		By consultancies
1	Meeting deadlines/reliability	1
2	Confidentiality	–
3	Enthusiasm and commitment	6
4	Accuracy of written material	2
5	Knowledge of relevant media	9
6	Written communication skills	7
7	Responsiveness	4
8	Confidence/trust in advice	3
9	Commercial realism	11
10	Continuity	15
11	Knowledge of target audiences	12
12	Oral communication skills	13
13	Appearance of staff	18
14	Problem solving skills	10
15	Knowledge of the industry	–
16	Creativity	16
17	Regular contact	8
18	Adequacy of consultancy resources	17
19	Management of budget	14
20	'Chemistry'	5

Source: Reproduced by permission of *IPR Journal*.

the generally accepted view of 'creativity' is that it involves processes like making constructive connections between apparently unrelated bits of information, or putting irrational ideas to practical use. You could assess the performance of a consultancy in these terms. 'Chemistry' is not only about people working well together; it is also to do with joint performance being better than the sum of the individual performances, and perhaps about relationships that do not depend entirely on the working environment for their success. Those aspects can be assessed.

■ Methods Used to Measure and Assess

Choosing the most appropriate and cost-effective methods for particular purposes comes with practice and experience, but you can learn a lot by watching, listening and reading. Some of the cases and other examples in the different chapters refer to measurement and evaluation. Chapter 4 describes the main kinds of research, types of data and common techniques for gathering information.

■ Media Measurement

Public relations objectives, strategies, stakeholders, budgets and programmes all vary from case to case, as the examples in this book demonstrate. What is measured and evaluated also varies, but there is one pretty well universal stakeholder: the media. Media coverage and how it is measured and assessed pre-occupies in-house PR departments, consultancies and clients. Measurement of quantity alone is no longer enough. (It never was, but at one time it was *all* there was.)

■ Evaluation the Paragon Way

Paragon Communications, in association with Research Services, devised a low-cost benchmarking system they call *Perceptions and Attitudes Monitor*. This draws on up to seven modules.

1. *Validation* of messages, principal media and techniques
2. *Media*: telephone questionnaire of up to 25
3. *Decision makers/opinion formers*: telephone questionnaire of up to 50
4. *Consumers*: computer-based omnibus covering 2000 households
5. *Employees*: postal questionnaire sent to home addresses
6. *Special events*: telephone research among those who were present and those who weren't
7. *Sponsorship*: continuous tracking research involving 6250 consumers each year.

Changes in perception of, and attitudes towards, the client and key competitors are measured over the period of the PR campaign, against benchmarks and quantified objectives. Paragon's *Media Coverage Analysis* is in terms of:

- total audience reach
- Cumulative Opportunities to See
- target audience reach
- impact (size, content, position)
- frequency in key target media during period of campaign
- delivery of agreed messages
- cost per thousand COTS of total audience reach

Additional measurements of quantity and quality are taken as needed: for instance, number and characteristics of people attending an event, or sales leads generated.

Paragon pays particular attention to differentiating between results due to public relations and those attributable to other causes. This can be especially important when comparing a client's visibility and standing with competitors.

■ Evaluation the Infopress Way

Infopress Communications offer a separate media analysis and evaluation service developed to help clients' PR and marketing communications staff to:

- determine media profile
- manage their PR programmes
- measure the effectiveness of media relations activities
- track issues
- monitor competitors' strategies

The media sectors to be analysed are agreed with the client, making sure that the coverage being evaluated is actually read or watched by the target audiences, and that the media sample is genuinely representative. Corporate and marketing messages are identified. Details of competitor companies are noted. Independent evaluators are briefed on the agreed evaluation criteria, and are sent cuttings and tapes on a regular basis.

The Infopress independent evaluators measure the volume of coverage, the number of namechecks (company or brand) in each item, and any other specified variables. Cuttings and tapes are given a score for each of the agreed messages, ranging from +10 (the exact message) to −10 (the exact opposite); 0 means a neutral piece. It is important that bad coverage is highlighted, as well as good.

Evaluators, who do not know the identity of the client, compile computerised scores and return them electronically to Infopress, where they are converted by computer into easy-to-read, easy-to-understand, tables.

This combination of independent evaluation by people and processing by computer provides real management information, such as messages or namecheck trends over the year for each media sector, total effectiveness of all message deliveries in all media month by month, analysis of the attitude of a single journalist of special importance to the client; all compared with similar analyses of key competitors, and all produced speedily and accurately.

However, Infopress argue that media analysis should be only part of the evaluation process. As Dermot McKeone, Deputy Chairman of the Infopress Group, points out, 'PR people get involved in many different activities other than press relations, and each of these activities deserves its own evaluation method.' McKeone urges you to make sure you evaluate all the elements of your PR programme, basing your evaluation criteria on the programme objectives and making sure that evaluation judgements are carried out by people who are unbiased.

■ Evaluating Classic FM the Media Measurement Way

Media Measurement notes that 'pervasive editorial coverage enhances advertising responses by 30 per cent and more' and aims to measure, monitor and evaluate the effectiveness of product PR. Through its Press Relations Performance Review the company identifies core journals and their potential interest in the product, monitors progress of the PR programmes in terms of key messages played back, circulation reached, beneficial/neutral/adverse comment and other factors.

Evaluations compare the client's coverage with the competition, looking at penetration of available articles, credited mentions, column centimetres, share of the circulation and so on.

Media Measurement evaluated the Classic FM campaign described in Chapter 1. Over the launch period of four weeks in late August and early September 1992, a total of 376 articles was reviewed, taken from 267 newspapers and magazines. Classic FM was mentioned in 373; other broadcasters in 231.

The combined length of all the articles analysed was 10 258 column centimetres (ccm) of which 3707 ccm were wholly attributable to coverage of Classic FM and 1877 ccm exclusively to other broadcasters.

A total of 184 articles (1141 ccm) concentrated on Classic FM's new approach to broadcasting. *The Times* and *Guardian* each published 22 articles. Combined circulation was 68 512 000. In the first week of the campaign 11 085 000 opportunities to read about Classic FM were created. Figure 14.1 charts the media coverage peaks during the launch period and compares Classic FM sources with others.

■ Equivalent Advertising Value

There is a tendency, and certainly a temptation, to assign a so-called EAV to quantitative measurements of media coverage. You can see why this should be so. It is fairly easy to do. Figures can look convincing.

An independent media-buying house estimated the advertising value of media coverage of Lightwater Valley Ultimate Theme Park at £400 000. The public relations budget was £30 000. That's a ratio of better than 13:1. Does that mean that public relations was 13 times more cost-effective than advertising? No, it does not. Media exposure is not advertising, does not perform the same functions as advertising, has different communication values from advertising, and is not perceived by the public as being interchangeable with advertising. A far better measure of the effectiveness of the Lynx Public Relations campaign for Lightwater Valley is that attendance went up by 25 per cent during the first year.

The Banana Group quotes impressive looking EAVs for media coverage of its Bananergy campaign. That is perfectly legitimate, and what many clients and employers expect. To me, the direct measurement of actual consumption of bananas, as shown in Figure 14.2, is more relevant and a lot more convincing.

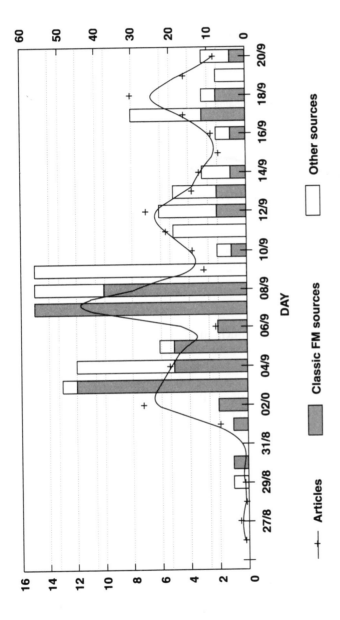

Explanatory note: left-hand scale and vertical bars refer to individual articles and sources; right-hand scale and continuous line graph refer to coverage peaks during the launch.

Source: Reproduced by permission of Media Measurement.

Figure 14.1 Classic FM: analysis of press coverage

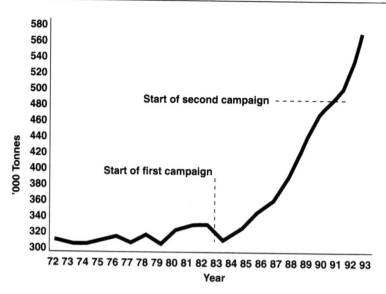

Source: Customs and Excise: and trade estimates. Reproduced by permission of The Banana Group and Beechey Morgan Associates.

Figure 14.2   Banana consumption, 1972–93

There is no way of knowing how much advertising expenditure would have been needed to achieve the same results for Lightwater Valley and the Banana Group. Indeed, who can say whether advertising would have done it at all?

Cohn & Wolfe's *Insurance Checks* campaign for Abbey National, described in Case 9.1, Chapter 9, had four distinct PR messages and media objectives. Table 14.2 summarises the results of the campaign in terms of media mentions of these messages.

Other results to note are that 14 979 readers, listeners or viewers wrote in to Abbey National asking for one or more of the Insurance Checks, and in the process made themselves prime candidates for the database. Judging by the number of unsolicited calls from journalists, Abbey National was fast becoming the leading authoritative source of media information on insurance matters generally.

■ More to Life than Media

The effectiveness of Shandwick Communications' award-winning awareness campaign for Compaq Computers was measured in three ways: media coverage, brand exposure and public attendance. The central strategy was to

Table 14.2 Insurance check programme summary

Publication	Circulation	No. of articles	Equivalent advertising cost (£)	No. of AN mentions	Photography/ cartoon	Key PR objectives and messages				
						A	B	C	D	Total
Nationals	26 152 686	28	80 805	67	7	13	7	17	26	63
TV/radio	15 451 631	81	81 989	229+	n/a	79	n/a	78	27	184
Daily regionals	8 384 851	95	36 098	256	39	77	35	83	50	245
Weekly regionals	3 896 286	82	7989	112	2	64	6	78	1	149
Consumer/trade	4 582 816	22	30 373	55	13	18	6	16	15	55
Total	58 468 270	308	237 254	719+	61	251	54	272	119	696

A Abbey National leads the feature/is a key insurance provider
B Communicates information on Abbey National products/uses product information
C Positions Abbey National as an authority on insurance/uses research
D Adds value to Abbey National product/offers Insurance Check

Source: Reproduced by permission of Cohn & Wolfe.

sponsor the Grand Slam Cup for professional tennis, 1990–94, and to promote the tournament through media relations, hospitality and an internal communication programme.

Measurement of media coverage showed that broadcasts of the tournament reached 80 countries in 1990, rising to 120 by 1994. Measurement of brand exposure showed that the Compaq brand was on screen for 42 per cent of the time. Measurement of public attendance showed that the 32 500 spectators present at the tournament in 1990 increased by more than 55 per cent, to 52 500, in 1994.[7]

Here are four ways of evaluating the success of a healthcare campaign, but only one involves media measurement:

- the amount of media coverage containing the key messages of the campaign
- the level of demand for campaign literature from the general public and health professionals
- increased consumer understanding and awareness
- any observed changes in consultations with GPs[8]

When Quality Street twistwrap chocolates were relaunched through radio birthday messages and weekend 'I'm sorry' slots, three methods were used for evaluating the campaign.

1. Statistical analysis showed that the target of three branded mentions per radio spot was exceeded in most cases.
2. Direct response analysis to radio programmes showed an average 3000 letters a week from listeners. Four stations reported that their telephone lines went down due to the sheer weight of phone-ins.
3. The client's own image tracking study showed that over a long period the product's 'gift worthiness attributes' improved.
4. Quality Street became the brand leader in the twistwrap market with a 49 per cent share.

Radio also came into a sustained UK awareness campaign for the National Peanut Council of America (NPCA), involving women's magazines, Oracle on Channel 4 television and radio features. In addition every British middle school and teacher training college was mailed with a compilation of reviews by health professionals of NPCA's resource pack, *Choosing Food*. A further 2600 copies of the pack were sent in response to requests from teachers and home economists, who also received a questionnaire. Returns showed that 87 per cent found pupils gained an understanding of the nutritional content of peanuts, 75 per cent thought their pupils likely to choose peanuts and peanut butter as a health snack and 72 per cent reckoned that students became more aware of the USA as a major provider of peanuts.

Both campaigns won awards for Welbeck Golin/Harris, the consultancy chosen by Rowntree Mackintosh and the NPCA.

■ A Campaign to Change the Law

So far we have looked at the measurement of results in a range of familiar areas like computers, entertainment, food and money. This next example is a little different.

PORTFOLIO
Case 14.1 – Bail bandits

Analysis
Although police in Avon and Somerset were solving twice as many crimes in 1990 as in 1980, crime was rising to such an extent that the overall detection rate had actually fallen. Research showed that between 24 and 34 per cent of all crimes in Avon and Somerset (39 per cent in Bristol) was committed by people on bail.

Objectives

1. To persuade the government to amend the Police and Criminal Evidence Act (PACE) and give police explicit powers to detain offenders expected to re-offend if granted bail
2. To press the government to provide a deterrent by introducing a new offence of offending on bail.

Strategy

1. To make the problem more visible
2. To enlist the support of influential third parties
3. To establish the Chief Constable as the spokesman, and to reflect his personality and commitment in the style of the campaign
4. To find a more catchy name for 're-offenders on bail'.

Budget
None. The police state that all costs were borne out of the normal overheads of the Department.

Programme

1. Reoffenders on bail were retitled 'Bail Bandits'.
2. Key magistrates, probation service leaders and other third parties were briefed to give informed, constructive and supportive comments if approached by the media.
3. A feature article about the initial research, published in the *Police Review*, reached an influential readership of chief police officers, Home Office ministers and officials, MPs and others interested in police affairs.

4.   Local and national media were invited to a press conference and briefed on the campaign and research results. Filming opportunities were provided (a look at the cells, an offender being charged). Striking examples were provided of major Bail Bandits.

5.   The Avon and Somerset Police Authority and local MPs received special briefings.

6.   The Association of Chief Police Officers, the national representative body, was asked to support and extend the campaign through comparable research in other forces.

7.   Every opportunity to exploit the campaign was seized: for instance, publication of crime statistics; actual cases of Bail Bandits re-offending when on bail; Home Secretary's visit to Bristol.

8.   The Police Federation, which represents the majority of police officers, debated the issue at its national conference, creating a platform for further publicity and public discussion.

9.   Employees of the Constabulary were kept informed throughout.

Results

1.   The term 'Bail Bandits' was instantly adopted by the media, the Home Secretary and others.

2.   The campaign was supported by MPs, the Police Authority, the Association of Chief Police Officers, the Police Federation and the Association of County Councils.

3.   Six months after the campaign began, the Home Secretary announced that the Government would introduce measures to tackle the Bail Bandit problem, including tougher penalties for reoffenders on bail.

4.   A working group, which included a senior Avon and Somerset officer, was set up to review PACE in relation to bail.

5.   Fifteen months after the campaign launch, the Home Office gave police explicit powers to detain criminals they suspect will re-offend if given police bail.

6.   IPR Sword of Excellence Award for Public Affairs, 1993.

Evaluation

In the words of Avon and Somerset Constabulary, 'all objectives were achieved'.[9]

■ The Royal Tournament

The objectives of Kestrel Communications' 1993 PR and marketing campaign for the Royal Tournament were specific and quantified: so many bums on seats, so much net revenue. Some of these resulted from public relations and some from marketing activities, as detailed in Case 3.5, Chapter 3. Here let us evaluate the results by identifying sources of greatest revenue. The net cost per visitor was £2.10 on a seat occupancy of 85 per cent. Table 14.3 shows the cost of some major paid media expenditure, how many visitors each attracted and what the net cost per visitor was in each case.

Table 14.3 Cost per visitor of major media, Royal Tournament, 1993

Medium	Cost	Number of visitors	Cost per visitor (£)
Mailing 2	£25 000	27 939	0.89
Earls Court Poster	£1200	1162	1.03
Mailing 1	£25 000	20 830	1.20
Fax Shot	£6542	5114	1.28
Radio Times	£8874	3835	2.31
You Magazine	£6120	2389	2.56
Sunday Mirror	£1445	469	3.08
Sunday Express	£6460	1309	4.94
Womans Own	£1275	224	5.69
Mailing 3	£25 000	3126	8.00
TV	£100 000	8466	11.81

Source: Reproduced by permission of The Royal Tournament.

A breakdown of 47 different sources of ticket bookings shows £288 343 from the first mailing, £370 663 from the second and £40 900 from the third. A further £269 158 came from counter sales, £117 384 through agents, £200 496 from group bookings, over £135 000 from the Services, other uniformed organisations and ex-Service associations, and £49 990 from the *Radio Times*. A door-drop test in north-west London compared leaflets inserted into free newspapers with solus drops (30 000 each). Inserts came out significantly ahead in the test, and the actual inserts campaigns generated £116 152 of revenue for an outlay of £33 500. The QTV test (advertising on screens in London post offices) was not successful and the idea was abandoned.

■ Getting Results for Charity

In Chapter 1 we considered the need for public relations objectives to be realistic: for example, aiming to change awareness of a particular product in a well defined market sector is rather more realistic than aiming to change the world. Equally important is the realism of the strategy chosen to achieve the objective.

PORTFOLIO
Case 14.2 – Huge celebrity involvement

If your aim was to raise money in order to prevent the death of premature babies or brain damage to them, I doubt if having fun would be the first thing on your mind; yet that is exactly the strategy chosen by Tommy's Campaign, a national charity based at the Guy's and St Thomas' Hospital Trust in London.

The target was to raise £5m through what the Campaign Chairman called 'well managed, frenetic activities' and *PR Week* labelled 'gimmicky ideas . . . a glitzy approach'.

Was it a sound concept to raise money for research into a serious, often tragic, problem, by having fun? Let's look at some of the things that went on.

At the Silverstone circuit, glamorous and famous women and men drove high speed cars on RAC Lady's Day and in the TAG McLaren Petit Prix.

Potty Challenge engaged Brownies and Guides in activities countrywide that may better be imagined than described.

In National No-Menacing Week children were bribed to be well behaved, and competed for the Good as Gold awards.

Guests for Tommy's Wine Dinner paid for their meal tickets with cases of fine wine that were then auctioned at Sotheby's.

Supermarkets and restaurants were among the retail outlets whose staff shaved their heads and swopped their uniforms to raise money.

A sumptuous Christmas Ball, a Stamp Appeal on national radio, a television 'Challenge' stunt, personal appearances by pop stars and football heroes: there was no doubt, and *PR Week* admitted, that 'column inches have been extensive and celebrity involvement huge'. The question is, did it work?

The answer is that it certainly did. Run 'more or less autonomously by the charity's own PR department', the Campaign raised more than £2m in the first 18 months, funded clinical equipment and research projects, and was well on the way to establishing a Centre for Fetal Health, and endowing a Chair.

To quote from the Campaign Chairman's Summary: 'The success is the result of some innovative and attractive fund raising ideas, a highly professional dedicated team of paid and voluntary staff, and some very hard work from many loyal supporters.'[10]

■ Evaluating Community Relations

In Chapter 7, we worked out some principles of good community relations and looked at some practical case histories. It is not always easy to measure and evaluate the effectiveness of such activities. Is there anything we can learn about that from other countries?

When Alastair Bruce was in the USA on a study tour in 1993, he noted that company commitment to community relations was very strong there. Full time community relations professionals were well established, and both they and the considerable number of employee volunteers tended to be well trained and worked to verifiable criteria.

At Texas Instruments, for example, community relations is treated in the same way as any other business activity, with defined objectives, key processes, targets and quantifiable measures. All this is regularly summarised in single-chart presentations. Every volunteer activity, says Bruce, is given a quantified cash value, which in 1993 was based on a nominal rate of $12 an hour. Texas Instruments compare their community involvement with that of other leading companies, using benchmarks established through standard questionnaires.

BP America, like its UK parent, is actively involved in education partnership programmes. These are evaluated in terms of the benefits to the company and to the education sector.[11]

Before researching the results of your own company's community relations, you should research local needs and concerns. Then, when you analyse findings, be sure that you are noting not only what the media say people are saying, or even just what people actually *are* saying, but what people do.

A three-cornered tug-of-war is going on in community relations, between self-esteem, altruism and commercial advantage. Get any one of these wrong and you are in trouble. It is only when *feeling good*, *doing good* and *doing well* are in balance (see Figure 14.3) that community relations can be truly effective, and that is another prime job for public relations. The ultimate aim of any public relations programme is to change behaviour to mutual advantage. That is what is evaluated.

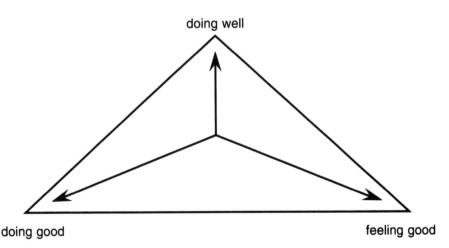

Figure 14.3 The community relations triangle

■ Accelerating a Revolution

Revolutions in technology come thick and fast. Many of them have their brief day before vanishing forever. Those that endure can take some time to become established. It is partly a matter of standards. Whatever country your car was made in and whatever company supplies the fuel you put in it, you know where you are with 4-star. Because petrol comes in a limited range of grades, competition is greater, development is easier and manufacturers, suppliers and users all benefit; not so with computer systems, whose standards are still being agreed.

PORTFOLIO
Case 14.3 – Open Systems are go

In the world of computer systems, products from one manufacturer do not necessarily work with those from another, though this is now beginning to change.

Open systems standards give common interfaces between parts of an IT system and so allow programs to be run on different computers. The decision to use IT is a strategic one, and Open Systems (OS) as a guiding principle has four main benefits: investment protection; system management; portability; interoperability.

Analysis
Independent research by the Policy Studies Institute in May 1989 showed:

- low levels of awareness and understanding of OS amongst corporate policy makers
- limited appreciation of the technical scope and application of OS to business needs
- lack of practical information and guidance, hindering IT professionals in planning and implementation
- in the market, the fragmented approach to promotion of OS caused confusion amongst users, dissipating valuable resources and effort

The DTI was a prime mover in accelerating the IT revolution and promoting OS by changing awareness, understanding and behaviour.

Objectives

1. To make corporate policy makers in 50 000 IT users *aware* of OS.
2. To give key decision makers in 5000 of the larger IT users (the 'core audience') a good *understanding* of OS.
3. To persuade 1000 of the most influential to *adopt and use* OS.

Budget
Phase 1: £2.1m over four years (about 17.5 per cent of the total research/operational/promotional budget).
Phase 2: Approximately £750 000 over two years (about 37.5 per cent of the total).

Consultancies
P Four Consultancy Limited, a management consultancy in marketing, with technical input from KPMG Management Consulting and Hoskyns.

Validation of target audiences
On a sectoral basis, P Four Consultancy undertook a fairly complex ranking and correlation exercise, measuring interest in OS and ability to invest in them, and arrived at a broad audience size of 53 000, in line with the DTI's original brief.

Phase 1 programme: technology transfer

1. About 30 one-to-one board level presentations to senior executives of suppliers, users and IT consultancies.
2. Major conference for 200 senior businessmen, addressed by Secretary of State.
3. Contact with suppliers, consultants, trade bodies and academic institutions to encourage them to promote OS to customers and members; provision of promotional material. Contract made with between 2000 and 3000 organisations, with members, subscribers and so on running into hundreds of thousands.
4. About 50 case studies/practical guides were written and produced.
5. Total of 750 000 publications, including bulletins, leaflets, brochures, reports, audio tapes and videos.
6. Targeted direct mail campaign: 22 shots over five years to core audience.
7. Advertisements in key business and IT media, with reply coupons. 3300 responses. Budget £380 000.
8. Regular briefing of journalists and provision of feature material.
9. Quarterly Bulletin distributed to all 13 000 people on DTI's OS database. By 1991 this had grown to 22 000 contacts, of whom 9000 were therefore inquirers.
10. Programme of 20 management and IT seminars/conferences, two exhibitions and 100 visits to prospective users.
11. 100 speeches.
12. Special effort to manufacturing industry: 100 000 publications, seminars for 7000 delegates, briefings, workshops, mobile demonstrations.
13. Full-scale demonstration projects at Aston University, Northampton Health Authority, the AA, and Lucas EVI Systems. In addition, the Open Systems in Manufacturing sub-module had its own demonstration projects including British Aerospace, Guinness and Rolls-Royce.

14. International contacts in more than a dozen countries.

Phase 2 programme: information exchanges

1. Open Systems information Service (OSiS) on-line, dial-up information services for non-specialists. Customers handled by NCC, database by Level 7.
    Initially sponsored by IBM, ICL and Bull, with DTI support, OSiS is intended to become self-financing from subscribers and advertisers.
2. Open Exchange, to allow users to share solutions to IT integration problems, using electronic bulletin boards.
3. Publication of authoritative document sponsored by ICL, IBM, Hewlett-Packard and Digital, explaining benefits of OS to business managers, IT users, IT professionals and systems developers.

Results

Phase 1   – Increase in awareness from 21 per cent to 70 per cent of the 50 000 broad audience
          – Of those who were aware of/understood the concept, 25 per cent claimed to be actively involved in adopting Open Systems
          – 50 per cent had been prompted to consider OS
          – 47 per cent had read about OS in DTI publications

All based on a sample of 600 executives. Evidence from the study confirmed that more than 1000 organisations were engaged in taking action on OS.

Phase 2   – OSiS: membership is growing at an increasing rate, thereby attracting new information providers, and this in turn is attracting new members. According to P Four Consultancy, it is obviously a 'chicken and egg' process: the more members the greater the interest by providers; the more information there is, the more perceptions of the value of the service increase amongst potential users.
          Satisfaction levels are very high.
          – Open Exchange: whilst progress in this area has been slow, those user groups that have used the service have generally been pleased with the structure/mechanism, and problems have been solved. This was one of the objectives of the service.
          – *The Characteristics of Open Systems* has been viewed by industry as being one of the most valuable documents to come out of the programme, because it explains the concept in easy to understand terms. It was also very successful, with two reprints and one revision. The document in a further updated form is also available on OSiS.[12]

Evaluation
An ambitious campaign. According to Peter Judge's magisterial critique:

> The DTI had set itself goals and it seems to have met them . . . In its own terms the campaign was clearly a success . . . Open Systems have advanced by leaps and bounds in recent years. Some standards . . . have not achieved the mass market DTI expected, even with heavy promotion . . . The continued availability of over-optimistic Open Systems Intercommunication (OSI) literature from DTI remains a weakness . . . however, early over-emphasis on OSI did not ruin the campaign . . . Other factors were driving suppliers towards Open Systems . . . DTI's campaign encouraged users to trust Open Systems . . . the level of public support was instrumental in persuading suppliers of the inevitability of Open Systems standards of one kind or another . . . Without the campaign, Open Systems would still be important. But it seems likely that users would not have moved so far in adopting it . . . We can only wait and see whether users take up the service which is delivered.[13]

At the time of going to press, the jury was still out.

■ A Really Significant Figure

The St John Ambulance Breath of Life campaign had some clear objectives and impressive results.

Objective:	To teach as many members of the public as possible the Breath of Life techniques for resuscitation of heart attack victims.
Results:	180 000 trained in one week alone. 1.7 million requests for information.
Objective:	To persuade the government to subsidise Breath of Life courses long term.
Results:	£80 000 Department of Health grant to pilot government-sponsored courses.
Objective:	To increase revenue from regular courses.
Results:	Paid courses up by 60 per cent on previous year.
Objective:	To attract volunteers and donations.
Results:	Recruitment doubled in some areas. £55 000 received in additional donations. The campaign won an IPR Sword of Excellence award in 1994.

All these figures are very impressive, but perhaps the most significant of all was the figure 4: that was the number of lives saved in just the first couple of months, lives that would otherwise have been lost.[14]

■ Verification

At the beginning of this chapter, evaluation was defined as the measurement of achievement against intention. Here is one final checklist to assist you in the process.

PORTFOLIO
Checklist 14.1 – The acid test

1. What were your strategic objectives? Were they quantified?
2. What were your tactical objectives? Were they quantified?
3. Was the whole PR programme carried through on time? to budget?
4. Were all target audiences reached?
5. Was each programme item cost justified?
6. Was everything done as well as it could be?
7. Were the strategic objectives attained? How was that measured?
8. Were the tactical objectives attained? How was that measured?
9. Where measurement was not practicable, what assessments were made?
10. What did the results tell you?
11. What use did you make of the new information?

In Conclusion

If you aim to dispense with method, learn method.
If you aim at facility, work hard.
If you aim for simplicity, master complexity.

Wang An-chieh of Hsiu-shui[1]

Any profession, trade or business that can be defined by case histories, or learned from checklists and guidelines, would not be worth following. There is much more to public relations than any book, course or syllabus can cover.

So this final entry for your personal portfolio is, like all the others, a signpost to help you find your own way, a hook on which to hang your own experience, a touchstone against which to test your own ideas. No more than that, and, I hope, no less.

■ THE FINAL PORTFOLIO

The mustard seed method of the management and practice of public relations applied to the IPR Sword of Excellence Guidelines.

Information

1. *What is your present position?*
   What is going well? What can be done better? What are the constraints? What strengths can be used to advantage? What disadvantages must be overcome? Have you identified all the problems? And all the opportunities? Have you established your benchmarks? What else do you need to know?

2. *What do you want to achieve?*
   How far removed are your objectives from your analysis? What specific changes are called for? What specific results are you aiming at? Have you quantified them? How do your PR objectives relate to the business objectives of the organisation? Are you being realistic?

Planning

3. *How are you going to bridge that gap?*
   What are the strategic decisions that will take you from where you are now (your analysis) to where you want to be (your objectives)? Do you have a

tactical plan for carrying out the strategy? What is your timescale? How will public relations be coordinated with other disciplines such as marketing?
4. *What do you need to be able to do the job?*
   Whether you are managing a complete campaign or handling press inquiries, have you secured your resources, such as information; staff; outside help (for example, PR consultancy); money; equipment; materials; skills; knowledge? Do you treat yourself as a resource? Have you worked out your budget?

Action

5. *Do you know the limits of your own authority?*
   Who has authority over you? What can you delegate? What must you refer upwards or sideways? What is your spending authority limit? Do you know the difference between responsibility and accountability? Who carries the can in the end?
6. *What will you actually do?*
   What is your detailed programme of action? What techniques will you use? How will you select the appropriate media? Are financial control systems in place? Do you know the difference between budget tracking and budget control?

Measurement

7. *How will you measure your effectiveness?*
   What can you measure? How do you assess something that can't be measured? What methods will be used when comparing achievement with intentions? Will strategic and practical results be measured? How will cost-effectiveness be evaluated? What use will be made of the information? What feedback systems are in place?

Remember

8. Always tell the truth.
   Never deceive yourself.
   Always check your sources.

Appendix A: Sources of Information

Industry Organisations, Professional Institutions and Other Representative Bodies

Association of Business Communicators
3 Whitehall Court
LONDON SW14 2EL
Tel: 0171 925 1331 Fax: 0171 925 1331

Association for Business Sponsorship of the Arts (ABSA) and Business in the Arts
Nutmeg House
60 Gainsford Street
Butlers Wharf
LONDON SE1 2NY
Tel: 0171 378 8143 Fax: 0171 407 7527

    ABSA (Scotland)
    Tel: 0141 204 3864
    ABSA (North) 01422 367860
    ABSA (Midlands) 0121 634 4102
    ABSA (Wales)
    Tel: 01222 221382

Advisory Committee on Business and the Environment (ACBE)
Department of the Environment
Environmental Protection Division
2 Marsham Street
LONDON SW1P 3EB
Tel: 0171 276 3788 Fax: 0171 276 3731

British Institute of Professional Photography (BIPP)
Fox Talbot House
Amwell End
WARE
Herts SG12 9HN
Tel: 01920 464011 Fax: 01920 487056

Chartered Institute of Journalists
2 Dock Offices
Lower Quays Road
LONDON SE16 2XL
Tel: 0171 252 1187 Fax: 0171 232 2302

Chartered Institute of Marketing
Moor Hall
COOKHAM
Berks SL6 9QH
Tel: 01628 524922 Fax: 01628 531382

Communications, Advertising and Marketing Foundation (CAM)
Abford House
15 Wilton Road
LONDON SW1V 1NJ
Tel: 0171 828 7506 Fax: 0171 976 5140

Confederation of British Industry (CBI)
Centre Point
103 New Oxford Street
LONDON WC1A 1DU
Tel: 0171 379 7400 Fax: 0171 240 1578

Confédération Européenne des Relations Publiques (CERP)
35–41 rue de Verdun
92150 Suresnes
France
Tel: 00 33 46 97 20 00 Fax: 00 33 46 97 20 10

Incorporated Society of British Advertisers Ltd (ISBA)
44 Hertford Street
LONDON W1Y 8AE
Tel: 0171 499 7502 Fax: 0171 629 5355

Institute for Employment Studies (formerly Institute of Manpower Studies)
Mantell Building
University of Sussex
Falmer
BRIGHTON BN1 9RF
Tel: 01273 686751 Fax: 01273 690430

Institute of Management (IM)
Management House
Cottingham Road
CORBY
Northants NN17 1TT
Tel: 01536 204222 Fax: 01536 201651

Institute of Manpower Studies – see Institute for Employment Studies

Institute of Public Relations (IPR)
The Old Trading House
15 Northburgh Street
LONDON EC1V 0PR
Tel: 0171 253 5151 Fax: 0171 490 0588

International Public Relations Association
Case Postale 2100
CH–1211 Geneva 2
Switzerland
Tel: 00 4122 791 0550 Fax: 00 4122 788 0336

International Public Relations Foundation
White Cottage
Rusper Road
NEWDIGATE
Surrey RH5 5BE
Tel: 01306 631 354

Marketing Research Society
The Old Trading House
15 Northburgh Street
LONDON EC1V OPR
Tel: 0171 490 4911 Fax: 0171 490 0608

National Consumer Council (NCC)
20 Grosvenor Gardens
LONDON SW1W ODH
Tel: 0171 730 3469 Fax: 0171 730 0191

National Council for Vocational Qualifications (NCVQ)
222 Euston Road
LONDON NW1 2BZ
Tel: 0717 387 9898 Fax: 0171 387 0978

National Union of Journalists
Acorn House
314 Gray's Inn Road
LONDON WC1X 8DP
Tel: 0171 278 7916 Fax: 0171 837 8143

Public Relations Consultants Association (PRCA)
Willow House
Willow Place
Victoria
LONDON SW1P 1JH
Tel: 0171 233 6026 Fax: 0171 828 4797

Public Relations Educators' Forum
The College of St Mark and St John
Derriford Road
PLYMOUTH
Devon PL6 8BH
Tel: 01752 777188 Fax: 01752 761120

Royal Society of Arts (RSA)
8 John Adam Street
LONDON WC2N 6EZ
Tel: 0171 930 5115 Fax: 0171 839 5805

Appendix B: Additional Information Sources

Some Public Relations and Communications Consultancies Referred to in this Book

Band & Brown
18 Compton Terrace
Canonbury
LONDON N1 2UN
Tel: 0171 704 2010 Fax: 0171 704 2442

Beechey Morgan Associates
Althorp Studios
4–6 Althorp Road
LONDON SW17 7ED
Tel: 0181 682 2482 Fax: 0181 682 2488

Biss Lancaster
69 Monmouth Street
LONDON WC2H 9DG
Tel: 0171 497 3001 Fax: 0171 497 8915

Bruce Naughton Wade
Enterprise House
59/65 Upper Ground
LONDON SE1 9PQ
Tel: 0171 620 1113 Fax: 0171 401 8319

Bullet Communications
Vencourt Place
259 King Street
Hammersmith
LONDON W6 9LW
Tel: 0181 748 1551 Fax: 0181 748 3690

Burson Marsteller
24–28 Bloomsbury Way
LONDON WC1A 2PX
Tel: 0171 831 6262 Fax: 0171 430 1033

Casstallack
9 Lees Lane
Romanby
NORTHALLERTON
North Yorkshire DL7 8DA
Tel: 01609 777571 Fax: 01609 778320

Cicada Consultants
Elton Villas
Birstwith
HARROGATE
North Yorkshire HG3 2NF
Tel: 01423 770256 Fax: 01423 771712

Citigate Corporate
26 Finsbury Square
LONDON EC2A 1DS
Tel: 0171 282 8000 Fax: 0171 282 8010

Cohn & Wolfe
18 Clerkenwell Green
LONDON EC1R 0DP
Tel: 0171 608 1576 Fax: 0171 454 1470

Counsellor
Brands House
Kingshill Road
Four Ashes
HIGH WYCOMBE
Bucks HP13 5BB
Tel: 01494 711228 Fax: 01494 716626

Dewe Rogerson
31/32 London Wall Buildings
London Wall
LONDON EC2M 5SY
Tel: 0171 638 9571 Fax: 0171 628 3444

DTW Group
13 Thomas Street
HEATH & REACH
Beds LU7 OAN
Tel: 01287 610404 Fax: 01287 638263

Dunseath Stephen
5 Castle Terrace
EDINBURGH EH1 2DP
Tel: 0131 228 6262 Fax: 0131 228 6889

Edelman PR World Wide
Haymarket House
28/29 Haymarket
LONDON SW1Y 4SP
Tel: 0171 344 1200 Telex: 0171 344 1222

Financial Dynamics
30 Furnival Street
LONDON EC4A 1JE
Tel: 0171 831 3113 Fax: 0171 831 7961

Firefly Communications
25/4 The Coda Centre
189 Munster Road
LONDON SW6 6AW
Tel: 0171 381 4505 Fax: 0171 385 4768

Fishburn Hedges Boys Williams
1 Northumberland Avenue
Trafalgar Square
LONDON WC2N 5BW
Tel: 0171 839 4321 Fax: 0171 839 2858

Flora Martin Public Relations
38 Park Terrace Lane
GLASGOW G3 6BQ
Tel: 0141 353 1177 Fax: 0141 353 2277

GJW Government Relations
64 Clapham Road
LONDON SW9 0JJ
Tel: 0171 582 3119 Fax: 0171 735 9561

Good Relations
59 Russell Square
LONDON WC1B 4HJ
Tel: 0171 631 3434 Fax: 0171 631 1399

Handel Communications
7 Hillgate Place
LONDON SW12 9ER
Tel: 0181 673 0030 Fax: 0181 675 1738

Hill & Knowlton
5–11 Theobalds Road
LONDON WC1X 8SH
Tel: 0171 413 3000 Fax: 0171 413 3111

Infopress Communications
2/3 Salisbury Court
Fleet Street
LONDON EC4Y 8AA
Tel: 0171 353 2320 Fax: 0171 583 9437 E-mail: 87:SQQ982

Kate Graham Public Relations
Grampian Media Village
Grampian Television
Queens Cross
Aberdeen AB9 2XJ
Tel: 01224 642751 Fax: 01224 644347

KBH Communications Ltd
49/53 High Street
Kensington
LONDON W8 5ED
Tel: 0171 938 3911 Fax: 0171 938 4176

Kestrel Communications
Broadway House
The Broadway
Wimbledon
LONDON SW19 1RL
Tel: 0181 543 2299 Fax: 0181 543 2292

Ketchum Public Relations
5 Langley Street
Covent Garden
LONDON WC2H 9JA
Tel: 0171 379 3404 Fax: 0171 240 8311

Key Communications
Principal House
304 Upper High Street
THAME
Oxon OX9 2EL
Tel: 01844 215461 Fax: 01844 217265

Le Fevre Williamson Public Relations
Attlee House
St Aldates Courtyard
St Aldates
OXFORD OX1 1DQ
Tel: 01865 202666 Fax: 01865 202333

Lowe Bell Financial
1 Red Lion Court
LONDON EC4A 3EB
Tel: 0171 353 9203 Fax: 0171 353 7392

Lynne Franks PR
327–329 Harrow Road
LONDON W9 3RB
Tel: 0171 724 6777
Tel: 0171 724 8484

Magellan Medical Communications
40–42 Osnaburgh Street
LONDON NW1 3ND
Tel: 0171 465 8366 Telex: 0171 465 8367

Malcolm Hurlston Corporate Consultancy
2 Ridgmount Street
LONDON WC1E 7AA
Tel: 0171 637 4890 Fax: 0171 580 0016

Manning Selvage & Lee
199 Knightsbridge
LONDON SW7 1RP
Tel: 0171 823 9666 Fax: 0171 823 8089

Media Measurement
62 High Street
Stony Stratford
MILTON KEYNES MK11 1AQ
Tel: 01908 265011 Fax: 01908 262455

MultiStrategies
2 Ridgmount Street
LONDON WC1E 7AA
Tel: 0171 636 5214 Fax: 0171 580 0016

Norman Hart Associates
Ravenor House
13 Culverden Park Road
TUNBRIDGE WELLS
Kent TN4 9QX
Tel:/Fax: 01892 533066

Northern Lights
The Coach House
4 Rutland Road
HARROGATE HG1 2PY
Tel: 01423 562400 Fax: 01423 502782

Ogilvy & Mather Public Relations
33 St John Street
LONDON EC1M 4AA
Tel: 0171 253 5757 Fax: 0171 404 2878

Paragon Communications
Film House
142 Wardour Street
LONDON W1V 3AU
Tel: 0171 734 6030 Fax: 0171 437 6085

P Four Consultancy
8 Spice Court
Plantation Wharf
LONDON SW11 3UE
Tel: 0171 924 3233 Fax: 0171 978 5304

Quentin Bell Organisation
22 Endell Street
Covent Garden
LONDON WC2H 9AD
Tel: 0171 379 0304 Fax: 0171 379 7259

Radio Lynx
Unit 4
Chelsea Studios
92 Lots Road
LONDON SW10 0RN
Tel: 0171 351 4895 Fax: 0171 352 0771

Scope: Communications
Tower House
8–14 Southampton Street
Covent Garden
LONDON WC2E 7HA
Tel: 0171 379 3234 Fax: 0171 240 7729

Shandwick
18 Dering Street
LONDON W1R 9AF
Tel: 0171 355 1908 Fax: 0171 499 1752

Smythe, Dorward, Lambert
55 Drury Lane
LONDON WC2B 5SQ
Tel: 0171 379 9099 Fax: 0171 379 7156

Tenet Public Relations
99–101 Worship Street
LONDON EC2A 2BE
Tel: 0171 377 1076 Fax: 0171 377 2522

The Rowland Company
67–69 Whitfield Street
LONDON W1P 5RL
Tel: 0171 436 4060 Fax: 0171 255 2131

Trident Training Services
London House
68 Upper Richmond Road
LONDON SW15 2RP
Tel: 0181 874 3610 Fax: 0181 874 0014

Two-Ten Communications
Communications House
210 Old Street
LONDON EC1V 9UN
Tel: 0171 490 8111 Fax: 0171 490 1255

Welbeck Golin/Harris
43 King Street
Covent Garden
LONDON WC2E 8RJ
Tel: 0171 836 6677 Fax: 0171 836 5820

Westminster Communications
Cowley House
9 Little College Street
LONDON SW1P 3XS
Tel: 0171 222 0666 Fax: 0171 233 0335

Westminster Strategy
1 Deans Yard
Westminster
LONDON SW1P 3NR
Tel: 0171 799 9811 Fax: 0171 233 0124

■ Media Training

Accolade Communications
Tel: 0161 904 8112 Fax: 0161 904 0043

Arnold Harris Associates
Tel: 01582 478151 Fax: 01582 478131

Aziz Corporation
Tel: 01962 774766 Fax: 01962 774728

BBS Productions
Tel: 01179 429411 Fax 01179 426112

Corporate Vision Limited
Tel: 0171 734 2335 Fax: 0171 734 7030

Coulter Ford Associates
Tel: 01344 780240 Fax: 01344 780250

Fenwick Business Communications Ltd
Tel: 0171 497 4900 Fax: 0171 240 7311

Hillside Studios
Tel: 0181 950 7919 Fax: 0181 950 1437

InterMedia Training
Tel: 0171 233 5033 Fax: 0171 873 8631

Media First
Tel: 01635 872384 Fax: 01635 861505

Media Interviews
Tel: 01249 655275 Fax: 01249 443520

TRT Television and Radio Techniques
Tel: 0114 264 8900 Fax: 0114 264 5717

Vertex Communications
Tel: 0171 457 2021 Fax: 0171 248 3295

■ Workshops, Seminars, Short Courses, In-Company Training

British Association of Industrial Editors
Tel: 01732 459331

Chartered Institute of Marketing
Tel: 01628 524922

Doug Goodman PR
Tel: 0181 977 1105

Norman Hart Associates
Tel: 01892 533066

Henshall Training Centre, Stockport
Tel: 0161 440 8466

Industrial Society
Tel: 0171 839 4300

Institute of Management
Tel: 01536 204222

Institute of Public Relations
Tel: 0171 253 5151

London School of Public Relations
Tel: 0171 584 4070

Public Relations Consultants Association
Tel: 0171 233 6026

Trident Training Services
Tel: 0181 874 3610

■ Some Other Organisations Referred to in this Book

Audience Selection
14–17 St John's Square
LONDON EC1M 4HE
Tel: 0171 608 3618 Fax: 0171 608 3286

Benn's Media
Riverbank House
Angel Lane
TONBRIDGE
Kent TN9 1SE
Tel: 01732 362666 Fax: 01732 367301

Gallup Opinion Polls
Gallup House
307 Finchley Road
LONDON NW3 6EH
Tel: 0171 794 0461 Fax: 0171 433 3235

Livingstone Guarantee (was Livingstone Fisher)
Acre House
11–15 William Road
LONDON NW1 3ER
Tel: 0171 388 4242 Fax: 0171 383 3389

Market and Opinion Research International (MORI)
95 Southwark Street
LONDON SE1 OHX
Tel: 0171 928 5955 Fax: 0171 995 0070

National Magazine Co
National Magazine House
72 Broadwick Street
LONDON W1V 2BP
Tel: 0171 439 5000 Fax: 0171 437 6886

Neilsen
Neilsen House
London Road
Headington
OXFORD OX3 9RX
Tel: 01865 742742 Fax: 01865 742222

NOP Research Group
1 & 2 Berners Street
LONDON W1P 4DR
Tel: 0171 612 0100 Fax: 0171 612 0547

Price Waterhouse
Southwark Towers
London Bridge Street
LONDON SE1 9SY
Tel: 0171 939 3000 Telex: 884657 PRIWAT G
Telecopier: 0171 378 0647

Willott Kingston Smith
10 Bruton Street
LONDON W1X 7AG
Tel: 0171 304 4646 Fax: 0171 304 4647

Appendix C: Professional Conduct

■ The Institute of Public Relations

The Old Trading House
15 Northburgh Street
LONDON EC1V 0PR
Tel: 0171 253 5151 Fax: 0171 490 0588

■ Objectives

1. To provide a professional structure for the practice of public relations.
2. To enhance the ability and status of our members as professional practitioners.
3. To represent the interests of our members.
4. To provide opportunities for members to meet and exchange views and ideas.
5. To offer a range of services of professional and personal benefit to members.

■ Code of Professional Conduct

■ Conduct Concerning the Practice of Public Relations

A member shall:

1.1 Have a positive duty to observe the highest standards in the practice of public relations and to deal fairly and honestly with employers and clients (past and present), fellow members and professionals, the public relations profession, other professions, suppliers, intermediaries, the media of communications, employees and the public.

1.2 Be aware of, understand and observe this Code, any amendment to it, and any other codes which shall be incorporated into it; remain up to date with the content and recommendations of any guidance or practice papers issued by IPR: and have a duty to conform to good practice as expressed in such guidance or practice papers.

1.3 Uphold this Code and cooperate with fellow members to enforce decisions on any matter arising from its application. A member who knowingly causes or allows his or her staff to act in a manner inconsistent with this Code is party to such action and shall be deemed to be in breach of this Code. Staff employed by a member who acts in a manner inconsistent with this Code should be disciplined by the member.

A member shall not:

1.4 Engage in any practice nor be seen to conduct him or her self in any manner detrimental to the reputation of the Institute or the reputation and interests of the public relations profession.

■ Conduct Concerning the Public, the Media and Other Professionals

A member shall:

2.1 Conduct his or her professional activities with proper regard to the public interest.
2.2 Have a positive duty at all times to respect the truth and shall not disseminate false or misleading information knowingly or recklessly, and take proper care to check all information prior to its dissemination.
2.3 Have a duty to ensure that the actual interest of any organisation with which he or she may be professionally concerned is adequately declared.
2.4 When working in association with other professionals, identify and respect the codes of those professions.
2.5 Respect any statutory or regulatory codes laid down by any other authorities which are relevant to the actions of his or her employer or client, or taken on behalf of any employer or client.
2.6 Ensure that the names of all directors, executives, and retained advisers of his or her employers or company who hold public office, are members of either House of Parliament, local authorities or of any statutory organisation or body, are recorded in the IPR register.
2.7 Honour confidences received or given in the course or professional activity.
2.8 Neither propose nor undertake, or cause an employer or client to propose or undertake, any action which would be an improper influence on government legislation, holders of public office or members of any statutory body or organisation, or the media of communication.

■ Conduct Concerning Employers and Clients

A member shall:

3.1 Safeguard the confidences of both present and former employers or clients: shall not disclose or use these confidences to the disadvantage or prejudice of such employers or clients or to the financial advantage of the member (unless the employer or client has released such information for public use, or has given specific permission for disclosure), except upon the order of a court of law.
3.2 Inform an employer or client of any shareholding or financial interest held by that member or any staff employed by that member in any company or person whose services he or she recommends.

3.3 Be free to accept fees, commissions or other valuable considerations from persons other than an employer or client, if such considerations are disclosed to the employer or client.

3.4 Be free to negotiate, or renegotiate, with an employer or client terms that are a fair reflection of demands of the work involved and take into account factors other than hours worked and the experience involved. These special factors, which are also applied by other professional advisers, shall have regard to all the circumstances of the specific situation and in particular to:

   (a) the complexity of the issue, case, problem or assignment, and the difficulties associated with its completion;
   (b) the professional or specialised skills required and the degree of responsibility involved;
   (c) the amount of documentation necessary to be perused or prepared, and its importance;
   (d) the place and circumstances where the work is carried out, in whole or in part;
   (e) the scope, scale and value of the task and its importance as an activity, issue or project to the employer or client.

A member shall not:

3.5 Misuse information regarding his or her employer's or client's business for financial or other gain.

3.6 Use inside information for gain. Nor may a member of staff managed or employed by a member directly trade in his or her employer's or client's securities without the prior written permission of the employer or client and of the member's chief executive or chief financial officer or compliance officer.

3.7 Serve an employer or client under terms or conditions which might impair his or her independence, objectivity or integrity.

3.8 Represent conflicting interests but may represent competing interests with the express consent of the parties concerned.

3.9 Guarantee the achievement of results which are beyond the member's direct capacity to achieve or prevent.

■ Conduct Concerning Colleagues

A member shall:

4.1 Adhere to the highest standards of accuracy and truth, avoiding extravagant claims or unfair comparisons and giving credit for ideas and words borrowed from others.

4.2 Be free to represent his or her capabilities and service to any potential employer or client, either on his or her own initiative or at the behest of any client, provided in so doing he or she does not seek to break any existing contract or detract from the reputation or capabilities of any member already serving that employer or client.

A member shall not:

4.3 Injure the professional reputation or practice of another member.

■ Interpreting the Code

5.1 In the interpretation of this code, the Laws of the Land shall apply.

■ Educational Qualifications

The following have been approved by the Institute of Public Relations as acceptable educational qualifications for Membership. At least four years' substantial PR experience is also required.

BA(Hons) in Public Relations, Bournemouth University	– 4 year sandwich
CAM Diploma in Public Relations CAM Foundation	
Post Graduate Diploma, Media and Public Relations University of Wales, Cardiff	– 1 year full time
Diploma in Public Relations, Institute of Technology, Dublin	– 1 year full time
BA in Communication, Napier University, Edinburgh	– 3 year full time
Combined Honours Degree in Public Relations, Lancashire Business School, University of Central Lancashire	– 3 year full time
BA(Hons) in Public Relations, Business School, Leeds Metropolitan University	– 3 year full time OR 4 year sandwich
MA in Public Relations, Department of Retailing and Marketing, Manchester Metropolitan University	– 1 year full time
BA(Hons) in Public Relations, Exeter University, College of St Mark & St John, Plymouth	– 3 year full time
MSc in Public Relations, School of Management, Stirling University	– 1 year full time OR 3 year distance learning
Watford/PRCA Diploma in International Public Relations, West Herts College	– 1 year full time

All the above are also accredited by the Confédération Européenne des Relations Publiques (CERP)
35-41 rue de Verdun
92150 Suresnes
France
Tel: 00 33 46 97 20 00 Fax: 00 33 46 97 20 10

■ The Registration of Professional Lobbyists

In conjunction with the PRCA, the IPR launched a new register of professional lobbyists on 27 September 1994.

■ Background

The IPR believes that regulation of lobbyists is really a matter for Parliament but, despite the recommendation to establish a statutory register by the Select Committee on Members' Interests in July 1991, Parliament still considers that this would best be achieved by self regulation.

The IPR represents the majority of public relations practitioners in the UK, many of whom are directly or indirectly engaged in lobbying activities. Lobbying is conducted by individuals acting on behalf of employers or clients and these individuals should be registered within a self-regulatory scheme.

The IPR intends to introduce a register for its members engaged in lobbying activities, drawing on the successful Canadian model introduced in 1988, to demonstrate its commitment to high professional standards and greater transparency in this growing area of public relations practice.

While principally concerned with lobbying activities in relation to the House of Commons, registration will also apply to members making approaches to local government, the EU and the Parliaments of other countries.

It is in the public interest that the relationships between members of the IPR, MPs and outside interests are conducted on a basis of openness and integrity.

■ Definitions

Lobbying is the specific effort to influence public decision making either by pressing for change in policy or seeking to prevent such change. It consists of representations made to any public office holder on any aspect of policy, or any measure implementing that policy, or any matter being considered, or which is likely to be considered, by a public body.

Lobbyists fall into two main categories.

1. *Consultants*   Individuals who, for pay, provide certain types of lobbying services on behalf of a client.
While this covers professional lobbyists such as public relations consultants, it can also include lawyers, accountants and other professional advisers who provide lobbying services for their clients.

2.   *In-house*   Employees whose job involves a significant amount of lobbying for
                          their employer.
                          *This covers those for whom lobbying is a substantial part of their
                          job requirement, if their activities are carried out frequently, or if
                          they account for a large part of the time they spend on the job.*

A *client* is the individual, organisation or corporation on whose behalf lobbying activities are undertaken and who would be the true beneficiary of the undertaking if successful.

Pay is defined as money or anything of value, including a contract, promise or agreement to pay money or anything of value.

■ Registration

☐ *Consultant Lobbyists*

Members of the Institute who are consultant lobbyists are required to submit a registration form when they lobby on behalf of a client, providing information about the client or, in any case where the client is not the ultimate beneficiary of any service provided, the name of such beneficiary. Apart from the initial setting-up of the register the onus is on the consultant lobbyists to amend or update their entry as and when changes take place.

Those from other professions engaged in lobbying, such as lawyers and accountants, can be included in the Institute's Register but would be required to become Affiliate Members of the Institute and therefore subscribe to the Code of Conduct.

☐ *In-house Lobbyists*

Members of the Institute who are in-house lobbyists are also required to submit a registration form when they lobby on behalf of, or of benefit to, their employer, providing information about their organisation. Apart from the initial setting-up of the register the onus is on in-house lobbyists to ensure they amend or update their entry as and when changes take place.

☐ *Issue or Subject of Lobbying*

Members are required to make a clear declaration of the issue or subject of any lobbying activity on the registration form together with the period for which the activity is being undertaken. This may take the form of a general statement of interests for an organisation where an ongoing corporate programme of contact between a lobbyist and holders of public office is to be undertaken. If a specific campaign on a single issue is to be conducted then a further, more detailed, registration form is required.

☐ *Confidentiality*

While the introduction of the Register is intended to make professional lobbying more open to public scrutiny, it is recognised that there may be exceptional circumstances where the premature disclosure of a client's or employer's interest may need to be subject to confidential disclosure. For example, this would apply to a contested take-over bid where lobbyists would also have to work within Stock Exchange rules. In such a situation the member would need to advise the Executive Director that a breach of confidentiality would affect the client's or employer's interest and agree to lodge an unopened letter, with instructions, as part of the registration process.

☐ *Registration Fees*

There are no registration fees.

☐ *Registration of Holders of Public Office*

The Institute's Code of Professional Conduct requires all members to ensure that the names of all directors, executives and retained advisers of their employers or company who hold public office, are members of either House of Parliament, local authorities or of any statutory organisation or body, are recorded in the IPR register. The collection of this information will now be formalised both through the annual gathering of information for the register of members as well as through the registration of professional lobbyists process.

All those who register as lobbyists will be clearly identified in the Institute's annual Handbook which includes the register of IPR members and is publicly available. A copy of the Handbook and the Institute's Register of Professional Lobbyists will be deposited annually with the House of Commons Library. In addition, all entries for registration will be available for inspection by prior arrangement with the Executive Director, and copies will be provided upon payment of a reasonable fee to cover costs of reproduction. It shall be the duty of all members of the Institute to ensure that their entries are clear, accurate and up-to-date.

Registration does not create any special privileges at the expense of the general public and shall not give the right to any preferential access to the Houses of Parliament, its services and facilities, or to Parliamentary Papers. However, members may wish to draw attention to the commitments they have entered into by membership of the IPR, the requirement to uphold the Code of Conduct and by registering their lobbying activity for public scrutiny.

■ A Statement on Editorial and Colour Separation Charges

WE THE UNDERSIGNED, the five major organisations representing journalists, public relations practitioners and advertisers in Britain, are united in condemning the fast-growing practice of publishers to charge for colour separations and editorial space to those freely-offering material to journals, now endemic in the Trade and Technical field.

Under the auspices of the Institute of Public Relations, as representatives of the Chartered Institute of Journalists, The Incorporated Society of British Advertisers, the National Union of Journalists, the Public Relations Consultants' Association and the Institute (IPR), we have agreed the following:

1   Charging for colour separations, for news items and similar material *where this is not an advertisement, advertorial or other overtly sponsored feature* is a radical departure from established publishing practice and appears to have no justification. It blurs the distinction between advertising and editorial, and undermines a central argument for public relations;

2   Each of the undersigned PR and journalist organisations has carried out a nationwide survey of its own members on this matter and the findings mutually reinforce the views expressed in this joint statement;

3   These findings also indicate that the total amount now collected in colour separation (and allied) charges by British journals from all sources runs into millions of pounds annually and is causing many businesses to switch cash from advertising budgets into these growing editorial support costs since editorial exposure is often considered more valuable;

4   Established reputable journals – particularly trade papers – with trusted editorial standing are losing credibility by pursuing a practice begun by newer opportunist publications operating as "free sheets", catalogues and publicity vehicles;

5   Certain identified publishers are requiring journalists to "sell" colour separations to public relations practitioners – both consultants and company executives – at the expense of editorial integrity and the basic elements of a free and independent press;

6   The practice is misleading in a manner which may be seen to be calculated, and is already eroding readership trust in the journals affected;

7   Most charges applied are not standardised nor published, and do not reflect the actual cost to a publishing house of making colour separations. They have been proven to be open to negotiation and are frequently offered on an "under the counter" basis, sometimes with the promise of special positioning of the editorial material in question;

8   Our members' reports show the charges to be a hidden form of income for publishers who implement the practice in place of copytasting and accepted norms of editorial responsibility;

9   In many cases, the practice is similar in approach and outcome to the corrupt media deals which have become institutionalised in some countries abroad. **It is in breach of all the Codes of Practice adopted by the organisations contributing to this statement;**

10   The practice creates intense difficulties, even hardship for both journalists and public relations practitioners;
For Journalists who suffer pressure from employers requiring duties which are in conflict with personal commitments to accepted editorial principles;
For PR practitioners whose clients or employers expect them to obtain media exposure through their own creativity and skills rather than hidden payments.

11   The value, to both advertisers and readers, of journals known to offer paid space under the guise of conventional selected editorial is already diminishing, and will continue to do so. The term "puff papers" is now gaining currency;

12   The joint signatories to this statement invite the Periodical Publishers' Association and The Newspaper Society to join them in condemning the practice and seeking by discussion and further concerted action to bring it to a halt.

■ Public Relations Consultants Association

Willow House
Willow Place
Victoria
LONDON SW1P 1JH
Tel: 0171 233 6026 Fax: 0171 828 4797

■ Professional Charter

A member firm shall:

1.1   Have a positive duty to observe the highest standards in the practice of public relations. Furthermore a member has the responsibility at all times to deal fairly and honestly with clients past and present, fellow members and professionals, the public relations profession, other professions, suppliers, intermediaries, the media of communication, employees, and above all else the public.

1.2   Be expected to be aware of, understand and observe this code, any amendment to it, and any other codes which shall be incorporated into this code, and to remain up-to-date with the content and recommendations of any guidance or practice papers issued by the PRCA, and shall have a duty to conform to good practice as expressed in such guidance or practice papers.

1.3   Uphold this code and cooperate with fellow members in so doing by enforcing decisions on any matter arising from its application. A member firm that knowingly causes or permits a member of its staff to act in a manner inconsistent with this code is party to such action and shall itself be deemed to be in breach of it. Any member of staff or a member firm who acts in a manner inconsistent with this code must be disciplined by the employer.

A member firm shall not:

1.4   Engage in any practice nor be seen to conduct itself in any manner detrimental to the reputation of the Association or the reputation and interests of the public relations profession.

■ Conduct towards the Public, the Media and Other Professionals

A member firm shall:

2.1   Conduct its professional activities with proper regard to the public interest.

2.2 Have a positive duty at all times to respect the truth and shall not disseminate false or misleading information knowingly or recklessly, and to use proper care to avoid doing so inadvertently.

2.3 Have a duty to ensure that the actual interest of any organisation with which it may be professionally concerned is adequately declared.

2.4 When working in association with other professionals, identify and respect the codes of these professions and shall not knowingly be party to any breach of such codes.

2.5 Cause the names of all its directors, executives, and retained consultants who hold public office, are members of either House of Parliament, are members of local authorities or of any statutory organisation or body, to be recorded in the relevant section of the PRCA Register.

2.6 Honour confidences received or given in the course of professional activity.

2.7 Neither propose nor undertake any action which would constitute an improper influence on organs of government, or on legislation, or on the media of communication.

2.8 Neither offer nor give, nor cause a client to offer or give, any inducement to persons holding public office or members of any statutory body or organisation who are not directors, executives or retained consultants, with intent to further the interests of the client if such action is inconsistent with the public interest.

■ Conduct towards Clients

A member firm shall:

3.1 Safeguard the confidence of both present and former clients and shall not disclose or use these confidences, to the disadvantage or prejudice of such clients or to the financial advantage of the member firm, unless the client has released such information for public use, or has given specific permission for its disclosure; except upon the order of a court of law.

3.2 Inform a client of any shareholding or financial interest held by that firm or any member of that firm in any company, firm or person whose services it recommends.

3.3 Be free to accept fees, commissions or other valuable considerations from persons other than a client, only provided such considerations are disclosed to the client.

3.4 List the names of its clients in the Annual Register of the Association.

3.5 Be free to negotiate with a client terms that take into account factors other than hours worked and seniority of staff involved. These special factors, which are also applied by other professional advisers, shall have regard to all the circumstances of the specific situation and in particular to:

    (a) the complexity of the issue, case, problem or assignment, and the difficulties associated with its completion;

    (b) the professional or specialised skills and the seniority levels of staff engaged, the time spent and the degree of responsibility involved;

    (c) the amount of documentation necessary to be perused or prepared, and its importance;

    (d) the place and circumstances where the assignment is carried out, in whole or in part;

(e) The scope, scale and value of the task and its importance as an issue or project to the client.

A member firm shall not:

3.6 Misuse information regarding its client's business for financial or other gain.
3.7 Use inside information for gain. Nor may a consultancy, its members or staff directly invest in their clients' securities without the prior written permission of the client and of the member's chief executive or chief financial officer or compliance officer.
3.8 Serve a client under terms or conditions which might impair its independence, objectivity or integrity.
3.9 Represent conflicting or competing interests without the express consent of clients concerned.
3.10 Guarantee the achievement of results which are beyond the member's direct capacity to achieve or prevent.
3.11 Invite any employee of a client advised by the member to consider alternative employment; (an advertisement in the press is not considered to be an invitation to any particular person).

■ Conduct towards Colleagues

A member firm shall:

4.1 Adhere to the highest standards of accuracy and truth, avoiding extravagant claims or unfair comparisons and giving credit for ideas and words borrowed from others.
4.2 Be free to represent its capabilities and services to any potential client, either on its own initiative or at the behest of the client, provided in so doing it does not seek to break any existing contract or detract from the reputation or capabilities of any member consultancy already serving that client.

A member firm shall not:

4.3 Injure the professional reputation or practice of another member.

Sample PR Ltd
1 Trust Lane
ASHFORD
KENT

Dear Mr Blofeld

This agreement confirms the appointment of
Sample PR Ltd

. . . .
(hereafter referred to as "the Consultancy")

as Public Relations Consultants to
Blofeld Ltd
(hereafter referred to as "the Client")

to carry out an agreed public relations programme, details of which are attached and initialled by the respective parties.

This agreement will commence on 1st January 199 . . . . for a period of . . . . .
. . . . year and will continue in effect unless terminated under the provisions of Clause F of this Agreement.

The Consultancy's service fees, exclusive of VAT, and based on management, executive and administrative time in the UK, will be calculated at the rate of:

£ . . . *per annum paid in four equal quarterly instalments in advance.*

The Consultancy reserves the right to negotiate a revised fee structure if the client changes its requirements so as to involve changes in the agree workload during the period of this agreement.

These fees apply only to work carried out in the United Kingdom, they do not apply to supervision of work performed abroad which will be subject to separate fee arrangements.

Items marked * will be subject to a handing charge of . . . . 17.65% . . . . (see Clause 14 of the Trade Standard Terms of Business).

The Client agrees to pay immediately on presentation any interim invoices in respect of advance or instalment payments required to be made to suppliers.

The Consultancy's service fees are payable:

By Banker's Standing order on the . . . . day of the quarter to which the fee relates.

Disbursement and expenses invoices are payable:

Within . . . . days of the date on which they are rendered

This agreement may be terminated at any time after an initial period of . . . . months by either party giving not less than . . . . months written notice of termination.

In the event of termination of this agreement, for whatever reason, the Client will be responsible for fees due to the Consultancy including costs, expenses and disbursements incurred by the Consultancy on behalf of the Client up to and including any notice period.

On satisfaction by the Client in full of its payment obligations, the Consultancy will co-operate so far as practicable in enabling the Client to take over any contract and arrangement with third parties, and will transfer to the Client any unused materials purchased on behalf of the Client.

The parties will agree to any additional compensation payable to the Consultancy in the event that detailed creative or other work for a future programme or project prepared by the Consultancy at the request of the Client during the period of this Agreement are subsequently implemented in whole or in part by the Client or his agent.

The following Trade Standard Terms of Business are deemed to be an integral part of this contract.

For and on behalf of *Sample PR Ltd* . . . .

Date: . . . .   Signature. . . . .

For an on behalf of *Blofeld Ltd* . . . .

Date: . . . .   Signature. . . . .

Figure C.1   Sample contract

■ The Institute of Management

Management House
Cottingham Road
CORBY
Northants NN17 1TT
Tel: 01536 204222 Fax: 01536 201651

■ Overall Goals

The Institute of Management will:

- encourage high standards of management education
- help to develop the potential of managers throughout their careers
- undertake and promote relevant management research
- represent managers in areas of policy

To achieve these goals the IM will:

- focus on four distinct areas of activity

    (a)   research;
    (b)   management development;
    (c)   membership and member services;
    (d)   representation.

- operate primarily in the UK and countries where it has branches. Where appropriate it will seek to extend its influence abroad, particularly into the rest of Europe.

■ Code of Conduct

At all times a member shall uphold the good standing and reputation of the profession of management; and while practising as a manager shall:

- have due regard for and comply with relevant law
- not misuse or abuse power or position
- follow the Guides to Professional Management Practice, as approved by the Council
- have a duty to provide information on request to any committee or sub-committee of the Institute established to investigate any alleged breach of this Code

■ Professional Duties

1. A professional man or woman is one who justifiably claims to provide an expert service of value to society, and who accepts the duties entailed by that claim, including:

   (a)   the attainment and maintenance of high standards of education, training and practical judgement, and
   (b)   honouring the special trust reposed by clients, employers, colleagues and the general public.

2. The professional discharge of such duties within management entails:

   (a)   the application of expert knowledge and judgement in the field of operations;
   (b)   the motivation and control of the activities of others, and
   (c)   a contribution to the joint achievement of objectives of the organisation, so far as this is possible and proper.

3. The discharge of one's duties as professional manager also involves the acceptance and habitual exercise of ethical values, among which a high place should be accorded to integrity, honesty, loyalty and fairness.

4. It is usual for professional managers to encounter circumstances or situations in which various values, principles, rules and interests appear to conflict, and may be difficult to harmonise in practice. No ready answer can be given for all such conflicts. The best resources which can be brought to bear are the professional and personal characteristics and qualities already identified.

5. Nevertheless, there are certain recurring situations which could give rise to concern, in which the best professional judgement and practice should normally be considered to be as described in the Guides to Professional Management Practice.

■ Guides to Professional Management Practice

■ As regards the Individual Manager

The professional manager should:

(a)   comply with any contract of employment or other agreement existing between an employer and the manager, allowing due reservation for matters of conscience;

(b)   identify and attempt to resolve conflicts of values, including ethical values, using a carefully reasoned approach;

(c)   pursue integrity and competence in all managerial activity;

(d)   take active steps for continuing development of personal competence;

(e)   take responsibility for safeguarding the security of confidential information;

(f)   exhaust all available internal remedies for dealing with matters perceived as improper, before considering any other action;

(g)   openly declare any personal interest which might be seen to influence managerial decisions.

■ As Regards Others Within the Organisation

The professional manager should, in addition to the above:

(a)   take full account of the needs, pressures and problems of others, and not discriminate on grounds other than those demonstrably necessary to the task;

(b)   seek to avoid asking others to do something which offends their conscience;

(c)   fully consider the mental and physical health, safety and well being of others;

(d)   encourage and assist others to development their potential;

(e)   be concerned with the development of quality in all management matters, including quality of life;

(f)   ensure that all are aware of their responsibilities, areas of authority and accountability and methods of their review and reward for contribution.

■ As Regards the Organisation

The professional manager should, in addition to the above:

(a)   agree and uphold proper lawful policies and practices within the organisation;

(b)   ensure the identification and communication of relevant policies, practices and information;

(c)   review organisation structure and procedures as to their suitability for achieving objectives;

(d) disseminate information on factors likely to require change in the organisation;

(e) seek to balance departmental aims in furtherance of the organisation's overall objectives.

■ As Regards Others External to, but in Direct Relationship with, the Organisation

The professional manager should, in addition to the above:

(a) ensure that the interests of others are properly identified and responded to in a balanced manner;

(b) establish and develop a continuing and satisfactory relationship based on mutual confidence;

(c) avoid entering into arrangements which unlawfully or improperly affect competitive practice;

(d) neither offer nor accept any gift, favour or hospitality intended as, or having the effect of, bribery and corruption;

(e) in the public interest, cooperate with others to uphold the law and to arrive at the truth in investigations and disciplinary processes.

■ As Regards UK Society and Environment

The professional manager should, in addition to the above:

(a) have due regard to the short and long term effects and possible consequences within society of present and proposed actions;

(b) be willing to contribute to and comment upon the manageability of proposed legislation and the running of social affairs;

(c) communicate to the public truthfully and without intent to mislead by slanting or suppressing information;

(d) seek to conserve resources wherever possible, especially those which are non-renewable;

(e) seek to avoid destruction of resources by pollution and have a contingency plan for limiting destruction in the event of a disaster.

■ As Regards Overseas Societies and Environments

The professional manager should, in addition to the above:

(a) be aware of the management implications of global environmental issues;

(b) decline to solve UK problems of pollution and processes by their export unchanged to the detriment of the quality of life of other societies;

(c) have due regard to the possibility that satisfactory practice in the UK might be offensive or misleading elsewhere;

(d) respect the customs, practices and reasonable ambitions of other peoples;

(e) wherever practicable, comply with the professional standards set out in the Code of Conduct and these Guides, but not necessarily be deemed to be in breach of obligations as a member of the Institute if complying with established overseas customs and practices which are inconsistent in detail with the foregoing.

Appendix D: Bibliography

The following reading list is published with the permission of the IPR, whose copyright it is.

Introductory Texts

Black, Sam, *Introduction to Public Relations*. Modino, 1989.
Howard, Wilfred (ed.), *The Practice of Public Relations*, 3rd edn. Butterworth Heinemann, 1988.
Jefkins, Frank, *Public Relations*, 4th edn. Pitman, 1992.
Lloyd, Herbert and Peter, *Teach Yourself Public Relations*. Hodder & Stoughton, 1989.

General Texts

Bartram, Peter and Colin Coulson-Thomas, *The Complete Spokesperson*. Policy Publications, 1990.
Black, Sam, *The Essentials of Public Relations*. Kogan Page, 1993.
Haywood, Roger, *All About Public Relations*, 2rd edn. McGraw-Hill, 1991.
Haywood, Roger, *Managing Your Reputation*, McGraw-Hill, 1994.
Jefkins, Frank, *Planned Press and Public Relations*, 3rd edn. Blackie, 1993.
Jefkins, Frank, *Public Relations Techniques*. Butterworth Heinemann, 1988.
Oxley, Harold, *Principles of Public Relations*. Kogan Page, rev 1989.
Ross Dina, *Surviving the Media Jungle*. Pitman, 1990.
Smythe, John, Colette Dorward and Jerome Reback, *Corporate Reputation: Managing the New Strategic Asset*. Century Business, 1992.
Stone, Norman, *How to Manage Public Relations*. McGraw-Hill, 1991.
White, Dr Jon, *How to Understand and Manage Public Relations*. Century Business, 1991.
Winner, Paul, *Effective PR Management*, 2nd edn. Kogan Page, 1993.

Financial Public Relations

Andrews, Kenneth, *The Financial Public Relations Handbook*. Woodhead-Faulkner, 1990.
Bing, Richard and Pat Bowman (eds), *Financial Public Relations*, 2nd edn. Butterworth Heinemann, 1993.
Graham, John and David Lake, *Investor Relations*. Euromoney Publications and Dewe Rogerson, 1990.

■ Local Government

Fedorcio, Dick, Peter Heaton and Kevin Madden, *Public Relations for Local Government*. Longman, 1991.

■ Government Relations

Connelly, John, *Dealing with Whitehall*. Century Business, 1992.
Miller, C, *Lobbying – Understanding and Influencing the Corridors of Power*, 2nd edn. Basil Blackwell, 1990.

■ Public Relations Techniques

Bernstein, David, *Company Image and Reality: A Critique of Corporate Communications*. Cassell, 1986.
Black, Sam, *Exhibitions and Conferences from A to Z*. Modino, 1989.
Ind, Nicholas, *The Corporate Image*, 2nd edn. Kogan Page, 1992.
Olins, Wally, *Corporate Identity*. Thames & Hudson, 1989.
Phillips, David, *Evaluating Press Coverage*. Kogan Page, 1992.
Sleight, Steve, *Sponsorship*. McGraw-Hill, 1989.

■ Internal Communication

Walters, Mike, *What about the Workers?* Institute of Personnel Management, 1990.
Wilkinson, Theon (ed.), *The Communications Challenge – Personnel and PR Perspectives*. Institute of Personnel Management, 1989.

■ Marketing Support

Wragg, David W., *Public Relations for Sales and Marketing Management*, 2nd edn. Kogan Page, 1989.

■ Case Histories/Studies

Black, Sam, *International Public Relations*. Kogan Page, 1993.
Moss, Danny, *Public Relations in Practice – A Casebook*. Routledge, 1990.
Nally, Margaret (ed.), *International Relations in Practice*. Kogan Page, 1992.

■ Annuals

Financial Times Public Relations Yearbook. Financial Times with The Public Relations Consultants Association.
Hollis Press and Public Relations Annual. Hollis Directories.
Hollis Europe Annual. Hollis Directories.

■ Periodicals

IPR Journal, formerly *Public Relations*, monthly, Institute of Public Relations.
PR Week, weekly, Haymarket Marketing Publications Ltd.
International Public Relations Review, quarterly, International Public Relations Association.

■ Out of print

Bland, Michael, *Be Your Own Man: A Public Relations Guide for the Small Businessman*, 2nd edn. Kogan Page, 1987.
Capper, A. and P. Cunard, *Public Relations Casebook*. Kogan Page, 1990.
Ellis, Nigel, *Parliamentary Lobbying*. Butterworth Heinemann, 1988.
Hart, Norman, *Effective Corporate Relations*. McGraw-Hill, 1988.
Hayes, Roger and Reginald Watts, *The Corporate Revolution: New Strategies for Executive Leadership*. Butterworth Heinemann, 1986.
Regester, Michael, *Crisis Management*. Hutchinson, 1987.
Regester, Michael and Neil Ryder, *Investor Relations*. Hutchinson Business Books, 1990.
Richardson, Tom, *Public Relations in Local Government*. Butterworth Heinemann, 1988.
Turner, Stuart, *How to get Sponsorship*. Kogan Page, 1989.

Other useful publications are mentioned in the text of this book or in the *Notes and References* section, pp. 285–291.

Notes and References

Introduction

1. Wang An-chieh of Hsiu-shui, *The Mustard Seed Garden Manual of Painting*, Chao shih, 1679. Modern translation by Mai-Mai Sze, Princeton University Press, 8th printing, 1992.
2. *Public Relations Qualifications and Professional Standards*, Institute of Public Relations, 1994.
3. IPR Sword of Excellence awards, 1993.

1 What Public Relations can do

1. P. W. Atkins, *The Creation*, W. H. Freeman, 1981.
2. Presentation at an Interact Seminar, 1988.
3. *IPR Journal*, January 1994.
4. *PR Week*, 20 May 1993.
5. IPR Sword of Excellence awards, 1993.
6. Ibid.
7. Norman Stone, *How to Manage Public Relations*, McGraw-Hill, 1991.
8. *PR Week*, 21 August 1994.
9. *IPR Journal*, January 1994.
10. Michael G. Morgan, 'Deciding to Visit the Osteopath', *Inter Medica*, Vol. 1, No. 11 (1993).
11. *PR Week*, 17 February 1994.
12. Case authenticated by Scope: Communications.
13. IPR Sword of Excellence Awards, 1993.
14. Acknowledgements to the Chartered Institute of Journalists.
15. *IPR Journal*, February 1994.
16. Trevor Morris, Managing Director, Quentin Bell Organisation.
17. *PC Answers*, August 1993.
18. *Kestrel in Focus*, No. 5 (Autumn 1993), Kestrel Communications.
19. Robin Leigh-Pemberton, Speech at Tallow Chandlers Hall, London, December 1991.
20. Tim Felton, *Horse and Hound*, July 1993.

2 Choosing and Using Public Relations

1. E. F. L Brech (ed.), *The Principles and Practice of Management*, Longmans, 1966.
2. IPR *Guideline No. 2 – Public Relations Practice: Its Role and Parameters*, 1991.
3. *Management Development to The Millennium*, Institute of Management, 1993.
4. Wendy Hirsh, *What Makes a Manager?*, Institute of Manpower Studies, 1988.
5. PRet Public Relations Education and Training Matrix, 1989.

6. Ibid.
7. This checklist is heavily indebted to *Best Practice – Managing Public Relations and the Client/Agency or Consultancy Relationship*, Incorporated Society of British Advertisers, 1994.
8. *PR Week*, 28 April 1994.
9. Ibid.
10. *IPR Journal*, January 1994.
11. *PC User*, 6–19 April 1994.

■ 3   Public Relations and Marketing

1. Professor Gilles Marion, Department of Marketing, Groupe ESGE, Lyon, in *Perspectives on Marketing Management*, edited by M. J. Baker, Vol. 3, John Wiley, 1993.
2. *IPR Journal*, June 1994.
3. *PR Week*, 26 May 1994.
4. *A Commonsense Approach to your Communications Budget*, British Business Press, 1986.
5. *PR Week*, 12 August 1994.
6. *PR Week*, 5 August 1993.
7. *PR Week*, 21 January 1994.
8. Case authenticated by Lambeth Children's Theatre Company.
9. *PR Week*, 5 August 1994.
10. Case authenticated by Welbeck Golin/Harris.
11. *PR Week*, 3 February 1994.
12. Case authenticated by Academy Computers.
13. Case authenticated by Infopress.
14. Case authenticated by The Royal Tournament.
15. *IPR Journal*, November 1994.
16. *Marketing: Communicating with the Consumer*, Mercury Books, in association with the CBI, 1989.

■ 4   Research and Public Relations

1. Roger Corbin, Nicklin Advertising, addressing the 2nd Business Advertising Conference, London, 1989.
2. Christopher West, 'Getting the Information', *Effective Industrial Marketing*, edited by Norman Hart, Kogan Page, 1994.
3. *A Guide to Market Research*, IPR Local Government Group, September 1993.
4. Acknowledgements to BT.
5. Case authenticated by Paragon.
6. Nigel Holmes, *Designer's Guide to Creating Charts and Diagrams*, Watson-Guptill, 1985.
7. *Marketing: Communicating with the Consumer*, Mercury Books, in association with the CBI, 1989.
8. Colin Morris, *What the Papers Didn't Say*, Epworth Press, 1971.

■ 5   Corporate and Financial Relations

1. Drawn from Concise Oxford, Pocket English and other dictionaries.
2. Wally Olins, *Corporate Identity*, Thames & Hudson, 1989.
3. Acknowledgements to *brand strategy*, *Checkout*, *Financial World*, Interbrand, Loughborough University Business School, *Management Today*, *Marketing* and Neilsen.
4. *brand strategy*, No. 54 (June 1993), Centaur Communications.
5. 'Backing the arts is good for business', *The Independent*, 9 December 1993.
6. Ibid.
7. *Setting Standards for the 1990s*, Association for Business Sponsorship of the Arts, 1990.
8. *The Conduct of Financial Communications*, IPR City and Financial Group, 1991.
9. *The Going Public Handbook*, Price Waterhouse, April 1994.
10. Case authenticated by Lombard Natwest.
11. Barrie Pearson, *Successful Management Buyouts*, Livingstone Fisher plc, 1993.
12. Case authenticated by GA Life.
13. Interact seminar, November 1988.

■ 6   Government Relations

1. Vladimir Tsimbalov, Head of Balt Art, the first PR agency to be set up in St Petersburg.
2. Sir John Hole, *The Civilisation of Europe in the Renaissance*, Harper Collins, 1993.
3. Maurice Ashley, *The English Civil War*, rev. edn, Alan Sutton Publishing, 1990.
4. S. T. Miller, *British Political History 1784–1939*, McDonald & Evans, 1980; Kenneth O. Morgan (ed.), *Oxford Illustrated History of Britain*, Oxford University Press, 1986; Sir Llewellyn Woodward, *The Age of Reform 1815–1870*, 2nd edn, Clarendon Press, 1992.
5. *PR Week*, 17 February 1994.
6. Case authenticated by The Rowland Company.
7. *PR Week*, 28 April 1994.
8. Acknowledgements to Peter Heaton, DTW Group.
9. *A Guide to PR Strategy*, IPR Local Government Group, September 1993.
10. *Public Relations in Local Government*, IPR, Spring 1993.
11. Acknowledgements to Westminster Communications.
12. Case authenticated by Wycombe District Council.
13. *The Observer*, 6 November 1988.
14. Case authenticated by Kestrel for Worldcom.

■ 7   Employee and Community Relations

1. Most of us have come across something like this in real life.
2. Acknowledgements to TSB and Dewe Rogerson.

3. *Effective Business Communication*, Association of Business Communicators, 1992.
4. IPR Sword of Excellence Awards, 1994.
5. Case authenticated by Jones Stroud Insulations.
6. *Guidelines for Business Sponsors of Educational Material*, NCC, 1988.
7. *The Independent*, 30 August 1993.
8. Alastair Bruce, *Community Relations Study Tour to the USA: Challenges for UK Managers*, Bruce Naughton Wade, 1994.
9. *Management Today*, August 1994.
10. Acknowledgements to Cherwell District Council, Oxfordshire.
11. *New Scientist*, 24 July 1993.
12. *The Environment Business Guide*, DTI Publications, September 1993; *Environmental Guidelines for the Professional Manager*, Institute of Management, April 1994.
13. Peter Hunt, Shell UK Community Relations Department. Talk to Greater London Group of IPR, June 1993.

■ 8   The Third Sector

1. Sir Dennis Landau, Chairman, Unity Trust Bank plc, addressing Forum for the Social Economy, London, 1993.
2. Based on material provided by Malcolm Hurlston Corporate Consultancy.
3. *Daily Express*, 30 June 1993; *Sunday Times*, 22 August 1993.
4. *Top-ix News*, Spring 1994.
5. Case authenticated by RAC Rescue.
6. Norman Stone, *How to Manage Public Relations*, McGraw-Hill, 1991.
7. Acknowledgements to the Mothers' Union.
8. *Community Affairs Briefing*, December 1993, Burson Marsteller.
9. From 'Non-Profit Organisations' (p. 135) onwards this chapter draws on material provided by Jane Hammond, Trident Training Services.

■ 9   Customer and Consumer Relations

1. David Perkins, 'Loyalty Marketing Services', *Management Today*, January 1994.
2. A. Bullock, O. Stallybrass, S. Trombley (eds), *Dictionary of Modern Thought*, Fontana, 1988.
3. Case authenticated by Cohn & Wolfe.
4. *brand strategy* No. 54 (June 1993) Centaur Communications.
5. Bernard Dubois and Renato Zancan Marchetti in *Perspectives on Marketing Management*, edited by M. J. Baker, Vol. 3, John Wiley, 1993.
6. David Jobber 'What Makes People Buy?', *Effective Industrial Marketing*, edited by Norman Hart, Kogan Page, 1994.
7. Acknowledgements to Confédération Européenne des Relations Publiques and Kymi.
8. *Meetings and Incentive Travel*, May/June 1994.
9. *The Independent*, 17 March 1992.
10. *Professional Manager*, Institute of Management, January 1994.

11. *Management Today*, January 1994.
12. *Caring for Customers*, Southern Electric Consumer Service, July 1994.
13. *Management Today*, January 1994.
14. Case authenticated by Polaroid.
15. Case authenticated by Stafford-Miller Ltd.
16. Case authenticated by Beechey Morgan Associates.

■ 10   Media Relations

1. Quoted in Nicholas Coleridge's *Paper Tigers*, Heinemann, 1993.
2. IPR Student Group's 'Meet the Press' event, reported in *Public Relations*, January 1994.
3. Survey by Grice West, reported in *Public Relations*, January 1994.
4. *Recommended Practice Paper No. 1 – The News Release*, IPR, 1991.
5. *Press Attitudes to News Sources and the Role of PR*, Two-Ten Communications, 1993.
6. Adrian Berkeley, LLB, FRSA, in *The 1994 Directory of Professional Photography*, British Institute of Professional Photography, 1994.
7. *Sunday Times*, 1 May 1994.
8. The Radio Lynx Syndicated Tape Survey 1994.
9. *Paraphrase*, Issue 14, 1993.
10. *PC Answers*, August 1993.
11. Frank Jefkins, *Press Relations Practice*, Intertext, 1968.
12. *Advertorials – the Readers' Perspective*, National Magazines and the Research Business Group, 1993/4.
13. *Sunday Times*, 20 March 1994.
14. *PR Week*, 29 July 1993.
15. Acknowledgements to the Association for Business Sponsorship of the Arts.
16. IPR Guideline No. 4, *The Use and Misuse of Embargos*, IPR, 1991.
17. Acknowledgement to the IPR as the co-signatories of the joint statement.
18. Fred Plester, *Bedfordshire on Sunday*, Editor of the Year 1987 and 1988.

■ 11   Organising and Training for Excellence

1. *Springs of Jewish Wisdom*, Burns & Oates, 1969.
2. Case authenticated by Scope: Communications.
3. Charles Handy, *Gods of Management*, 3rd edn, Century, 1991.
4. Ibid.
5. Wendy Hirsh, *What Makes a Manager?*, Institute of Manpower Studies, 1988.
6. PRet Public Relations Education and Training Matrix, 1989.
7. Case authenticated by Brent Council.
8. Acknowledgements to Cicada Consultants, National Council for Vocational Qualifications and Nigel Bain Consultancy.
9. *Boardroom Briefings*, Institute of Management, 1993.
10. *Management Development to the Millennium*, Institute of Management, 1993.
11. Acknowledgements to IPR Education and Training Committee.

12. *PC User*, 20 April 1994.

■ 12   Paying for Public Relations

1.   I think I may have been the first to say this.
2.   *PR Week*, 20 and 27 January 1994.
3.   *Marketing Week*, 28 May 1988 and *PR Week*, 3 February 1994.
4.   Case authenticated by Eureka! For Children.
5.   *The Independent*, 29 January 1994.
6.   Case authenticated by Beauty International.
7.   *Marketing Services Monitor*, June 1994.
8.   Acknowledgements to the PRCA and the Incorporated Society of British Advertisers.
9.   *Marketing Business*, Chartered Institute of Marketing, June 1993.

■ 13   Public Relations in a Crisis

1.   Sam Wauchope, managing director, Acorn Computers, *The Independent on Sunday*, 15 November 1992.
2.   James Gleick, *Genius*, Little, Brown, 1992.
3.   Quoted by permission of Kate Graham, Kate Graham Public Relations.
4.   Malcolm Browne, 'The Disaster Business', *Management Today*, October 1993; Jane Bird, 'Better Safe than Sorry', *The Sunday Times*, 28 November 1993.
5.   Ray Morley, *Crisis – a Timetable for Recovery*, Commercial Union, 1993.
6.   *PR Week*, 20 May 1993.
7.   Source: the financial press.
8.   Smythe, Dorward, Reback, *Corporate Reputation*, Century Business, 1992.
9.   *PR Week*, 8 April 1993.
10. IPR Sword of Excellence Awards, 1993.
11. Ibid.
12. Acknowledgements to Kate Graham, Kate Graham Public Relations.

■ 14   Evaluation

1.   Julia Thorn, Chairman and Chief Executive, Paragon, at Interact seminar, 1991.
2.   Radio Lynx Report, *Music Marketing Services*, 1994.
3.   IPR Sword of Excellence Awards, 1993.
4.   Norman Stone, *How to Manage Public Relations*, McGraw-Hill, 1991.
5.   Edmund Capon, *Qin Shihuang – Terracotta Warriors and Horses*, International Cultural Corporation of Australia, 1983.
6.   *IPR Journal*, April 1994. Research conducted by Gillian Hogg for Stirling University, supported by the IPR's Scotland Group and Scottish Enterprise.
7.   IPR Sword of Excellence Awards, 1993.
8.   Nicola Ilett, director of Bullet Communications, special report on Healthcare, *PR Week*, 9 September 1993.

9.   Case authenticated by Avon and Somerset Constabulary.
10.   Case authenticated by Tommy's Campaign.
11.   Alastair Bruce, *Community Relations Study Tour to the USA: Challenges for UK Managers*, Bruce Naughton Wade, 1994.
12.   Case authenticated by DTI and P Four Consultancy, with input from technology consultant Peter Judge.
13.   Peter Judge, *The Road to Open Systems*, DTI, 1994.
14.   IPR Sword of Excellence Awards, 1994.

■ In Conclusion

1.   Wang An-chieh of Hsiu-shui, *The Mustard Seed Garden Manual of Painting*, Chao shih, 1679. Modern translation by Mai-Mai Sze, Princeton University Press, 8th printing, 1992.

Index

Abbey National 37, 144–6, 172, 236–7
abbreviations, list of xvii
ABC *see* Association of British
  Communicators
ABFD *see* Association of British Factors
  and Discounters
ABSA (Association for Business
  Sponsorship of the Arts) *see*
  sponsorship
abstinence 11
Academy Computers 43–4, 163, 202–3
ACBE *see* Advisory Committee on
  Business and the Environment
added value 143–7
admiration 70
advertising
  brands 69
  cannot do job of PR 15, 33
  corporate identity 67
  equivalent advertising values 159, 234,
    236
  expenditure related to PR 200
  Highland Spring 47
  knocking copy 14
  PR cannot do job of 15
  Royal Tournament 48, 241
  in third sector 139
  WDC 102
advertorials 46, 94, 175–7
Advisory Committee on Business and the
  Environment (ACBE) 127
AEEU *see* Amalgamated Engineering and
  Electrical Union
Amalgamated Engineering and Electrical
  Union (AEEU) 110
Amanda Barry 205
America *see* USA
American Express (Amex) 45, 123–4
Amex *see* American Express
analysis xxiii, 13, 249
  Abbey National 144, 237
  Academy Computers 43
  advertorials 176, 177
  Avon & Somerset Constabulary 13,
    239
  Banana Group 157–8

Brent Council 188–9
Classic FM 235
consultancy earnings 27–8
consultancy staff earnings 210–11
consultancy staff levels 28
DML 96
DTI Open Systems 244
EC 106
Eureka! 203
GA Life 86
in-house earnings 210–11
Lambeth Children's Theatre
  Company 38–9
Lombard Natwest 80
markets 36–41
national press preferences 169
perception 60
Polaroid 154
Polo Mint 41
RAC 133
regional press preferences 170
Royal Tournament brief 47–8
Royal Tournament receipts 240–1
salary costs 210
Shell Select 58
Stafford-Miller 156
WDC 101
Anti-Corn Law League 92–5
Apple Computers 37, 197
Argent Group 200
assessment *see* evaluation
Association for Business Sponsorship of the
  Arts (ABSA) *see* sponsorship
Association of British Communicators
  (ABC) 112
Association of British Factors and
  Discounters (ABFD) 80
Atkins, P. W. 1
attitude 1, 8, 10, 57, 186
Audience Selection 53
audio visuals 112–5, 189–90
audit
  communications 59
  performance 100
  PR 62–3
Avenger 11

Avon & Somerset Constabulary 13, 52, 95, 239–40
awareness 5, 6, 16, 101, 102

Babycham 72
Band & Brown 205
BAIE *see* British Association of Industrial Editors
Bail Bandits 52, 239–40
Banana Group 33, 53, 157–9, 234, 236
Bananergy *see* Banana Group
Banbury 125–6
Bank of England 17
bar charts 61
Barnardos 7, 136
Barnes, Paul 99
Baxters of Speyside 105
Bayeux Tapestry 91
BDA *see* British Dental Association
BDHF *see* British Dental Health Foundation
Beaumont & Sons 197
Beauty International 205–6
Beechey, Jane 158
Beechey Morgan Associates 40, 54, 158, 236
behaviour 1
believability *see* credibility
Bell, Quentin *see* Quentin Bell
Benn's Media 161
Berkeley, Adrian 168
Best of Britain 75
BIMBO *see* management buy-in and buy-out
Biss Lancaster 7
Black Box 33
Blain, Gordon 121
Bodyshop 45
Bose 40
BP 243
brainpower 21
brands 36, 41, 68, 69–72
Breath of Life *see* St John Ambulance
Brech, E. F. L. 18
Brent Council 112, 152–3, 188–90
Brent Walker 95
briefing *see* press
British Aerospace 6, 57
British Airways 6
British Association of Industrial Editors (BAIE) 44
British Dental Association (BDA) 156
British Dental Health Foundation (BDHF) 146, 157

British Maritime Charitable Foundation 5
broadcasting 170–2
    Classic FM 12, 13, 233–5
    Kiss 100 FM 42
Bruce, Alastair 122, 243
Bruce Naughton Wade 122
Brunel University, 101
BT 55, 154, 202, 205
budget 198–213
    Abbey National 145
    Academy Computers 44, 202
    Apple Computers 37
    Argent Group 200
    Armand Hammer 207
    Assi Doman 207
    Association of Contact Lens Manufacturers 204
    Avon & Somerset Constabulary 239
    Bahamas Tourism Office 207
    Banana Group 158
    Beauty International 206
    Billington Sugar 206
    Black Country Development Corporation 204
    Bose 40
    Brent Council 100, 190
    BT 202, 205
    Budget Rent-a-Car 207
    Capital Regions, USA 205
    CBFA 132
    checks 212–3
    Cinergi 199
    Classic FM 13
    competitive 200–1
    confidential 80, 97
    control 209–11
    D-Day 198
    DML 97
    DTI 208, 245
    Easington District Council 202
    East Sussex County Council 202
    EC 107
    Elgie Stewart Smith 88
    Endeso 200
    Endsleigh 178
    Eureka! 203
    European Association of Aesthetic Medicine 201
    Food and Drink Federation 207
    Football League 178
    French Government 208
    GA Life 86
    Gateway 2000 205

budget (*cont.*)
  guesswork 208
  Guys 40, 201
  Hay Personnel Services 205
  Health Education Authority 204
  Henkel 205
  Hertsmere Council 96
  Hippo Club 74
  IBM 199, 205
  Investment in People 205
  Jersey 205
  K'Nex 200
  LCTC sponsorship 39
  Lincolnshire University 205
  Lightwater Valley 234
  Lloyds Bank 73
  local government 99–101
  Lombard Natwest 80
  London Clubs 205
  Malaysian Timber Council 207
  Mazda Cars 205
  McDonalds 208
  Mobil 116
  Mondex 205
  motor cycling 207
  Motorola 205
  NCH Action for Children 204
  Neilsen 204
  Northern Telecom, 200
  Pfizer 207
  Polaroid 155
  Police Federation, 8, 207
  Polo Mint 42
  principles 199–201
  RAC 134
  related to advertising 200
  related to turnover 199
  RNIB 200
  Robinsons 207
  Romania 200
  Rover Tomcat 75
  Royal Mail Stamps 37
  Royal Tournament 48, 208, 241
  RTZ 74
  Shell Select 58
  Solent & Severn Inns 204
  Southern Electric 204
  Smith, W.H. 208
  Stafford-Miller 156
  Station Bravo 205
  task-directed 201
  Taunton Cider 36
  Telewest 200
  Tring International 205

  TSB 112
  TUC 204
  Vidal Sassoon 42–3
  Visionware 38
  VNRs 172
  Warner Brothers 204
  WDC 101, 202
  Whirlpool 207
  zero-based 201
budget brackets 201–8
  under £50,000 202–4
  £50,000–£100,000 204–6
  over £100,000, under £350,000 206–7
  £350,000–£750,000 207
  over £750,000 207–8
Burson Marsteller 204, 205
business
  market 36
  objectives *see* objectives
  sponsorship of educational
    material 121–2
Business in the Community 119
Business Users Group 154–5
buyers
  educational 121–2
  family 147–8
  industrial 148
  influences 36, 147–151
  key 150–1
buy-in and management buy-out
    (BIMBO) 81–3

cable TV 122
CAD *see* Computer Aided Design
Cadburys 70
Calder, Ritchie xx
Cameron Choate 207
Canning, Alison 28
Care for the Family 11
Careline 153
caring PR 7
Carlos, Dave 11
case histories, list of xiv
catalogues 32–3
cause-related marketing 44–5
CBFA *see* Co-operative Bank Financial
    Advisers
CBI *see* Confederation of British Industry
CDC *see* Cherwell District Council
CERP *see* Confédération Européenne des
    Relations Publiques 150
Certificate of Excellence *see* Sword of
    Excellence
Chanel 174

change 8, 9, 22, 61, 66, 123–4
Charge Against Hunger 45, 123
charities 241–2
Chartered Institute of Journalists
 (CIoJ) 13, 182, 271
Chartered Society of Designers 69
charters 99, 152, 190
charts 60, 61
checklists, list of xv
chemistry 231
Cherwell District Council (CDC) 125–6
Chinese Whispers 115
choosing a design consultancy 68–9
choosing a PR consultancy 23–6
Christian Aid 139–40
Chrysler 10, 11
CIoJ *see* Chartered Institute of
 Journalists
Cinergi 199
Citigate 204, 221
City & Financial Group 17, 76
Civil War 91–2
Clapham omnibus 98
Clarke, Alison 8
Classic FM 12, 13, 233–5
Clear English award 87
Cleveland Supertram 126
client matching 27
Clothes Show 71, 206
Cobden 93–4
Coca-Cola 69, 70
codes of conduct
 Institute of Management 277–81
 Institute of Public Relations 265–73
 Public Relations Consultants
  Association 27, 273–7
Cohn & Wolfe 28, 37, 144, 236, 237
colour separations 181–2, 271–3
combination research *see* research
Commercial Union 216–18
commissioning photography 168
communicating with staff 109–118
communications audit *see* audit
Communications Group *see* The
 Communications Group
Communist Manifesto 95
community relations 12, 109, 118–28
Community Relations Triangle *see*
 triangles
Compaq Computers 236, 238
competitive budgeting *see* budgeting
competitors 153–4
computer aided design (CAD) 43, 44, 163
Computer Associates 59–60

Computers for Schools 124
condoms in soup 105
conduct, professional *see* codes of
 conduct
Confédération Européenne des Relations
 Publiques (CERP) 150
Confederation of British Industry
 (CBI) 49, 63–4
consultancies 23–32, 67, 68–9, 211–12
 list of 255–64
consultation 124–7
consumers 35–50, 141–9
 advertorials, perception of 175–6
 Apple Computers 37
 bananas 157–9
 brand rankings 69
 Business Users Group 154–5
 Corn Laws 92–4
 Cow & Gate 146
 crises affecting 225–6
 EC 33, 64, 106–8
 GA Life 86–7
 Highland Spring 47
 NCC 74, 121–2, 138–9
 personal finance products 85
 Polaroid 154–5
 Polo Mint 41
 research 52–3
 Securicor 143
 Shell Select 57–9
 Toyota 103
contracts 96
control/benefit relationship 130, 131
Co-operative Bank 140
 Financial Advisers 132
Cope Matthews 47
Corbin, Roger 51
Corn Laws *see* Anti-Corn Law League
corporate
 design 5, 67–8, 68–9
 identity xxii, 66–7, 71
 image xxii 12, 66
 relations 66–90
 values 67–8
cosmetic surgery 40, 201
cost
 analysis of Royal Tournament 240–1
 control 209–11
 going public 77
 justification 208–9
 materials 212
 overheads 209–11
 salaries 210–11
 services 212

costing procedures 209
COTS *see* opportunities to see (OTS)
Counsellor 53, 156
Cow & Gate 146
creativity 193–5, 231
credibility 14, 15, 36, 151–2
credits 178–9
creosote 14
crisis PR 214–27
  aftermath 226–7
  definitions 214
  Commercial Union 216–8
  Hoover 224
  management 224–6
  Piper Alpha 215
  planning 216, 218, 221, 223, 224, 225
  recovery from 215–6, 227
Croft, Roger 33
CPS *see* Crown Prosecution Service
Crown Prosecution Service (CPS) 124–5
cumulative opportunities to see
  (COTS) *see* opportunities to see
  (OTS)
Customer Pledge 58–9
customers 35–50, 141–59
  business 36–7, 149–50
  centres 156–7
  competitors 153–4
  corporate 66–90
  crime 224
  in a crisis 220–1, 224
  dissatisfied 141
  enhancement 143
  environment 127
  intermediary 45–6
  Kymi 149
  internal 151–2
  local government 99–101, 189–90
  marketing 7, 35, 49
  M & S 70–1
  price 71
  quality 142
  Toyota 68
  value 142
  voters 151
customising 143–4
Customs and Excise 152
cycle of change *see* change

D-day commemorations 198–9
Das Kapital 95
data
  primary 52–3
  qualitative 54
  quantitative 54
  secondary 52
David Clark Associates 204
deadlines 180–1
decision making 15, 103–4, 147–8
Decision Making Unit (DMU) 148
Dennis Davidson Associates 204
Department of Trade and Industry
  (DTI) 43, 127, 208, 244–7
design 47, 67–9
Design Council 69
Designosaurs 43
desk research 52, 58
Devonport Management Ltd
  (DML) 96–7, 208
Dewe Rogerson 111, 200
Dickens, Charles 95
Digital 73
dinosaur effect 43
direct marketing 40
disasters *see* crisis
distinctiveness 79–81
DML *see* Devonport Management Ltd
DMU *see* Decision Making Unit
Dobie, Clare 88
Downing Street, No 10 36, 47, 97
Dr Barnardo's *see* Barnardos
DTI *see* Department of Trade &
  Industry
Dunseath Stephens 223–4

earnings
  consultancies 27–8, 211–12
  consultancy staff 210–12
  in-house staff 210–11
Easington District Council 202
East Sussex County Council 202
EAV *see* equivalent advertising value
editorial integrity 46, 98, 175, 177, 181
Edsel 10
education *see also* training
  integrity 74
  involvement 119–22
  qualifications 190–1, 268–9
  sponsorship 74, 121
Egyptians 91
Elgie Stewart Smith 5, 88
Elstree Studios 95
e-mail 34
embargo 180
employee relations 109–17
Endsleigh *see* Football League
Energis 153–4
Engels, Friedrich 95

enhancement 143
environment 127–8
equivalent advertising value (EAV) 159, 234–6
Essex Brewer *see* Ridleys
Eureka! for Children 6, 203–4
Europe 21, 22, 23, 64, 102–3, 104, 106–8, 130, 149–50, 190, 207, 208, 252, 253, 259
evaluation 2, 17, 228–48, 250
 Abbey National 145–6, 237
 Academy Computers 202–3
 assessment 13, 230–1
 Anti-Corn Law League 94
 Avon & Somerset Constabulary 13, 240
 Banana Group 159, 236
 community relations 242–3
 DTI 247
 GA Life 87
 Lightwater Valley 234
 Lombard Natwest feedback 81
 measurement 228–34
 media 232–8
 process 228
 real reward 121
 Royal Tournament 241
 strategic 12
 WDC 102
events 138, 172–4
exhibitions 139
expectations 24, 35, 141, 231
expenses 139–40

face-to-face discussions 54
factoring 79–80
Farrant, Emma 197
feature articles 167–8
fees 211–12
fever charts 61
figures, list of xiii
Financial Dynamics 200, 221
financial relations 66–90
financial sector 76–90
Finland 149–50
Firefly Communications 37
Fishburn Hedges 7, 204
Fleming, Lesley 44
Flora Martin PR 43–4, 163, 202
flotation 76–9
 timetable 78–9
Football League 178
Ford 10–11
 Focus on 177

Forum for the Social Economy 130
Fox, George 90
Fraser, Liz 28
French Academy 14
function of PR *see* public relations
fundraising
 events 138
 NCH Children in Action 202

GA Life *see* General Accident Life
Gallup 58, 87
Garvey, Steve 172
Gantt charts 61
Gaymers 72
GCI 207
General Accident Life (GA Life) 52–3, 86–7
General Motors 11
generic PR 157–9
Gettysburg 95
Giovanni Botero 91
GJW Government Relations 99
Goldesgeyme, David 73
good practice *see* codes of conduct
Good Relations 38
government relations 91–108
Graham, Kate 215, 225
graphs 61
group discussion 54
Group 4, 219–20
Guardian Direct 174
guidelines, list of xvi
Gummer, Peter 36
Guy's Hospital 40, 201, 242

Häagen Dazs 7
Hammond, Jane 140
Hampstead Health Authority 7
Handel Communications 36, 204
Handy, Professor Charles 186
Hanna, Vincent 49
Hard Times 95
harmonisation 105
Hart, Norman xix
Haywood, Roger 16–17, 107
Health Education Authority 204
Hertsmere Council 95–6
Highland Spring 36, 46–7
Hill & Knowlton 40, 207
Hippo Club 74
histograms 61
Hoffnung, Gerard 142
Hogg, Gillian 24, 231
Hoover 224

hostile takeover bids   *see* takeovers
house journals   111, 138
House of Commons   *see* Parliament
house style   66, 69
Hunt, Peter   128
Hurlston, Malcolm   130

Ian Smyth Associates   205
IBM   70, 199, 246
ICL   229, 246
IES   *see* Institute for Employment
    Studies
IM   *see* Institute of Management
in-house PR   23–32, 35, 210–11
Incorporated Society of British Advertisers
    (ISBA)   182, 212, 271
infomercials   46, 177
Infopress   34, 36, 47, 59–60, 126, 154, 233
information super highway   34
information technology   197, 244–7
inheritance generation   88
Institute of Journalists   *see* Chartered
    Institute of Journalists
Institute for Employment Studies (IES)   21
Institute of Management (IM)   21, 127–8,
    193
Institute of Manpower Studies   *see*
    Institute for Employment Studies
Insurance Checks   144–6, 236–7
Institute of Public Relations (IPR)   xxii,
    xxiii, 22, 49, 182, 196–7, 271
integrity
    editorial   46, 98, 175, 177, 181
    educational   74
    management   222
    professional   181, 267, 269, 275, 278,
        279
intermediaries   45
Intermedica   9–10
internal PR   6–7, 12, 57, 109–18, 149
    principles of   111, 115–18, 137
internal customers   *see* customers
international research   63
interviews   172
involvement   36, 120
IoJ   *see* Chartered Institute of Journalists
IPR   *see* Institute of Public Relations
IPR Journal   24, 190, 231
ISBA   *see* Incorporated Society of British
    Advertisers

Jewish wisdom   183
Jobber, Dr David   148
Jones, Dr Hilary   158

Jones Stroud Insulations   120–1
Judge, Peter   247
Junior Champs   30–2
Just-Add-Oil   7

KAP hypothesis   9–10
KBH Communications   12–13
Kestrel Communications   6, 16, 33, 38, 48,
    107–8, 208, 240–1
Ketchum PR   207
key buyers   150–1
Key Communications   205
kidnapping   224
Kiss 100 FM   42
K'Nex   200
knowledge   22, 183, 187
Kodak   79
Koestler, Arthur   193
KPMG   245
Kwik-Fit   223–4
Kymi   149–50

Lambeth Children's Theatre Company
    (LCTC)   38–9
language   103–8, 153
Landau, Sir Dennis   129
Law Society   132–3
LCTC   *see* Lambeth Children's Theatre
    Company
Leedex PR   204
Leeds University   86
LeFevre Williamson   80, 208
Leicester School of Engineering   203
Lightwater Valley   223, 234, 236
Lincoln, Abraham   95
line graphs   61
Livingstone Guarantee   81–2
Lloyds Bank   73
lobbying   94, 98, 239–40, 269–71
local government   99–102, 202
Local Government Group   99, 100
Lombard Natwest   79–81, 208
London Fashion Show   42
Lorenzo de Medici   91
Loughborough University   70
Lowe Bell   198, 205
Lynne Franks PR   43, 205
Lye, Kate   222
Lynx PR   223, 234

Maastricht   102
Magellan Medical Communications   201
mail order   32–3
mailings   48, 107

management
  buy-in 81–3
  buy-out 81–3
  in the 21st century 21, 196
  integrity 222
managing PR 2, 19, 20, 28, 29
Manning Selvage & Lee 207
Marion, Professor Gilles 35
market
  analysis 36–41
  business 36
  financial services 85
  intermediaries 45–6
  review driven 88
Marketing Opinion Research International
  (MORI) 5, 8, 15, 207
marketing 7
  and corporate identity 67
  mix 69
  and PR 7, 35–50
Marketing Guild 62
Marks & Spencer 70–1
Mars 174
Marx, Karl 95
MBI *see* management by-in
MBO *see* management buy-out
McDonalds 70, 208
McKeone, Dermot 233
McNally, Tom 219
measurement *see* evaluation
media 137, 160–82
media credits 178–9
media listings 160–1
Media Measurement 13, 233–5
media measurement *see* evaluation
Medical Imprint 207
membership survey, IPR 49
message 12, 15
Michael Peters 47
Microsoft 16, 40
Middle Ages 91
Mills, Barbara 124
Mirage International Systems 174
mission statements 67, 72
Mobil 106, 116
MORI *see* Marketing Opinion Research
  International
Morris, Colin 64
Mothers' Union (MU) 137
motivation 12, 22, 45
MU *see* Mothers' Union
multi-dimensional perception 59
multipliers 210–11
MultiStrategies 131

Murdoch, Rupert 160
mustard seed method xxii, 249
Muzack, W.A. 56

Names in the News 62
National Breakdown 143
National Consumer Council (NCC) 74,
  121, 122, 138–9
National Heritage, Department of 198–9
National Magazines 176
national newspapers, PR input to 169
National Opinion Polls (NOP) 53
National Peanut Council of America
  (NPCA) 238
National Union of Journalists 182, 271
National Vocational Qualifications
  (NVQs) 190–1
NCC *see* National Consumer Council
NCH Action for Children 204
Neilsen 204
Nescafé 70
Nestlé 70
Newcastle University 53
niche products 7–8, 15
Noble, Mary 174
non-profit organisations 135–40
NOP *see* National Opinion Polls
Northern Lights 6, 52–3, 86–7, 203
Northern Telecom 200
NUJ *see* National Union of Journalists
NVQs *see* National Vocational
  Qualifications
Nynex Cablecomm 219

objectives xxiii, 4–11
  Abbey National 144, 237
  Academy Computers 43
  Anti-Corn Law League 92
  Avon & Somerset Constabulary 239
  audio visuals 112
  Banana Group 158
  Beauty International 205
  Brent Council 189
  budgets 210
  business 5
  changes as 8–9
  DML 96
  DTI 244
  EC 106
  Eureka! 203
  events 173
  flotation 76–7
  GA Life 86
  Hertsmere Council 95

objectives (*cont.*)
  Kymi 149
  Lambeth Children's Theatre
      Company 38
  lobbying 98
  Lombard Natwest 80
  media credits 178
  Polaroid 154
  Polo Mint 41
  privatisation 76–7
  quantifying 228–9
  RAC 134
  realistic 4–7
  report writing 84
  Royal Tournament 48, 240
  St John Ambulance 247
  Shell Select 58
  speechwriting 89
  sponsorship 75
  Stafford-Miller 156
  takeover bids 221
  third sector 130
  Tommy's Campaign 242
  Toyota 110
  unclear 198
  unusual 11
  verification of 248
  WDC 101
  Zola's 14
Ogilvy and Mather 16
ohp *see* overhead projector
Olins, Wally 67
once-removed network 45
one-to-one 54
open systems 208, 244–7
opinion 8
opinion formers 36
opportunities to see (OTS) 59, 108, 206,
    232
Opposition, The 9
organising PR 183–97
  Toyota 184–5
Outstanding Consultancy Awards xxiii,
    42, 97, 135, 146, 175
overhead projector 112–13
overheads 209–11

P-Four Consultancy 245
PACE *see* Bail Bandits
Paragon 57–8, 88, 116, 135, 206, 213, 226,
    229, 232
Parliament 47, 91, 98–9
Patten, John 126
Pearson, Barrie 82

Peel, Sir Robert 94
Pepsi Cola 220
perception 1, 5–6, 35, 45, 59–60, 157
performance
  audit 100
  criteria 69–70
  indicators 100
  skills 186, 188–90
  telephone 55–6
Perkins, David 141
Perrier 36, 46–7, 221
personal finance 85–8
personal maturity 22
personal portfolios
  how to organise 2–4
  list of cases xiv
  list of checklists xv
  list of guidelines xvi
personality of the brand 41, 72
Peter Roderick PR 174
photography 80, 168
pie charts 61
Piper Alpha 215
PIPPIES (persons inheriting parents'
    properties) 88
P & O Events 48
planning 11–13, 107–8, 249–50
  Classic FM 12–13
  Commercial Union 216–18
  crisis 215–27
  EC 107–8
  Kymi 149
  RAC 134
Plester, Fred 182
Polaroid 154–5
Police and Criminal Evidence Act *see* Bail
    Bandits
Police Federation 8, 207
Police Superintendents, Association of 9
Policy Studies Institute 244
Polo Mint 41–2
portfolios *see* personal portfolios
postal surveys 54
practice, codes of *see* codes of conduct
PRCA *see* Public Relations Consultants
    Association
Premier Relations 204
Prendergast, Peter 108
press 162–70
  articles 167–8
  briefings 88
  national 169–70
  notices 162–6
  regional 170, 180

sponsorship 180
weekend 168–9
pressure groups 21, 92–9, 138
Preston, Peter 35
PRet *see* Public Relations education and training
Price Waterhouse 77–9
pricing
  competitive 71
  predatory 71
primary data *see* data
privatisation 76, 79
product
  demonstration 173–4
  marketing 37–43
  niche 7–8, 15
  placement 46
  purity 221
  taken to media 174
  tampering 220–1
  unconvincing 16
  withdrawal 220, 221
professional conduct *see* codes of conduct
professional integrity 181, 267, 269, 275, 278, 279
professional organisations 186
Professional Practices Committee, IPR 181–2
programmes 11–13, 107–8, 250
  Abbey National 145
  Academy Computers 44
  Anti-Corn Law League 93
  Avon & Somerset Constabulary 239–40
  Banana Group 158–9
  Beauty International 206
  Brent Council 189–90
  DML 97
  DTI 245–6
  EC 107–8
  Eureka! 203
  GA Life 86–7
  Highland Spring 47
  Kymi 149–50
  Lombard Natwest 80–1
  Polaroid 155
  Polo Mint 42
  RAC 134–5
  radio *see* broadcasting
  Royal Tournament 48
  Shell Select 58–9
  Stafford-Miller 156–7
  television *see* broadcasting

WDC 101–2
provisos, media 180–1
proxy 72
Prudential 143
pseudo research *see* research
public relations
  and advertising 15, 200
  business function 1–2
  definitions xxii
  education and training 22, 140, 183–97, 261–3, 268–9
  flotation 77–9
  functions 1–34
  generic 157–9
  knowledge 22, 183, 187
  management function 18–19
  and marketing 7–8, 35–50
  no substitute for policy 16–17
  organisation 183–97
  skills 22–3, 186–97
  Public Relations Business *see* The Public Relations Business
Public Relations Consultants Association (PRCA) xxiii, 22, 27, 42, 182, 271
Public Relations education and training (PRet) matrix 22, 190
publics *see* stakeholders
purchasing *see* buying

Qin Shihuang 230
QTV, 48, 241
qualitative data *see* data
quality 12, 46, 71
Quality Street 238
quantitative data *see* data
Quentin Bell Organisation 205
questionnaires *see* research

RAC *see* Royal Automobile Club
radio *see* broadcasting
Radio Lynx 171, 229
reassurance, 32–3
recruitment 21–3
reference banks 193–5
refreshing the brand, 41
regional newspapers, PR input into 170
Register of Professional Lobbyists 98, 269–71
reports 83–5
Representation Plus 205
representative bodies, list of 251–4
reputation xxii, 1, 14, 16–17, 63, 71–2, 76, 85, 87–8, 141

research 51–65
    Avon & Somerset Constabulary 52
    Banana Group 53, 158
    checklist 65
    combination 53
    cost-free 62
    decision making 147–8
    desk 57, 58
    Eureka! 203
    Foodlink 207
    GA Life 52–3, 86–7
    Gallup 58, 87
    international 63–4
    kinds of 52–4
    Lombard Natwest 80
    MORI 207
    Neilsen 204
    NOP 53
    Open Systems 245
    planning 51–2
    Polo Mint 42
    primary 52–3
    pseudo 64
    purpose 51
    Royal Tournament 58
    secondary 52, 58
    Shell Select 58
    Stafford-Miller 53, 156
    syndicated 53
    techniques 54
    telephone 54–6
    training 196–7
    WDC 53, 101–2
results 2, 23, 250
    Abbey National 145–6, 236, 237
    Academy Computers 44, 202
    Anti-Corn Law League 94
    Avon & Somerset Constabulary 240
    Banana Group 159
    Beauty International 206
    Black Box 33
    Brent Council 190
    Classic FM 13
    Commercial Union 218
    community relations 242–3
    DML 97
    DTI 246
    EC 108
    Eureka! 203–4
    GA Life 87
    Hertsmere Council 96
    Highland Spring 47
    Jones Stroud 120–1
    Kymi 150

    Lombard Natwest 81, 170
    Polaroid 155
    Polo Mint 42
    RAC 135
    Royal Tournament 49, 241
    St John Ambulance 247
    Shell Select 59
    Stafford-Miller 157
    Tommy's Campaign 242
    Toyota 12
    WDC 102
    Zola 14
Reuters 172
reviews of financial products 88
Richmond Towers 206
Ridley, the Essex Brewer 175
Rifkind, Malcolm 96
Ritchie Calder xx
RNIB *see* Royal National Institute for
    the Blind
roadshows 78, 205–6
Rodgers, Peter 88
Romania 200
Romans 91
Rootes Group 10–11
Rosyth Dockyard 96–7
Rowland Company *see* The Rowland
    Company
Rowntree Mackintosh 238
Royal Automobile Club (RAC) 116,
    133–5
Royal Mail 37
Royal Mint 5–6
Royal National Institute for the Blind
    (RNIB) 6, 200
Royal Tournament, The 6, 38, 47–9, 208,
    240–1
RTZ 73–4

St John Ambulance 247
St Michael 70
safe sex 11
Sainsbury 146–7
salary costs 210–11
Salvoni, Janet 213
sans frontières 116
Saturday editions 168–9
Savonarola 91
Scope: Communications 12, 68, 103,
    184–5, 205
Scottish Vocational Qualifications
    (SVQs) 190
secondary data 52
Securicor 143–4

Select Committees 98–9
Sensodyne *see* Stafford-Miller
Shandwick 5–6, 27, 36, 204, 205, 219–20, 229, 236
Shell Select 57–9
Shingles, Geoff 73
Single Market 106
skills 22–3, 186–197
Skipjack tuna 146–7
slow burn 33
SMARTS Advertising and Design 43
Smith, W.H. 70, 208
Smythe, Dorward, Lambert 222
social economy 130–1
social contribution 119
Southern Electric 153, 204
speech writing 88–90
speeches, Anti-Corn Law League 93
spelling 192–3
sponsorship 39, 68, 72–6, 120–2, 138–9, 178–80
  ABSA 75, 178–9
  checklist 75–6
  corporate 72–6
  credits 178–9
  Digital 73
  educational 74
  Football League 178
  Hippo Club 74
  Lambeth Children's Theatre Company 38–9
  Lloyds Bank 73
  national expenditure 72–3
  NCC guidelines 74, 121–2
  principles of 74–6
  reasons for 73–4
  regional press 180
  Rover Tomcat 74
  RTZ 73–4
  third sector 138
Spreckley Pittham 207
staff communication *see* internal PR
staff newspapers 111, 138
staffing levels 28–9, 100
Stafford-Miller 53, 156–7
stakeholders
  checklist of 19–20
  definition of 19
  decision making 37
  range of publics 1
Strachan, Valerie 152
strategic image statement 72
strategy xxiii
  Abbey National 144

Academy Computers 43
Anti-Corn Law League 93
Avon & Somerset Constabulary 239
Banana Group 158
Beauty International 206
brands 36
Brent Council 189
Classic FM 12
DML 96–7
DTI 244
EC 107
Lombard Natwest 80
Polaroid 154
Polo Mint 41
RAC 133
Shell Select 58
Stafford-Miller 156
Tommy's Campaign 242
Toyota 12
WDC 101
Stratton, Dr Peter 86–7
Stuarts 91
supertram *see* Cleveland
SVQs *see* Scottish Vocational Qualifications
Sword/Certificate of Excellence xxiii, 35, 87, 97, 135, 146, 159, 190, 238, 240, 247, 249
symmetrical PR 19
syndicated research *see* research
syndicated tapes 145, 171–2

tables, list of xii
  using 61
takeovers 221–2
targeting 38, 80, 160–3
task-driven budgeting *see* zero based budgeting
Taunton Cider 36
Taylor, Professor Lawrie 58, 59
Telecom Gold 34
telephone performance rating 55
telephone questionnaires 54
television *see* broadcasting
Telewest 200
Tenet Public Relations 28
Terry's Suchard 150–1
Tesco 40–1, 124
Texas Instruments 243
Text 100 16, 205
The Communications Group 200, 205
The Public Relations Business 40
The Rowland Company 96–7, 205, 208

The Ultimate Roller Coaster　*see*
　　Lightwater Valley
third party endorsement　15, 36, 38, 58–9,
　　86–7, 95, 139
third sector　129–40
　definition　130
Thorn, Julia　226, 228
Time Warner　45, 123
Time to Read　45, 123
timescale of change　9
timetable
　flotation　78–9
　RAC　134
　strategic　12
Tommy's Campaign　242
tone of voice　15, 55, 116, 118
Top-ix　133
top-up society　58
topicality　36
Toyota　12, 68, 70, 102–3, 110, 119, 184–5
training　183–97, 261–3, 268–9
　matrix　22, 190
　in the Third Sector　140
　in the 21st century　196–7
translation　105–6
triangle
　community relations　243
　of influence　147–8
Tribe perfume　205–6
Trident submarine　96–7
Trident Training　140
truth
　credibility rankings　15
　reasons for telling　xxiii–xxiv
TSB　111–12
Tsimbalov, Vladimir　91
Tudors　91
Turner, Yvette　38
Two-Ten Communications　169–70

United Parcel Service (UPS)　229
Unix　38, 197

UPS　*see* United Parcel Service
USA　122–4
using PR　*see* function of PR

value　142–4
values　8
verification　5, 245, 248
Vidal Sassoon　42
video　48, 112–15, 189–90
　news releases (VNR)　58, 107–8, 172,
　　202
virtuous circle　70
Visionware　38
visual reference banks　194–5
VNR　*see* video news releases
vocational qualifications　*see* NVQs and
　　SVQs
voters　151

Wang An-chieh　xxii, xxiii, 249
Warner Brothers　204
Wauchope, Sam　214
Welbeck Golin/Harris　7, 8, 36, 41–2, 175,
　　238
Westminster Strategy　9
Windows　16, 38
Wolfgang Amadeus Muzack　56
Worcester, Robert　5, 8
Worldcom　33, 64, 106–8
writing
　accuracy　191
　articles　167–8
　business plan　82–3
　press notices　165
　reports　83–5
　speeches　88–90
　style　90, 191–2
Wycombe District Council (WDC)　53,
　　101–2, 202

zero-based budgeting　*see* budgeting
Zola, Emil　13–14